Xmas, 1940
from
Yoneko Miyagi

D1131991

LIVING BIOGRAPHIES OF
Great Composers

Sibelius

LIVING BIOGRAPHIES OF
Great Composers

By HENRY THOMAS AND
DANA LEE THOMAS

Illustrations by
GORDON ROSS

Garden City Publishing Co., Inc.
NEW YORK

COPYRIGHT, 1940
BY GARDEN CITY PUBLISHING CO., INC.
14 WEST 49TH STREET, NEW YORK, N. Y.

CL

PRINTED IN THE UNITED STATES OF AMERICA

Contents

CONTENTS

Introduction

THERE are two types of biography. The first type is the story of a man's mortal life. The second is the picture of his immortal personality. It is this second type that we have tried to produce in the *Living Biographies of Great Composers*. This book, like the other books in the present series, is intended to be a collection of *personality portraits*.

The masses of the people have always been interested in the personality portraits of their leaders. To paraphrase Shakespeare, the private affairs of the great are the public concern of us all. No imaginative race has ever contemplated the creation of the universe without an attempt to understand the Creator. And so the poets and the myth-makers of the world have supplied mankind with the living biographies of the gods.

In like manner, as we listen to the wonder of music, we seek to understand the fountain from which it flows. And lo, we find at the source of this divine fountain not a god, but something far more miraculous—a man! A man who interprets the thoughts of God into human song. And it is this interpretative power of the great composer that raises his personality upon an immortal plane.

INTRODUCTION

Yet the mere *power* to interpret is in itself not enough to immortalize the composer. As we shall see in the following chapters, the great composer is also possessed of a *determination* to interpret—that stubborn, instinctive, sublime perseverance, in spite of all odds, to bestow his dreams upon a thankless, contemptuous, and often antagonistic world. The other day we observed an ant with a bit of leaf in its mouth—a tremendous load for its strength—trying to toil up the slope of a lawn. A teacher friend of ours placed a rock in its path. The ant was baffled for a moment, and then it proceeded to make its way around the rock. The teacher went on to put other obstacles in the way of the ant, but in every instance the ant persisted in climbing either around or over the obstacle and to go ahead toward its original goal. "I am trying to experiment on the ant," said the teacher. "I want to see how persistently he can fight against odds."

"And to what purpose do you want to see that?" we asked.

"To the purpose that mankind may learn wisdom and strength from the ant," replied the teacher.

An Eastern legend has it that God puts obstacles into the path of genius that the angels may learn wisdom and strength from mankind. This wisdom and strength—in the language of art we call it beauty—is the stuff which goes into the making of the great composers. It is this quality which transforms a human sufferer into a divine teacher.

H. T.

D. L. T.

BACH

Great Compositions by Bach

CHORAL:
St Matthew Passion.
St John Passion.
Mass in B minor.
Christmas Oratorio.
Bauern Cantata.
Caffee Cantata.

INSTRUMENTAL:
Brandenburg Concertos for Orchestra (1–6).
Concerto in the Italian Style.

Sonatas for Violin and Piano (1–6).
Suites for Orchestra (1–4).
Chromatic Fantasy and Fugue.
The Well-Tempered Clavichord (Books I and II).
French Suites (1–6).
English Suites (1–6).
"Goldberg" Variations (1–32).
The Art of the Fugue.
Musikalisches Opfer for Harpsichord.
Preludes, Fugues, Toccatas, etc.

Bach

Johann Sebastian Bach

1685–1750

IT WAS as if music and not blood flowed in the veins of the Bachs. The first of them was a miller who played the flute. We know as little about the quality of his music as we know about the quality of his grain. "At any rate," remarked Johann Sebastian of him, "he must have learnt to keep time to the beating of his wooden sails in the wind."

Of the other members of the Bach musical dynasty fourteen were accomplished organists at Jena, Anstadt, Ohrdurf, Magdeburg, Mülhausen, Weimar and Lahm; twelve were cantors or musical directors; one was official court musician to Count Ludwig Gunther at Anstadt; one was musician to the Duke of Saxe-Eisenach; another, to the Duke of Saxe-Meiningen; a third, to Count Hohenlohe; and still another, Kapellmeister to the Duke of Weimar. At least ten of the Bachs were composers of choral preludes, cantatas, masses, suites, fugues and concertos; two of them were notable players on the oboe; three played the viola da gamba; and two were experts on the violin. For several generations, indeed, every professional musician within certain districts of Germany had come to be known as a "Bach."

II

"THE OBJECT of all music should be the glory of God," observed Johann Sebastian. "Any devout man could do as much as I have done, if he worked as hard." Sebastian had been brought up, good Lutheran that he was, in the protestant tradition of hard work. You cannot hope to become one of God's elect on high if you do not consecrate yourself to a long and laborious candidature here on earth. Hard work meant lifting your load from the ground, hoisting it up on your shoulder and bearing it steadily upward in your journey to the Lord's shrine. Life was a hard struggle. There were tremendously heavy forces endeavoring to keep man down in the dust from which stemmed his mortality. But, of course, the true path of man was forward and upward—and this in spite of his load, indeed *because* of his load. . . .

Sometimes the greatest obstacles against a man's progress are not impersonal but human forces, thought Bach. The stupidities of your fellow men. It is they who keep you down with their ridiculous rules and regulations. He had, for example, been installed as organist in the Church of Anstadt. It was a fine organ that belonged to the church. It responded like a sensitive animal to his touch. But the church officials did not respond as cordially. They did not like the way he accompanied the congregation in their hymns. And they had never experienced any trouble with their other organists. It was a perfectly simple matter to keep in step with the congregation and to play the same tunes all the time. They sent him a formal complaint. "For years our organists have played the Sunday choral music without variations. But you persist in making variations and intermixing many strange sounds that confound the entire congregation." What in the world was he doing to the sacred strains of their music? Furthermore, he had been appointed with

[4]

the understanding that he would rehearse the choirboys and teach them patiently. But up to that time he had remained selfishly with his organ and hadn't spent a minute with the boys. "Therefore you are to declare whether you will rehearse the scholars in the future or not. If you aren't ashamed to take your wages, you mustn't be ashamed to teach the scholars."

Well, that dispute was soon ended. The church officials got rid of their "lazy" organist. Bach secured a position in another church. Not a bad salary here. The wandering organist couldn't complain. Eighty-five gulden, twelve bushels of corn, six trusses of brushwood. They even sent him a wagon to transport his furniture to the new town. And as a bonus, for he seemed a rather likable fellow, the town council offered him three pounds of fish every year.

But imagine his audacity! As soon as he caught sight of the organ he declared that he didn't like it. It was too small. It had been good enough for all the other organists. *They* hadn't complained about the insufficiency of the pressure on the pipes and the inadequacy of the wind passage. What if the thirty-two-foot stop was missing? *They* hadn't turned up their noses. What manner of man was this, anyhow? He actually wanted a peal of bells—a Glockenspiel—connected to the pedals. The members of the council breathed a sigh of relief when Bach left the position.

Yet people began to whisper that he was a good organist. He had a giant fist. He could stretch twelve notes with his left hand while he performed running passages with his three middle fingers. Some said he could trill with his thumb and forefinger and at the same time play a melody with his fourth and fifth fingers. And what a physique! He was bigger and huskier than any other organist in Germany. And a merry and companionable fellow for all that. Ready to hold his own with anybody over a mug of beer. None of your temperamental and weazened and aloof little old musicians, but a man of the people—hale and hearty and tough-muscled, like a blacksmith presiding over the bellows of a forge rather than the pipes of an organ. Looked as if he would be more at home fanning a flame instead of pumping a current of air.

And they never forgot how he had put that upstart French organist, Jean Louis Marchand, in his place. The story was told in family circles from one generation to the next. Louis had regarded himself as the world's foremost player. The court at Versailles had turned his head. And when he came to Germany the princes showered him with medals for his performances. There arose a rumor among people who like to discuss such matters that he was a finer performer than Sebastian. But Bach's friends would concede nothing. They persuaded Bach to write a letter to Marchand, challenging him to a musical duel. Marchand accepted the challenge graciously enough. A jury of musicians was polled and a time and place were set. A large audience gathered to witness the contest. Bach arrived promptly. But where was Marchand? He had taken the first coach out of Germany back to his beloved France. The reputation of Bach was now beyond dispute.

But fame is a capricious wind. The weather-vane of public approval began suddenly to veer away from Sebastian. People said that too many honors were turning Bach's head, that he was becoming too puffed up with his own importance, that when he played the organ he was so busy admiring the ring he had received from the heir to the throne of Sweden that he forgot to watch the keyboard. It was too bad, whispered some of his slanderers, that Sebastian couldn't meet the great Handel. For then he would be able to realize his own littleness.

They especially resented what they were pleased to call his unreasonable arrogance. Once, when he applied for a position as church organist, he was told that he must pay a sum of money into the church treasury—a necessary and time-honored custom. Upon his refusal to comply with this custom, the presiding officer admonished him sternly that "if one of the angels of Bethle-

[6]

hem came from heaven . . . and desired to be organist of St Jacob's Church but if he had no money to pay into the treasury, there would be nothing else for him to do but to fly back to heaven." But Sebastian apparently was no friend of the angels. For he persisted in his stubbornness and declined the job.

And when he did get his next job his thoughts—it was rumored —were intent upon the wine cellar of the church instead of being centered upon higher things. "We can't make head or tail out of him. From day to day he grows stouter out of sheer laziness. Original compositions? Fiddlesticks! Let him attend like an honest man to his regular duties—duties for which he is being paid. Let him spend more time with the choirboys instead of going off—heaven alone knows where. Let him play the organ and fear the Lord and be satisfied with his salary—or else we'll get another organist in his place."

Someone had the audacity to whisper, "My good friends, you do not understand this Bach. He is a genius."

"Genius? We can't use genius. What we need is a cantor who is able to play the church music in a respectable and conventional manner."

III

BUT APART from such disputes, it was a happy life he led. A life brimful of music. Organist at Ohrdurf, Anstadt, Mühlhausen, Lübeck, Leipzig; musician to the Weimar court; favorite of Frederick the Great. For many years King Frederick, that mercurial soldier-poet-musician who was laying the foundations for a mighty German empire, had been urging Bach to give a performance on the organ at Berlin. And at last Sebastian agreed to enter the earthly Valhalla and to soothe the battle-scarred Warrior King with his strains. When Frederick received word of his arrival his old eyes lit up. "Gentlemen," he said to his assembled courtiers, "this is an eventful day. Sebastian Bach is here!" The old organist entered the court in his traveling clothes and

[7]

shuffled through one room after the other, with the entire court at his heels, sitting down and performing in turn on each of the emperor's seven pianos. Frederick had heard that Bach was "somewhat of a composer of music." Bach modestly acknowledged this. "Write me out the subject for a fugue, and I shall try to develop it into six parts," he suggested. Frederick wrote a theme on paper. The old musician, with hunched and tired shoulders but with fingers that had never lost their youth, sat down at the keyboard and transformed the emperor's theme into a thousand cascades of melody. Frederick shouted in admiration, "My God, there is only one great Bach!"

One great Bach, but many little ones. His procreative powers were as prolific as his creative. Twice married, he raised a family of twenty children. Playful as a boy himself, he was always in the presence of youngsters. For, in addition to his family brood, he was surrounded by a host of pupils. From all over Europe they flocked to learn the mystery of his technical magic. They adored him and tried to catch something of his own skill as they practiced the finger exercises he gave them. He was an eccentric old loon with a welter of novel ideas. For example, he taught them to use the thumb and the little finger as well as the other three fingers on the keyboard—an almost unheard-of departure from the conventional way of playing the scales. And with what amazing results!

But it was hard work, this constant use of the entire hand, with the wrist and the elbow held always horizontally to the keyboard. And so whenever the pupils grew tired of their monotonous practice he would jot down melodic little preludes for them to play as a relaxation. And sometimes he would take up one of his more complicated keyboard pieces and improvise upon it in a sort of reverie. Then at the end, "You must learn to play it like me, Christoph Transchel. That is how it sounds." This, indeed, is how it sounded; but what was a poor devil of a pupil to do with a madman who improvised in keys that were complete strangers to the human ear and who leaped about recklessly from key to key without the slightest halt in the flow of his melody?

Yet there were some who understood him. For example, his sons Johann Friedrich and Karl Emanuel. These two boys had inherited the madness in his blood. No wonder they were fond of one another, this father and these sons. They would sit for hours in the parlor and sing chorales without end. Or each would pick up an instrument and improvise a theme in harmony and counterpoint, blending with the others into an orchestral salvo of music. As for the other members of the family, they too belonged within the charmed circle of musical understanding. Why, the very letters of their surname, B-A-C-H, spelled out a melodic succession.

A family of strange talents and sensitive nerves, these Bachs. Especially Father Sebastian. If you felt music keenly, too keenly, you had to be quick tempered toward those professional organists whose every clumsy note stabbed you to the heart. You couldn't help tossing your wig at their heads and telling them they ought to be shoemakers instead of musicians. And this gave you the reputation for being a nasty old crank. Nasty old crank indeed! What could these numskulls understand of your superior vision? You sat at the organ along with a thousand others, but you did not feel the same dull things that they felt. They sat with both their feet on the earth and looked with a fixed horizontal stare at the blank walls ahead. You did so, too, at first. But one day a strange thought disturbed you, and then it all became as clear as day. Man must look not only straight ahead, but up. Are not all the churches built to glance at the sun? The very plan of life—for we stand upright on two legs—is along vertical lines. And so must it be with music. Just as the child tilts its face to seek guidance from its father, so must the melody that man sings look upward, ever upward. The notes ascend the scales and climb the dizzy octaves, and then swoop down to catch their breath. The structure of music, like the structure of churches, must be along the lines of ascent and descent. The melody must form a highway from earth to heaven and from heaven back to earth. As one group of notes enters upon its journey along the highway a second group prepares to follow in its wake. And as soon as this second group has taken to the road a third and a fourth group prepare to follow in their turn. And at any given moment of this eternally recurring ascent and descent scores of little troops of notes are in various stages of the journey, either on the way upward or on the way downward again to take by the hand new parties on the glorious trip. And though each party sets out from the terminal with measured punctuality—that is, on a strict time schedule and at equal intervals—some of the more impetuous notes overtake the more sluggish notes, so that there is a constant intermingling and helter-skelter motion up and down the scales. Flights and pursuits and captures and escapes—the origin of Sebastian Bach's fugues.

But Bach is not content to leave matters like this. He must see to it that there shall be no confusion, no discord, in this constant succession and interpenetration of sound. The notes must live together with one another in complete harmony.

Yes, that was the word—harmony. But how could this be brought about? Here the organist profited by his own experience. At home, when the numerous members of the family gathered in the parlor of a Sunday, they did a great deal of talking and singing. Each one had his own little repertoire of ideas and each would utter these ideas boldly in the face of the others. No one who wished to speak was the least bit stifled. Everyone was free to express himself to his heart's content. More often than not, several would find themselves speaking all at once. Yet such was their good will that the general spirit was one of the utmost harmony. Each individual opinion was an important contribution to the mutual understanding of the entire family.

When they sang their chorales the principle was the same. Each voice would freely improvise its own melody, and all the voices would blend into a concordant unit.

And this precisely was the principle he applied to the harmonizing of his compositions. The upward aspiration of man—the upward aspiration of music. But while man still finds himself on earth, hampered in his ascent by the horizontal ceiling of his own mortality, the society in which he dwells must be a free, a harmonious, a democratic society. For in the beauty of diversity alone lies true unity. Such was the spirit of the composer organist as he wrote his church cantatas and his Passion music. For this musician at the enchanted instrument spoke directly to the common man through the universal language of his preludes and his fugues. "In the architecture of my music I want to demonstrate to the world the architecture of a new and beautiful social commonwealth. The secret of my harmony? I alone know it. Each instrument in counterpoint, and as many contrapuntal parts as there are instruments. It is the enlightened self-discipline of the various parts—each voluntarily imposing on itself the limits of its individual freedom for the well-being of the community. That is my message. Not the autocracy of a single stubborn melody on the one hand. Nor the anarchy of unchecked noise on the other. No—a delicate balance between the two—an enlightened freedom. The science of my art. The art of my science. The harmony of the stars in the heavens, the yearning for brotherhood in the heart of man. This is the secret of my music."

IV

BODY WORN OUT, eyes failing, head bent down with the weight of his sixty-five years. And yet he could not believe that his end was near. There was so much work still to be done. Another chorale to be written, another concerto, another fugue. But now his eyesight is nearly gone. He must dictate the music. "Out of the depths we call unto Thee." The last call, and then there will be silence.

Well, he was content. He had done a good job. At thirty-eight he had reached the height of his creative powers. He had written the *St Matthew Passion* and the *St John Passion*—tremendous musical dramas depicting the sufferings of Christ. There had been Passion music before him, just as there had been Greek tragedy before Aeschylus—simple Christian canticles and Greek folk choruses. But Bach, like Aeschylus, transformed this heterogeneous folk tradition into a homogeneous and personal art form. And that stately *Mass in B minor*, dedicated to the Catholic king of Poland. Yes, he had served God well with his music. Two hundred compositions for the organ, preludes, fugues, cantatas for orchestra and voice and concertos for string and wind instruments. And his music, like his character, had been hearty, unpretentious, devout. Simple as the song of the birds to the rising and the setting sun.

And now, after a tranquil day, the tranquillity of the night. He died quickly, of an apoplectic stroke. He was buried in St John's churchyard, to be forgotten for over a hundred years. The Leipzig *Chronicle* carried the following brief obituary notice:

July 28, at eight in the evening, the learned musician, Herr John Sebastian Bach, composer to His Majesty the King of Poland, Kapellmeister to the courts of Gothen and Weissenfels, director and cantor of the school of St Thomas, died.

That was all. The town council expressed mild regrets. "Herr Bach was a great musician, no doubt, but we wanted a schoolmaster, not a musical director." His widow, left with the burden of her huge family, soon went through her husband's savings. She became an object of public charity and upon her death was buried in a pauper's grave. The music which Bach had written lay in obscurity in the cupboard of the St John's vestry. Whenever a pupil at the religious school desired some paper in which to wrap up his picnic sandwiches he went to the cupboard and tore a sheet from Bach's manuscripts. While Ludwig van Beethoven was composing the immortal notes of his *Fifth Symphony* the last surviving daughter of Sebastian Bach was living out her life in a poorhouse.

"You know, the old fellow was so modest he didn't know his own worth," remarked one of his admiring pupils to his companion at the grave of the master. "It may take centuries before the world becomes aware of him."

HANDEL

Great Compositions by Handel

VOCAL:

40 Operas, including *Rinaldo, Radamisto, Lotario, Faramondo, Xerxes, Julius Caesar, Dedamia.*

19 Oratorios, including *The Messiah, Esther, Deborah, Athalia, Saul, Samson, Israel in Egypt, Joseph, Belshazzar, Heracles, Judas Maccabaeus, Semele, Joshua, Solomon, Jephtha, Theodora.*

Musical Settings to Dryden's *Ode for St Cecilia's Day,* Milton's *L'Allegro* and *Il Penseroso.*

INSTRUMENTAL:

Organ Concertos (1–12).

Concerti Grossi for strings (1–12).

Sonatas for violin, viola, oboe, etc.

Various Suites for full orchestra, including *Water Music, Fireworks Music,* etc.

Many pieces for organ, including Preludes, Fugues, etc.

Handel

Georg Friedrich Handel

1685–1759

A MASQUERADE in Venice, the city of melody and madness. All the leading artists of Italy and many foreigners, too, are present. For this is the Carnival Week—the period in which all the beauty and the passion and the joyousness of the Old World have been gathered into this singing city of the lagoons. Seven opera houses are open every evening. Every day in the churches the holiday-hearted populace flocks to hear the orchestras, the organs and the choirs. All Venice is bathed in music and dancing and color and laughter and life.

Here, at the masquerade, the famous Alessandro Scarlatti is improvising at the clavier. The masqueraders have stopped their dancing. They are crowding around the clavier, listening with rapt attention to the dean of the Italian musicians. Many of them have already heard his latest and greatest opera, *Mitridate Eupatore*, that miracle of musical beauty and dramatic intensity. He is now playing variations upon some of the leading tunes of that opera—bubbling fountains and cascades of music that leap into life at the touch of his fingers.

And now he is through with his playing. The masqueraders

have burst into a tempest of cheers. In the midst of it a young man has taken his place at the clavier. He is a stranger at this masquerade, for nobody here seems to know him. Tall and awkward and homely, he appears to be scarcely out of his teens as he begins to move his clumsy overgrown fingers over the keyboard. The presumptuousness of him, to dare to play on the clavier after the great Scarlatti! The masqueraders have moved away and are now busy with their dancing.

But wait. There is something familiar about the tune he is playing. It is a new variation upon one of Scarlatti's songs. And, by Jove, an improvement upon Scarlatti himself! The notes are no longer a bubbling cascade. They are a constellation of dancing suns. The very heavens themselves seem to have broken into a wild and passionate whirl of blazing tones. Scarlatti leans forward with a look of amazement upon his noble face. "Ah, but this fellow can really play!" He turns to his son, who is sitting at his side. "Tell me, Domenico, do you happen to know who this young man is?"

"No, I don't. But to judge from his playing, he must be either the celebrated Saxon or the devil!"

II

THE "celebrated Saxon," Georg Friedrich Handel, was fond of traveling incognito and mystifying people. Though but twenty-two years old at the time of his visit to Venice (in 1707), he had already won a reputation as a musician of extraordinary genius. Yet, unlike Bach, he came of a very unmusical family. His father, Georg Handel, was a barber in the employ of the Duke Augustus of Saxony. He prospered in his tonsorial art and in 1665 was able to buy a luxurious house at Halle. He was married twice—the first time (in 1643) to the widow of a barber, and the second time (in 1683) to the daughter of a clergyman. His first wife, who was ten years his senior, bore him six children; and his second wife, who was thirty years his junior, bore him four children. Georg Friedrich was the second child of the second marriage. When he was born, on Monday, February 23, 1685, his father was sixty-three years old and his mother only thirty-three. From his earliest childhood Georg Friedrich was blessed with an old head and a young heart.

He showed an early aptitude for music. But his path to a musical career was not unobstructed. His father, highly successful himself in his bourgeois calling, was anxious to bring up his son to a similar trade or profession. Let young Georg be a barber or a lawyer—anything but a musician. For musicians at that period were regarded as a class of vagabonds, occupying a position even lower than that of servants. Most of the German servants, as Papa Handel pointed out, enjoyed the security of employment, while the vagabond musicians sang and starved their way over the gutters of Germany. Indeed, there were in Germany very few professional musicians. Some of the leading masters of the period, men like Kuhnau, Rosenmüller, Schütz, practiced law for their livelihood and composed music merely for their amusement. So let Georg learn to manipulate a razor or to write a law brief, instead of wasting his time thumping upon the clavichord.

But somehow, through some unknown strain in his blood from heaven knows what forgotten ancestor, the seed of music had found its way into Handel's heart and refused to be dislodged from there. The story is told—and there may be a germ of truth in it—that the little boy of six managed to smuggle a small clavichord into an out-of-the-way attic of his father's spacious home and that he stole into the attic at night to practice on the instrument while the family was asleep.

His father, in an effort to discourage him from this "unprofitable trade," once even threatened to cut off the child's fingers. But to no avail. Handel persisted in his desire to be a musician. And this desire was fed through a constant stream of music that managed to trickle into Handel's sensitive ears in spite of his father's objections. Every evening a chorale was played on the tower of the Liebfrauenkirche. At the Sunday services there were frequent performances of cantatas. And in the streets of Halle there were weekly renderings of the latest music offered by the church choirs and the town musicians.

When Georg Friedrich was seven years old his father took him on a visit to his cousin, Georg Christian Handel, the valet de chambre to the Duke of Weissenfels. One day, in the course of this visit, the boy managed to get into the chapel of the duke's estate where he sat down and began to play on the organ. The duke heard him, asked who he was and urged his father to encourage the child's undoubted talents. A duke's request was not to be taken lightly; and so, with great reluctance, Papa Handel upon his return to Halle placed his son under the charge of Friedrich Wilhelm Zachau, the able organist of the Liebfrauenkirche. He hoped, however, that this madness would be but a brief interlude in his child's life and that Georg Friedrich would soon see the light and turn from the silly business of spilling notes into men's ears to the more sensible business of scraping whiskers from men's chins.

His father was mistaken. Music turned out to be not a momentary diversion but a lifelong passion with Handel. Zachau was not only a great musician but an inspiring teacher. First of all he gave his young pupil a strong foundation in harmony, and then he taught him how to build the structure of his composition upon this foundation. He was a man of catholic tastes, and he imparted this catholicity to his impressionable pupil. He acquainted him not only with the various forms of music, but with the various tonal characteristics which each of these forms assumed in the different countries of Europe. Under the tuition of so thoroughgoing and enthusiastic a master Handel's genius developed into a growth of varicolored beauty. Handel's music is not typical of any time or place. It is universal. Hence its imperishable appeal.

[20]

The method of Zachau's teaching was practical as well as theoretical. He made Handel compose, in addition to the regular exercises, a complete motet or cantata every week. Crude as these must have been at the outset, they implanted in the young musician a lifelong habit of hard and sustained work. Handel was one of the most tireless composers in the history of modern music. And one of the most rapid. Whatever he undertook he brought to a speedy and satisfactory conclusion. For he had learned as a young pupil under Zachau not to waste any time in dillydallying.

But he was able to compose so swiftly and so expertly because he was blessed with an inexhaustible well of musical genius. And this well came rippling to the surface at an amazingly early age. At eleven he had already composed six sonatas for two oboes and a bassoon—the favorite instruments of his childhood. Years later, when these juvenile sonatas were discovered and brought to his attention, he laughingly remarked: "Yes, I used to compose like the devil in those days."

But his composition took only a part of his time. In his spare moments Handel learned to play the harpsichord, the violin, the oboe and the organ. And this was not all. His father still hoped to make a "respectable" citizen out of him, and so he sent him to the regular school where Handel mastered the "more sensible" subjects of the prosaic world.

While he thus sojourned in the borderland between the poetical dreams of his genius and the prosaic realities of his father's ambition his father died (February 11, 1697). Handel was now in a position to follow his own choice as to his future career. Yet for a time he allowed the dead hand of his father to guide him. He continued his schooling at the Lutheran Gymnasium for five years, and then at the age of seventeen he matriculated as a law student at the University of Halle.

But he stayed there only one year. The call of the music was too strong in his blood. In his spare moments during his college term he had frequently "filled in" for Christoph Leporin, official organist of the Cathedral; and when Leporin was finally dismissed for neglect of duty Handel was offered the post and accepted it.

The salary for this job, before Leporin's time, had been fifteen dollars a year, with free lodging thrown in. Leporin's predecessor had probably starved to death, as one of Handel's leading biographers, Chrysander, observes. When the post was offered to Handel the salary was raised to $37.50 a year— enough to starve on at a somewhat more respectable rate. But Handel, fortunately, was not obliged to suffer in order to develop his musical genius. For his father had left him a sufficient competence to live on. And so we find the young musician of eighteen established as the leading organist of Halle and the composer of several hundred cantatas.

But Handel was not satisfied with his local fame and his juvenile compositions. Having successfully tried out the wings of his genius at Halle, he was now ready for more extensive flights in wider fields. Accordingly, he bade his mother good-by (in the summer of 1703) and left his native city for Hamburg.

III

AMONG the first acquaintances that Handel made in the "Venice of Germany" was Johann Mattheson. This young man, who was four years his senior, was one of the most remarkable products of the German versatility of the eighteenth century. At the age of nine he had played the organ in several churches. At twelve he had mastered the harp, the double bass, the violin, the flute and the oboe. At thirteen he had begun the study of law and had learned to speak English, French and Italian. At fifteen he had been hired to sing the leading parts in the opera at Kiel. At eighteen he had produced an opera of his own. At twenty-two, when he met Handel, he was the secretary of the British Lega-

tion at Hamburg, the composer of several operas, masses, oratorios and cantatas and the author of a number of books on
music, philosophy and science. It was his ambition to produce
a book for every year that he lived. He more than fulfilled that
ambition; when he died at the age of eighty-three he had published eighty-eight books. Yet this man was no mere book-
worm or cloister musician. In spite of his amazing industry
he found plenty of time for diversion. He was an expert
swordsman, an excellent dancer and a general favorite with
the ladies.

Handel's friendship with Mattheson brought its practical as
well as its intellectual advantages. For Mattheson introduced
him to the British ambassador, Sir Cyril Wyche, a lover of music
who not only secured pupils and engagements for Handel but
who was later to pave the way for Handel's prolonged residence
in England.

Thanks to the help of his new friends Handel entered the
Hamburg orchestra as a second violinist. He was much more
expert, however, on the clavichord and the organ; and he was
anxious to secure the position of organist at some church. An
opportunity presented itself shortly at Lübeck, about forty miles
from Hamburg. Here at the Marienkirche was the famous old
organist, Dietrich Buxtehude, who was looking for a successor.
Both Handel and Mattheson entered into a friendly rivalry for
the position. But there was a serious drawback—in the person of
Buxtehude's unattractive and elderly daughter. In accordance
with the custom of the day, Buxtehude insisted that whoever
inherited his organ must also inherit his daughter. Mattheson
and Handel refused the offer. They didn't care to marry Buxtehude's organ only to have the daughter thrown in as a dowry.
They returned to Hamburg. (Two years later, it is interesting
to note, Bach also turned down the same offer and for the same
reason.)

Not long after their return the two young friends had a serious quarrel, and this quarrel was due directly to their friendly rivalry in music. The occasion was the performance of Mattheson's opera, *Cleopatra*, which Mattheson conducted and in which he played the part of Antony. When he was not on the stage he conducted at the harpsichord, and when he was called upon to sing on the stage he yielded his place at the harpsichord to Handel. On this occasion, when Mattheson returned to the instrument right after he had enacted the death of Antony, Handel was so engrossed in the music that he refused to give up his place. As they were leaving the theater Mattheson struck Handel, whereupon the latter challenged Mattheson to a duel. They fought this duel before a large crowd in the market place, and Handel escaped death only through a stroke of good luck. Mattheson, who was by far the better swordsman, had made a savage lunge at Handel's breast, but the sword snapped on a large metal button on Handel's coat. Whereupon the two young hotheads embraced and went off together to a rehearsal of Handel's first opera, *The Fortunes of Almira*.

Handel was not quite twenty when *Almira* was produced (January 8, 1705). This opera enjoyed so great a success that it was performed without interruption until February 25, when Handel's second opera, *Nero* or *Love Through Blood and Murder*, was produced—and with almost equal success. Mattheson sang the leading role in both these operas.

Handel no longer played the second violin in the orchestra. He was now able to make a fairly good living through his composition, his teaching and his performances on the harpsichord at the theater. He avoided the gay night life of the theatrical folk, worked hard, saved his money and prepared to travel patiently the long and painful road to artistic achievement.

But there were obstacles in the way. His rival musicians were jealous of his early success. The Director of the Hamburg Opera, Reinhard Keiser, refused to produce any more of Handel's works. Instead he tried to compose several operas of his own.

But in his effort to spite Handel's face Keiser bit his own nose. His music was unpopular, and the attendance at the theater began to fall off. Finally his debts became so burdensome that he was compelled to withdraw from the management of the theater.

The manager who succeeded Keiser was interested in farce rather than in opera. "Serious music," he said, "tires the audience." He made his debut with *Die Lustige Hochzeit* (The Merry Wedding). Halfheartedly he ordered one opera from Handel. But when this opera (*Florindo und Daphne*) was submitted to him he completely mutilated the score so as to make it "fit for pleasure-loving ears." There was nothing now to keep Handel any longer in Hamburg. He went to seek for his further inspiration in Italy, taking along with him two cases full of his musical compositions.

IV

HANDEL'S REPUTATION had preceded him to Italy. In Florence, in Rome, in Naples, in Venice—wherever he went he was enthusiastically greeted as "the celebrated Saxon." He became the close friend of the Scarlattis, father and son, both of whom held many contests of virtuosity with him. So profound was the admiration of the younger Scarlatti for Handel's genius that whenever he mentioned Handel's name he made the sign of the cross.

As for Handel, he was enchanted with Italy, the country in which music "bloomed like a flower under the open sky." He steeped himself in the melodies of the Italian operas, the cantatas, the oratorios, the masses at the Vatican; he composed several pieces after the Italian style; he almost yielded to the entreaties of the Roman priests that he give up his Lutheran faith and adopt Catholicism; he conceived a passionate love for Italian painting, for he was a poet of the eye as well as of the ear; and he planned to remain indefinitely in this "land of perpetual springtime" when an attractive offer from Agostino Steffani recalled him to Germany.

Steffani, the Kapellmeister of the Opera House at Hanover, was a more curious figure even than Mattheson. Priest, composer, mathematician, philosopher, critic, ambassador, singer and director of secular as well as of sacred music, he was the councilor of princes and the confessor of kings. Physically he was a little bit of a man—a miniature tornado of gaiety, as gentle as he was merry, as wise as he was gentle, as charming as he was wise. He met Handel in Rome during the winter of 1708–09, and he took him immediately under his protection. When he returned to Hanover he brought Handel along with him as his assistant Kapellmeister. Thirty-two years older than Handel, he proved to be not only his worldly wise employer but his spiritual and artistic guide. His music, to quote Romain Rolland, "was the most perfect picture of Italian song in a golden age." Regarded as the outstanding lyricist in the music of the seventeenth century, he bestowed upon Handel his inheritance of supreme lyricism. And Handel took this gift and enriched it through the medium of his own genius. As Chrysander remarks: "Handel walked in the footsteps of Steffani, but his feet were larger."

Yet this statement is only partially true. Handel walked in nobody's footsteps. His genius had marked out a path for itself. To be sure, he stopped occasionally on the roadside to pluck a familiar flower and to luxuriate in its perfume. But this was the greatest extent to which the music of others influenced his own music. Faint reminiscences, subtle blendings of half-forgotten memories into newer and richer ideas, but no direct plagiarism, no deliberate following in the footsteps of others. Handel is one of the most original of all composers.

V

SHORTLY after his return to Germany Handel paid a visit to England. He was only twenty-five at the time, but he had already acquired the reputation of a lifetime.

The arrival of Handel in London was like the sudden influx of fresh water into an arid valley. Purcell, that awkward but gentle voice of the wildwoods, "the miniature Mozart of England," had now been dead for fifteen years, and the English were athirst for new songs. Handel was received with open arms. The Director of the London Opera, Aaron Hill, begged him for something from his pen. Handel replied with alacrity, and within eleven days he wrote an opera for the London manager.

The success of this opera (*Rinaldo*) was enormous. One of its songs, *Cara Sposa*, became a popular household tune all over England. Another was adopted as the regimental march of the British Life Guards and was used, almost a quarter of a century later, as the highwayman's chorus in *The Beggar's Opera*. The publisher of *Rinaldo*, a man by the name of Walsh, made about ten thousand dollars on the opera. Handel, however, realized considerably less money on the venture. Indeed, Handel jokingly suggested that Walsh should compose the next opera and that he (Handel) should publish it. In this way, said Handel, they might come out even in the end.

He returned to Hanover for a short time, but he found that the opera in that city had fallen into a decline. He therefore turned his eyes again toward London. His music had taken root in that country and had found there a congenial soil. The English people liked his music, and he liked the English people. He asked for a leave of absence from Steffani. The latter obligingly consented, "on condition that he come back to Hanover after a reasonable time."

Handel arrived in London on his second visit toward the end of 1712. He stayed there—save for an occasional trip to Germany—for the remainder of his life.

VI

QUEEN ANNE OF ENGLAND, enchanted by his music, appointed him Official Composer to the British Court. Secure in this position, the young music laureate of England composed an occasional patriotic ode or cantata for the queen and spent the rest of his time composing nonpatriotic masterpieces for the general public. Though scarcely able at the start to speak the English language, he found himself perfectly at home in England. For his character, like his music, was cosmopolitan. His only nationality was the international brotherhood of the United Artists of the World. His home became the gathering place of all those who were able to translate their individual thoughts into the universal alphabet of beauty. Among his most intimate friends were Alexander Pope, the Lilliputian who wrote like an angel, and Jonathan Swift, the angel who had been born into a race of Lilliputians. He admired the flashing wit of the one and the biting satire of the other. And they, in turn, marveled at the sweeping impetuosity of his musical genius—the genius of a multitude of rivulets tumbling together into one mighty stream. Pope compared him to the mythical titan of Roman mythology —Briareus:

> Strong in new arms, lo! Giant Handel stands,
> Like bold Briareus with his *hundred hands*.

Handel's days were thus filled with music and the sunlight of appreciative friendship. His life was serene. "He was very regular and uniform in his habits," we are told. "He worked in his study every morning till dinnertime, when he sat down with the most talented men of any in the kingdom." In the afternoon he frequently went to listen to the organ recitals at St Paul's Cathedral. At times he would himself volunteer to play on the organ, and then the cathedral would be filled to overflowing. In the evening he generally accompanied the members of the cathedral choir to the Queen's Arms Tavern. In this tavern there was a large room with a harpsichord, and Handel would sit down at the keyboard and top off his day's feast of sacred music with a secular dessert.

"But now there arose a new king over Egypt, who cared not for Joseph." When Queen Anne died and George I came upon the throne Handel was obliged to seek for an independent livelihood. For King George, the imported Elector of Hanover, was angry at what he was pleased to call Handel's "desertion" from his native Germany. For a time he would have nothing to do with him. Fortunately, however, Handel secured an appointment as Kapellmeister at the castle of the Earl of Carnarvon. Here he had at his disposal a trained chorus and an excellent orchestra, as well as a cultured audience of the earl's artistic friends. And, most important of all, he had leisure to compose without the distraction of financial worry. He set to work enthusiastically, and within the next three years (from 1717 to 1720) his genius came to full fruition. It was at this time, as one of his biographers points out, that Handel "created a new style in music." He wrote operas that were like living, flowing streams as compared to the stagnant pools of the earlier operatic melodies. He composed anthems whose strong, open-air cadences were freed completely from the sentimental, stuffy, indoor pietism of the German church composers. And he began at this period to develop that strange, new, beautiful, exotic flower of music, the oratorio, a blending of the solemnity of the cantata with the lightness of the opera—a biblical drama in which the poem relates the story and the music supplies the scenery. His oratorios—*Esther, Saul, Samson, Israel in Egypt, The Resurrection, Judas Maccabaeus, Deborah, The Passion of Christ, The*

Triumph of Truth and *The Messiah*—represent the Musical Renaissance of Europe. For in them the somber spirit of the ancient Greek tragedies is reborn under the accelerated pulsations of modern life.

VII

HANDEL terminated his service under the Earl of Carnarvon at the end of a few years. For a new opera house had been opened in London, and he decided to try his fortune in the venture. What he succeeded in doing was to *sink* his fortune in that venture. He invested fifty thousand dollars—all his life's savings—in the opera; and when, after several unsuccessful seasons, he computed his assets and his liabilities he found that he had lost not only his original investment of fifty thousand dollars but an additional fifty thousand dollars that he had borrowed from his friends.

There were several reasons for his failure. In the first place, he was a good musician but a poor businessman. He spent all his time composing—averaging about two operas a year for twenty years, to say nothing of his prodigious output of other vocal and instrumental music. This left him no opportunity to look after the business end of the enterprise. Then, again, the rank and file of the people didn't care enough for serious music to make it pay. "What is necessary in music," said the London *Journal* (February 24, 1722), "is that it should chase away *ennui* and relieve clever men from the trouble of thinking." It was Handel's ambition to make men think instead of relieving them from thinking. On top of all that, the amateur aesthetes among the nobility considered it an interesting sport to arouse rivalries among the composers. Accordingly they encouraged another musician, the Italian Bononcini, to open a competitive opera house in London. The wits of the day, whose talent for doggerel was superior to their appreciation for music, amused the public with epigrams about this operatic rivalry. One of these silly

epigrams reduced both Handel and Bononcini to the status of
circus clowns:

> Some say, compared to Bononcini,
> That Mynheer Handel's but a ninny;
> Others aver that he to Handel
> Is scarcely fit to hold a candle.
> Strange all this difference should be
> 'Twixt Tweedledum and Tweedledee.

In such an atmosphere it was inevitable that both the rival
enterprises should go into bankruptcy.

But the most important factor in Handel's financial failure
was the jealousy that his genius aroused in hearts less gifted than
his own. There sprang up in London a veritable conspiracy to
disenthrone him from what his detractors regarded as his "un-
deserved power and fortune." A hailstorm of abusive articles
and pamphlets began to fall about his ears. They attacked his
operas because he wrote them, as they alleged, "to flatter his
own ears, even though they shocked the ears of the audience."
They vilified his oratorios because they were "neither fish nor
fowl, but a strange and undigestible concoction." On the nights
on which he produced his operas they deliberately arranged all
sorts of distractions—such as assemblies, card games, cockfights,
"batteries of female diversions" and the like—to keep the public
away from his theater. And "these joint endeavors of all ranks
and sexes," they gloated in one of their articles, "succeeded
well." His audiences grew "very thin," and Handel fell into
"a deep melancholy." They even accused him of immorality
with his actresses and of profanity because he allowed words
from the Bible to be sung in his oratorios.

Added to all these misfortunes was another—the incessant
piracy of his works by all and sundry. For at that period there
was no copyright protection either for music or for literature.
His onetime publisher, Walsh, was busy pillaging his songs and

getting rich on the profits. His most popular operas were being performed everywhere without so much even as a request for permission or a letter of thanks. No wonder, then, that his health broke down and his mind came close to the verge of giving way.

But he kept on fighting—not only for his own sake but for all poor musicians everywhere. Though frequently in need of charity himself, he organized and conducted several concerts for other needy composers. And he refused to take a penny out of the proceeds of these concerts.

At the time of his poverty he was offered the honorary degree of Doctor of Music at Oxford. But the honor would cost him five hundred dollars, and so Handel refused it. "Vhy de devil I trow my money avay for vat de blockheads give me?" he said in his broken English. "I no vant such honors."

Meanwhile his health and his fortunes had reached the lowest ebb. His right side had become paralyzed, and his money was all gone. His creditors seized him and threatened him with imprisonment. For a brief time he was tempted to give up the fight—but then he rebounded again to compose the greatest of his inspirations, the epic *Messiah*. And so tremendous were his recuperative powers that he wrote this entire work in three weeks.

There now came a brief bright period in his life. But it was like a lightning flash in the night. New wealth, fame, friendships with Fielding, Hogarth, Smollett, Colley Cibber, Arbuthnot and Gay, recognition from King George II, a statue erected in his honor at the Vauxhall Gardens—and then the dark. He was at work on the second act of his opera, *Jephtha's Daughter*, when his eyes grew suddenly dim. He kept at it slowly, laboriously, for several months. When he finished this work (August 30, 1751) he could hardly see the notes with a magnifying glass. He underwent an operation for cataract, but in vain. Within a few months his light had been, as he expressed it, "completely blotted out."

[*32*]

HANDEL

In the spring of 1759 there was a production of *Samson* at Covent Garden. Handel, sitting near the organ, broke down when he heard the words of the blind warrior who had been fighting all his life against the Philistines:

> Total eclipse, no sun, no moon,
> All dark amidst the blaze of noon.

When, at the end of the performance, he was led to make his customary bow to the audience he was greeted with a glorious, pathetic ovation of cheers and tears.

A few nights later he was present at a production of his *Messiah*. He suffered a fainting spell in the midst of the performance. He went home to his bed, never to rise from it again.

He expressed the wish that he might die on Good Friday, "in the hope of rejoining the good God, my sweet Lord and Saviour, on the day of His Resurrection." His wish was fulfilled, for it was in the early morning of Holy Saturday (April 14, 1759) that the singer and his Messiah met face to face.

HAYDN

Great Compositions by Haydn

VOCAL:

The Seven Words from the Cross.

Various Oratorios, including *The Creation, The Seasons.*

Several Cantatas, including *Ariana a Naxos, The Ten Commandments.*

14 Masses.

5 Grand Operas and 4 Comedies.

22 Arias, 36 Songs, etc.

INSTRUMENTAL:

125 Symphonies, including the *Surprise Symphony,* the *Farewell Symphony,* the *Clock Symphony,* the *London Symphony,* the *Oxford Symphony,* the *Military Symphony,* the *Toy Symphony,* etc.

About 30 Concertos for various string instruments with orchestra.

77 String Quartets, about 40 Piano Trios, 66 compositions for wind and strings, 12 collections of Minuets, numerous Sonatas for clavichord, etc.

Haydn

Franz Joseph Haydn

1732–1809

Haydn, like Handel, was a living proof of nature's contempt for the artificial classifications of human worth. Haydn's father was a wagonmaker and his mother was a cook; yet they had in their blood the seed of the nobility of genius.

Born on April Fool's Day in 1732, Franz Joseph fooled the world by raising the obscure name of the Haydns into the sunlight of undying fame. He was a humorous, elf-like, mischief-loving little fellow, and there was great need for a sense of humor in the poverty-stricken home of the Haydns. For sorrow and death were frequent visitors at this one-storied peasant's hut in Rohrau, Austria. Out of the twelve Haydn children by his father's first marriage six died in their infancy. And of the five children of his father's second marriage not one survived. Nature, in her reckless experimentations, breaks many bits of clay in order to produce one masterpiece.

Sepperl, as Franz Joseph was familiarly called by his parents, gave evidence of his musical talent at an early age. Thanks to a schoolmaster cousin who recognized this talent he was put into the choir of the Catholic church at Hainburg, a town situated about twelve miles from Rohrau.

Life at "the big city" was, for the little six-year-old choirboy, a mixture of music and mischief and hunger. He learned to sing his part in the masses; he amused himself by snipping off the tails from the wigs of the choristers in front of him—for which he often received a good thrashing; and he became an expert in maintaining upon a neighborly basis those two most inharmonious of neighbors—a cheerful heart and an empty stomach.

One day there was a procession in the streets of Hainburg. The regular drummer of the town was ill, and Haydn undertook to substitute for him. Unfortunately, he was so small that he couldn't carry the drum. Moreover, he had never played the drum in his life. But these were no drawbacks. The instrument was carried before him upon the back of a bigger boy—who, to add to the ludicrousness of the picture, happened to be a hunchback—and little Haydn marched through the entire parade beating perfect time to the music.

His musical precocity came to the attention of Johann Georg Reutter, the Kapellmeister of the Cathedral of St Stephen at Vienna. Herr Reutter, who happened to be visiting Hainburg in search of talent, gave Haydn an examination in singing. "Bravo!" he cried, delighted with the child's pleasant though feeble voice. "But how does it happen, my little man, that you can't sing a shake?"

"How do you expect me to sing a shake," replied Joseph, "when my teacher himself can't sing it?"

Reutter took the amusing little fellow to Vienna, taught him how to make the necessary vibrations in his throat for the ornamental trilling effect and enrolled him in the choir of the "foremost church in the Empire." The boys in this choir, lodged and fed and clothed—all too niggardly—at the expense of the congregation, were taught not only music but the four R's—reading, writing, arithmetic and religion. Occasionally the children were sent to some wealthy Viennese home, where they sang to the guests and helped in the kitchen in return for a square meal.

Haydn's voice, as he grew older, developed into a rich soprano, and this indirectly was the cause of his dismissal from the choir. Herr Reutter, anxious to retain the use of this soprano voice indefinitely, suggested the emasculation of the child. When his father flatly refused his permission the angry choirmaster set his young pupil adrift on the streets of Vienna.

And now began a period of vagabondage for the penniless and friendless youngster of seventeen. The winter was coming on—it was November 1749—and Haydn had nowhere to lay his head. For a short time he thought of going back to Rohrau. But his father was already overburdened with the support of his growing family. Haydn decided to stay and to starve at Vienna.

Luckily, he was able to save himself from starvation. He fell in with a musical acquaintance of his, a certain tenor by the name of Spangler. This good Samaritan, though poor himself, took Haydn into his garret home where he fed and lodged him until Haydn was strong enough to stand on his own feet.

And it was not long before Haydn was able to take care of himself. For Vienna at that time was a music-mad city. "At the hour when work ceased," wrote a traveler, "houses, streets and parks became one immense scene of dancing and merriment." Haydn made himself an intimate unit of that scene. He joined a band of serenaders and, violin in hand, strolled through the streets in the summer evenings, earning his bread like a gypsy and charming the young girls with his music even though he couldn't captivate their hearts with his homely little figure and his big bulbous nose. In the winter he earned his keep by playing in the taverns and composing minuets for the dances of the rich.

Indeed, it seemed that he had been born under a lucky star. And this star always managed to steer him toward the right sort of people. At six he had met the schoolmaster who had launched him on his musical career. At eight he had come under the guidance of Reutter, who had furthered his training as a singer, player and composer. At seventeen he had met Spangler, who had saved him from starvation. And now, at twenty-two, he made the acquaintance of Nicolo Porpora, the famous teacher and musical dictator of Vienna. Up to this point the musical education of Haydn had been desultory, for his earlier teachers had possessed neither the ability nor the inclination to give him a methodical training in harmony. But here was a chance for Haydn to ground himself, under a genuine master, in "the real foundations of musical composition."

Unable to pay for his lessons under this "patriarch of melody," Haydn became Porpora's valet. He brushed his clothes, combed his wig, submitted to his fits of temper, swallowed his vulgar insults and absorbed his musical knowledge.

It was probably through Porpora that Haydn made another of his lucky acquaintances. This time it was with an Austrian nobleman, Karl Joseph von Fürnberg. The Baron von Fürnberg was passionately fond of chamber music, and he engaged the young virtuoso as a violinist and composer. Under the patronage of this nobleman Haydn composed about eighteen string quartets—an experimental form of composition out of which later grew the structure of his famous symphonies.

Still guided by his lucky star, Haydn advanced from the Baron von Fürnberg to the Count Maximilian von Morzin, and from the Count Maximilian to Prince Esterhazy. With this final promotion (in 1760) the young composer found himself safely launched upon a successful career.

II

THE YEAR 1760 marked the beginning of Haydn's musical felicity—and his marital infelicity. For it was in that year that he acquired both a patron and a wife.

His wife was, so to speak, wished upon him. For some time he had been paying court to the young and attractive daughter of Johann Peter Keller, a wigmaker of Vienna. But when he proposed marriage to her she informed him that she had decided to enter a convent. The father, however, told Haydn not to despair. He had another daughter, old and unattractive, to be sure, but a good match for a musician nonetheless. In a moment of pique at the younger daughter's indifference Haydn accepted the older daughter—to his everlasting regret. Anna Maria Keller would have preferred a shoemaker to a musician for a husband. She might have understood the value of a shoemaker's leather, but she had no conception of the value of a composer's music sheets. Indeed, she frequently cut up his musical compositions into curling papers and pastry forms. And thus the immortality of Haydn's work depended upon the vagaries of a shrewish wife.

Haydn bore the shrewishness of his wife with a shoulder-shrugging resignation. Yet for a time he dreamed of deliverance. He had met a young Italian singer, Luigia Polzelli, who like himself was unhappily married. Haydn and Luigia fell in love with each other, and both expressed the hope that a double accident might leave them free to sanction their love with a legal marriage. Luigia Polzelli's husband died within a short time, and Haydn felt strengthened in his hope. "Dear Polzelli," he wrote, "Perhaps that moment may yet arrive which we have so often desired, when two pairs of eyes will be closed. Here is one pair shut! But what of the other? May it be as God wills!"

But God did not will it. Anna Maria's eyes remained open for a good many years to come. And when at last she died Haydn was sixty-eight and Luigia Polzelli was only forty—hardly the combination for a romantic love affair. Madame Polzelli married another man, and Haydn was left to end his days alone. He had missed his love, but he had found his peace.

[*41*]

III

BUT LET US RETURN to the palace of Esterhazy. When Haydn came to live at this palace it was as a glorified servant. In accordance with his contract he was expected to "know his place, to be quiet, sober and modest toward his superiors, to be always in uniform (as befitted a servant), to compose all the necessary music for His Highness's entertainment, to write nothing for anyone else without His Highness's permission, to obey with the greatest exactitude all the orders he may receive from His Highness and to take his meals with the other domestics."

In return for all this servitude Haydn received one supreme gift—tranquillity. He remained in the employ of the Easterhazys for thirty years—the most momentous and the most inspired period of his life. Prince Esterhazy died in the first year of Haydn's residence at his palace; and the prince's brother, Nicolas the Magnificent, took Haydn over to his own palace, enlarged his orchestra and increased his salary. With his musicians always at hand Haydn was able to test his music as he composed it, pruning it, revising, accepting, rejecting, adapting a passage to this or that instrument and balancing the whole into a perfect and harmonious unit. This was an opportunity which Haydn enjoyed to the full. "I not only had the encouragement of constant approval," he tells us, "but as conductor of the orchestra I could make experiments, observe what produced an effect and what weakened it, and was thus in a position to improve, alter, make additions and omissions and be as bold as I pleased." As for the inferiority of his social position, he accepted it, like the misadventure of his marital state, with a good-natured resignation. "It is indeed sad always to be a slave," he wrote, "but Providence wills it, and so I must bear it." After all, if the Esterhazys enslaved their artists, they were kind to their slaves.

[42]

Kind, but exacting. Nicolas Esterhazy forced Haydn to compose at a furious pace, to "break the legs of time," as he expressed it. He was himself a fairly good performer on the baryton —a musical instrument in which catgut strings and metal strings were set into sympathetic vibration with one another— and he made Haydn write almost two hundred pieces for this instrument. One day Haydn composed a baryton duet—a simple part to suit the limited capacity of the prince and a more difficult solo for the cellist of the palace orchestra, Adam Kraft. When Esterhazy saw the composition he flew into a rage. "In the future," he cried, "all solos for the baryton must be written for me! No man must be shown off as a better player than I!"

Haydn's lot was burdensome but not unhappy. His prominent position at the Esterhazy palace brought him to the attention of many distinguished foreign visitors who spread his music and his fame abroad. In addition to his liberal salary he was able to increase his earnings through private lessons which Esterhazy allowed him to give in his spare time. (One of his pupils was the young Beethoven.) He loved his music, he loved his pranks and, above all, he loved people. He was like a father to the members of his orchestra. Indeed, they affectionately called him "Papa Haydn." He lived simply, walked, fished and hunted for his amusement, sent generous sums of money to his relatives at home, smiled at his wife's vituperations, ducked her blows and composed music that was like the singing of the angels in their playful moments.

Yet his music, with all its playfulness, had something sad in it—the sadness of a voice singing in a gilded cage. For Haydn loved to travel, and his patron refused him even the privilege of a frequent visit to Vienna. It was on the occasion of one of these refusals that Haydn composed his *Farewell Symphony*. The season was late, and the members of the orchestra were homesick for their families. But the prince was stubborn in his determination to keep them at their work in his country palace. He invited his friends for a holiday concert. The last number on the program was this new *Farewell Symphony*. "A symphony in F sharp minor." A strange, surprising key, thought the audience. But they were to be still more surprised before the evening was over. The first Allegro went off without any undue incident. This was followed by the melancholy sweetness of the Adagio, a movement punctuated with the "sad sighs and complaints of mortals chained to their destiny." But the real surprise came in the Finale. A hundred bars of vigorous melody, like an angry protest—and then a sudden stop of all the instruments. When the playing began once more the melody was a muted fragment of the Adagio, distributed into four parts for violins. As the violins softly developed the theme the second horn and the first oboe blew out their candles and tiptoed out of the hall. Then the bassoon tried to join the melody; but after a few notes he gave up the attempt, blew out his candle and followed the others out of the hall. One by one the rest of the players muted their music, extinguished their lights and stole out. And now there are only three left—the first and the second violin, and Haydn. A slender silver rivulet of sound rippling away into the darkness, and Haydn sits alone with his head bent over his desk.

Haydn awaited his prince's reaction not without fear. But Esterhazy had relished the joke no less than the music. He told Haydn that the meaning of the symphony was quite clear to him and that they might all start on their vacation the next day.

His infrequent vacations at Vienna were like journeys to Paradise—days of good food, good music and good fellowship. Upon his return to Esterhaz from one of these vacations he wrote to a dear Viennese friend, "the noble, esteemed, and excellent Frau von Grenziger," a letter in which he regretfully compared his monotonous life at Esterhaz with the diversified pleasures of Vienna. "Here I am again in solitude—abandoned —like a poor orphan—almost without human companionship —sad—filled with the memory of happy days gone by . . . And who knows when these pleasant days will return? That happy company, a whole circle of friends united in heart and soul, all those delightful musical evenings . . . where are they now? They are past, and it will be long before they come again . . . Upon my return to Esterhaz, I found everything upside down . . . I could scarcely sleep . . . The wretched north wind woke me and nearly tore my nightcap from my head. In three days I lost twenty pounds in weight, for the excellent Viennese food is far away . . . Ah, if I only had now some of the delicacies of Vienna . . . that delicious soft beef instead of this slice of cow half a century old, those sweet pastries instead of these dried up apples and nuts . . . Here, at Esterhaz, nobody asks me, 'Will you have your chocolate with or without milk?' 'Do you prefer your coffee black or with cream?' 'What can I offer you, my dear Haydn? Will you have a vanilla or a pineapple ice?' . . . If I only had a bit of good Parmesan cheese . . . to help down the macaroni and spaghetti! . . ."

But these were only passing moods, like bits of clouds that sail over a smiling brook. The song in his heart kept rippling incessantly on, in music brilliant as the dancing of a sunbeam reflected from a mirror wielded by the hand of a mischievous boy. Always he catches us unawares with the sudden outburst of laughter, the puckish twinkling of the eye, the unexpected turn of the phrase, the echo of the hunting field, the imitation of the bear dance, the gossip of the birds. He sets the Ten Command-ments to music, and for the Sixth Commandment, *Thou shalt not steal*, he deliberately purloins a theme from Martini. He composes a *Children's Symphony*, and he introduces into it all sorts of toy instruments. He sits at his little square piano, composing his *Symphony in G major* (the "Surprise" Symphony). Suddenly his face lights up as he introduces an explosive fortissimo on the kettledrum in the midst of a subdued passage. "This will make the ladies jump!" he cries to his friend Gyrowetz, who happens to be present at the moment.

[45]

A playful child, a *devout* child. His music is a hymn to a generous Providence—a song bubbling up from a contented soul. "Since God has given me a joyful heart," he said, "He will forgive me for having served Him joyfully."

IV

HAYDN has been called the Father of the Symphony. This is not altogether correct. The father of a child is himself the child of a father. This is as true in the artistic as in the physical world. Haydn did not originate the symphony. The structure of the symphony is a natural development from that of the quartet. As early as 1744, when Haydn was only twelve years old, the symphonic form was already well known in Paris. In the following year the symphony was regarded in Germany as an established type of musical composition. At that time it consisted of three movements. The introduction of the minuet as a fourth movement followed only a few years later. When Haydn reached his maturity there were already hundreds of symphonies known in the leading musical centers of Europe. What Haydn did, therefore, was not to invent a new form of music but to bring an older and cruder form to a new high level of beauty. "His predecessors," writes Sir Hubert Parry, "had always written (their symphonies) rather carelessly and hastily. But Haydn . . . applied his mind more earnestly to the matter in hand and found out new ways of contrasting and combining the tones of different members of his orchestra and getting a fuller and richer effect out of the mass of them when they were all playing." Yet even the advanced symphonies of Haydn, as compared with the later elaborations of Mozart and of Beethoven, are modest little nosegays of melody, simple bits of native folk songs woven into garlands of imperishable fragrance.

If Haydn wasn't the Father of the Symphony, he was the godfather to the music of Mozart. Almost from childhood Mozart was an ardent admirer of "Papa Haydn." He played on several occasions at Esterhazy's musical evenings. He dedicated to Haydn a group of his earliest compositions. As for Haydn, he regarded Mozart with a truly parental solicitude. Indeed, he was one of the few contemporaries of Mozart who recognized the greatness of his genius. "I only wish," he wrote in one of his letters, "that I could impress upon every friend of mine, and upon the critics in particular, the same deep sympathy and profound appreciation which I myself feel for Mozart's inimitable music . . . The nations ought to vie with one another to possess such a jewel within their frontiers. It enrages me to think that the unparalleled Mozart is not yet engaged at any imperial court! Pardon my excitement; I love the man so dearly." When, in the springtime of his genius, Mozart was thrown with a number of paupers into an unmarked grave Haydn's grief was inconsolable. "Forgive me," he said to his friends. "I can't hold back my tears at the thought of my Mozart." As Mozart in his youth had composed under the influence of Haydn, Haydn in his old age began to compose under the influence of Mozart.

V

EVERY MORNING, before he sat down to work, Haydn prayed to God to give him talent for that day. If his work went well, he believed that God had listened to his prayer; if not, he smilingly remarked that God had punished him for his sins. He would have been happy to spend the rest of his days in this tranquil contentment, serving the Lord and pleasing his prince. But just as his old age was coming upon him he lost his position through the death of Esterhazy (September 28, 1790). Fortunately the prince had willed him a pension of a thousand gulden (about five hundred dollars) a year. He paid two visits to London, where he received the acclamations of the multitude and an honorary degree from Oxford—distinctions which might have been more palatable in the days of his stronger appetites but for which he was humbly grateful even at this late period of his life. And then, at the age of sixty-six, he composed his masterpiece, *The Creation*.

This oratorio, based upon Milton's *Paradise Lost*, is "half religious and half descriptive." It begins with a picture of chaos—a welter of discords, incomplete phrases, crashing dissonances, uncertainty, suspense. And then—a sudden harmonious blending of all the instruments and voices announcing the birth of the universe: "And then there was light!"

This is followed by a series of recitatives and choruses depicting the creation of the sun, the moon, the stars, the division between the day and the night, the unrolling of the heavens and the shaping of the earth, the birth of the flowers and the fishes and the insects and the birds and the beasts, and the magnificent Alleluia of the angels as they behold the earth and the heavens proclaiming the glory of God.

And then comes the creation of Man, and the song of Man—softer and sadder and tenderer, but no less beautiful than the song of the angels. The song of Man, the mortal echo of the immortal song of God.

VI

ON HAYDN's seventy-sixth birthday his friends arranged for him the pleasure of a final triumph. They took him in a wheel chair to a special performance of his *Creation*. Among those present was his now famous pupil, Beethoven. As Haydn entered the hall the entire audience rose to their feet. When the chorus reached that radiant passage, "And then there was light," the multitude burst into deafening applause. Haydn, overcome, rose to his feet and exclaimed: "Not I, but a Power from above created that." As he was being wheeled out of the hall at the end of the concert Beethoven bent down and kissed his hand.

His long, peaceful life was almost ended. But he was not allowed to die in peace. The fates had prepared for him a Surprise Symphony of their own, with the sudden crash of the cannon to break in upon the tranquillity of his old age. On May 10, 1809, the invading army of Napoleon had arrived at the gates of Vienna. In the course of the bombardment one of the cannon balls fell close to Haydn's house.

This was near the finale of the last movement of the symphony. Immediately after the bombardment Haydn took to his bed. Three weeks later it was over. "This miserable war," he said on his deathbed, "has been the end of me."

MOZART

Great Compositions by Mozart

VOCAL:

15 Masses.

Requiem (completed by his pupil Süssmayr).

Several Cantatas, including *Davidde Penitente, Maurer-Freude*, etc.

Operas, including *Don Giovanni, Cosi Fan Tutte, The Marriage of Figaro, Idomeneo, La Finta Giardiniera, The Magic Flute, The Abduction from the Seraglio.*

Various Arias, Songs, Canons, etc.

INSTRUMENTAL:

41 Symphonies, including the *Jupiter Symphony*, the *Haffner Symphony*, the *Prague Symphony*, the *Symphony in G minor*.

9 Marches, 25 Dances, 31 Serenades.

6 Concertos for the violin.

25 Concertos for the piano.

Various Concertos for the flute, the harp, the horn, the clarinet.

About 25 String Quartets.

Eine Kleine Nachtmusik.

Fantasies, Fugues, Variations, Minuets, Rondos, etc.

Mozart

Wolfgang Amadeus Mozart

1756–1791

MELODY is the essence of music." It is a fine charger gallop-
ing over the highways of sound. Anything else is just an old
plodding hack horse compared to her. The tune's the thing.
You do not learn a tune, you feel it. Bother learning! "*Chi sa
più, meno sa.*" Who knows most, knows least. "Come," said Papa
Mozart, "let us whistle a tune!"

Papa Leopold Mozart was official musician to the Archbishop
of Salzburg. Mama Mozart was the handsomest lady in town.
Little Wolfgang played the piano with genius. He loved the
tones of his "butter violin." People declared that the ears of this
child were magically sensitive. Before he could read he was able
to tell the pitch of an instrument to the eighth of a tone. What
large animated eyes! Almost too large for his face. "And tell us,
Papa Leopold," asked the people of Salzburg, "what do those
eyes see?" There is the light of genius in them. Musical genius.
They seem to say, "I cannot write poems. I cannot draw pictures. But I can make music, Papa Leopold. I am a born musician."

A strange little fellow, Wolfgang. Threw his arms around his

[*53*]

father and his mother and asked them a hundred times a day whether they still loved him. And when the father jestingly answered in the negative the little fellow's eyes glistened with tears. The lips quivered. What can you do with a child like that? Bandage his heart? Why, the sound of a trumpet would send him into a spasm of pain.

The world will go hard with this young man. But bother the world! Why waste time in mourning? Wolfgang is a child of genius. Let him make the most of it.

II

AT FIVE Mozart wrote a piano concerto that was too difficult for anyone to play. An amazing gift! Take the child on a tour through the grand courts of Europe. And take his little sister along. For she, too, is a child of genius. Much money will flow into your pockets, guldens and louis d'or and florins and ducats. Exploit the infants. People will go wild over the little mites and lavish them with bonbons and kisses. Papa Leopold saw to that. He took them to Munich to play before Maria Theresa, the Austrian queen. Then to Heidelberg, where Wolfgang's little fingers flew over the keyboard of the organ with such speed as to rob the audience of its breath. He took them to Frankfort to meet the great poet, Goethe, and then to France to amuse the entourage of Madame Pompadour. To London, to Holland. A journey of genius, kisses from empresses, bravos from kings. Mozart was the ninth wonder of the world! The "London Bach," son of the great Sebastian, said that many a court musician knew less music at the end of his career than Mozart knew at the beginning. What a large curly head! It seemed too large for his small body. And too wise, whispered the more discerning friends of the Mozart family. So brilliant a flame would all too quickly burn out the fuel of his delicate little body.

As the boy grew older he went to Italy, the land of sparkling

melodies, spirited arias, soft skies. This was a perfect country
for the development of Wolfgang's talent. *Per Die,* but it was the
home of music makers! He would write operas for the fat prima
donnas with the tinkling voices. He would pack the theaters
with his melodies and make his fame and fortune to the cheers
of the whole world. And all that when he was scarcely in his
teens! Was he too young for such dreams? Not at all. Operas were
not hard to write. Not when you had already conducted a solemn
mass in public though you were too small to be seen by most of
the congregation. Why, the writing of an opera was nothing to a
boy with such a genius. And such a memory! The notes of the
sacred *Miserere* as sung at St Peter's had never been written
down in score. That was forbidden. But the boy was so impressed with the music after he had once heard it that he wrote
the entire score down from memory. And the Pope, who was
blessed with a sense of humor, made him a member of the order
of The Golden Spurs, though he was scarcely fourteen. Henceforth he was known as "the Chevalier Mozart." And the Philharmonic Society in Bologna extended their membership to
him. After such recognition what was the writing of a mere
opera?

He wrote his opera on the subject of King Mithridates. It was
an instant success. "Long live the Little Maestro!" cheered the
spectators and stamped their feet. One of the critics wrote:
"The young Kapellmeister studies the beautiful in nature, and
then gives us back this beauty adorned with the rarest musical
grace." And the established composers grumbled into their
beards, "This young upstart musician will send us all into
oblivion!"

III

IT IS A SAD STORY when fame comes too early in life. As you grow
older the world has ceased to look upon you as a wonder child;
the bravos of the public have long since grown indistinct. There

was now a beard upon young Mozart's chin. He was a full-grown and a much more self-conscious artist. He had spent long, hard years of study since the miraculous dawn of his genius. "I assure you, dear friends, that no one has given so much care to the technique of composition as I. There is not a great master whose works I have not frequently and diligently studied."

And now that he had grown to be a man he realized how little do men appreciate one another. His day as a glamour child was forgotten. Employed now as concertmaster to the archbishop of his native town at twenty-five marks a month, he was dreadfully unhappy in his environment. The archbishop looked down upon him because of his youth. He had no faith in his musicianship. The fact that Mozart had missed the formal training of the conservatory was sufficient to discredit him in His Excellency's eyes. Repeatedly the archbishop told Mozart to go somewhere and "really learn music." Humiliated, Mozart determined to leave Salzburg and look for other employment. He who had written operas at fifteen and had been the toast of the world would surely be recognized again.

His father was more practical and more pessimistic. With moist eyes he gave his hand in farewell. "Cling to God, Wolfgang," he said; "you will learn bitter truths about men."

And indeed, Mozart was destined to be disillusioned from the very start. He went to Munich where as a child he had played before the Elector. At that time the great man had embraced him and thanked God for his genius. But now that Mozart looked for actual employment the Elector was cold. There was no vacancy, he maintained. Perhaps after Mozart spent a few years of study at the conservatory . . .

The young man went to Augsburg. Why didn't his masters invite the greatest talents in Italy, Germany, France, Spain and England to compete with him in any form of music? There was nothing he couldn't do. Why, he could furnish more thrills than

[56]

a magician if that was what people were after. Give him a theme in G minor, and he would improvise a fugue on the clavichord in the major key in a dozen different tempos, and then he would play the theme backwards in a serenade. That should certainly earn him the admiration of people who had jobs at their disposal. Or else, why not give music lessons? Really, now, wouldn't a thousand young ladies flock to him, fascinated by his gray-blue eyes and his waving hair? And in the intermission between lessons he would whirl each one around in his exquisite dancing. "Yes, I'll give lessons and become rich . . . But really a million other people are better suited for that. I am a composer and I have been born to be a Kapellmeister." He dare not bury the talents that God had given him.

But wait, a wealthy count has an offer for him. He urges Mozart to come to Munich and to write a German opera. This may bring to birth a national theater. Mozart is enthusiastic at the prospect. He will write four operas a year and he will receive a profit of several hundred dollars!

He was happy, for a while. But the count was unable to get together enough people to collaborate with him and the project fell through.

And so he resorted to music lessons. His stay in Augsburg, apart from his financial worries, was not unpleasant. For a naughty and winsome little cousin of his with a robust appetite for love kept him contented for a while. And when he left for Mannheim he carried away with him the memories of many a delightful caress.

And caresses were his only solace for poverty in Mannheim too. Mannheim, in the land of the soft south winds. The very air was melody and life—a wild pizzicato rhythm. Here he soon forgot his little cousin in the blandishments of his pupils—a swarm of free-loving girls attracted to him by the magic of his music. And one of them he singled out for his own—Rosa Cannbich, the daughter of the Kapellmeister. He knelt in adoration

[57]

at her feet. He wrote andantes to fit her moods. She was a goddess whispering him into the heavens of delight. But he was far too restless to remain long at her side. For there was someone else beckoning to him—Aloysia Weber, with the golden voice. All thoughts of Rosa left him when he saw Aloysia Weber.

The Webers were poor in the goods of the world. But they were rich in their love for music. Aloysia was studying for the opera. And Mozart bound her to his heart with an aria he dedicated to her. He hadn't a single quiet hour. Thoughts of Aloysia would not let him rest. Aloysia was planning to further her career by going to Italy. And he was ready to follow her and to "die at her side," if necessary. He would write her "a million operas" and sit entranced at her feet as she sang his songs.

He was rudely awakened from his fancies by Papa Mozart. What, follow that chit of a girl to Italy and serve her like a lackey? He had better attend to his own musical future! Italy was a dilettante's nonsense. Would he marry this Weber girl and die of poverty in a room full of suffering children? No, he must remain single and go to study in Paris. And during the period of his study he could give music lessons for a living. How could a giddy young girl hope to become successful in Italy in competition with the world's great prima donnas? *Narrischer Knabe,* foolish boy! You are far too ready to succumb to every attraction that throws itself as an obstacle in your path. Yield your body to the moment's pleasure if you must, but don't sell your soul into eternal bondage! No, you will go to Paris. And with your mother. For you are utterly incapable of getting along without her help. You don't understand the value of money. You don't even know how to pack your clothes properly.

Mozart listened to his father. "After God comes Papa," was his motto. He parted from Aloysia and went to Paris with his mother. And yet, "giving music lessons here is no fun," he wrote to his father. "It goes counter to my genius." You teach stupid young ladies to compose. They don't want to write operas or arias or symphonies. Merely sonatas for the piano. They can write a bass accompaniment to a minuet, but genuine melody not at all. They have no real talent, no musical ideas. They must be taught artificially. There are no results. You write a theme and beg them to make a variation on it. They enter upon mountains of labor and give birth to a little mouse. "All the Parisians are stupid and superficial when it comes to music." They show off at the pianoforte by playing so rapidly that they miss notes in every passage. And their audiences never notice the omissions. "At such speed you can use the hands indiscriminately. But you ask yourself—is that beautiful? The true art of sight reading consists in giving expression to every note tastefully and accurately, so as to create the impression that the player had composed the piece." *Parbleu!* If it were not for his flirtations and an occasional game of billiards, he might have died of boredom in this "City of Asses"!

His flirtations and his billiards and his music. He had begun to work on his symphonies, and to tell the truth he didn't know whether they pleased anybody. Whom should they please? Those French asses? He didn't much care. The sooner he could get away from Paris, the better he would like it.

And then two events occurred to bring his stay in Paris to an end. His mother died, and a vacancy arose in the position of Kapellmeister at Salzburg. His father urged him to accept the position; and Mozart, eager to be rid of Paris, jumped from the frying pan into the fire. He returned to the service of the archbishop. What a horrible place for a young artist! Paris with all its faults was heaven compared to Salzburg. Those Salzburgers were clodhoppers with deaf ears. "If we only had woodwinds in the town orchestra! You have no idea what a wonderful effect can be accomplished in a symphony scored for flutes and oboes and clarinets, as well as for strings. Our music would be so much more beautiful if only my townsmen would add these woodwind sections." But his townsmen care neither for wood-winds nor for violins nor for any other musical instruments.

Ah, but Munich and its people were different. They under-stood. Wolfgang was saved from his boredom at Salzburg by receiving a commission to write an opera. The Elector had un-bended at last. Mozart left for Munich and started on his opera, *Idomeneo*.

It was a work based upon an old legend of Crete. He wrote enthusiastic letters home to his father about the "superiority" of this music. His father, with the experience of his older years, replied that Wolfgang had better stop dreaming. "A plague upon superiority, my son. Write something popular instead. Think not only of the music lovers, but also of the unmusical public."

But Wolfgang was cocksure of himself. "Never you fear," he wrote to his father. "There is music in my opera for all sorts of people." The work was *bound* to be a success. "There is a fever in the poor boy's head. A youngster gets easily overheated when honor or fame is at stake! Careful, son, do not catch cold."

The opera was unsuccessful. Mozart was obliged to go back to Salzburg and to the service of Archbishop Hieronymus. It was a bitter pill to swallow. He wouldn't hesitate a moment to cast his job to the winds if it weren't for the fact that he wanted to please his father. There was a mutual and cordial dislike be-tween the archbishop and himself. He couldn't give concerts of his own, for the archbishop was jealous of his success. Every honor he received from the outside world was the occasion for a rebuke from Hieronymus. He had many better musicians at court than Mozart, he said. "What an impudence for this low fellow to demand independence for his silly compositions and his musical soirees!" Let the young man know his place—at the lower table together with the other "temporal and spiritual valets." At this table the young musician at least had the honor of sitting above the cooks.

But suddenly all this was changed—by the thrust of an aristo-cratic boot. One day a nobleman high in the service of the archbishop flew into a rage against the gentle composer and translated his temper into a vigorous kick. Down the stairs toppled Mozart and out into the world again.

IV

He journeyed to vienna. He was now twenty-five, a man of full-grown genius and cynical disgust. His face was thinner and there was little of laughter in his eyes. But with all that, he still clung to his undying faith in his own destiny. He was still young. He wrote popular music. Eventually he *must* be recognized, in spite of all his disappointments.

And now at last there was one person who was willing to share his disappointments and his faith. "Who is this latest object of my love?" he wrote his father. "Not Aloysia Weber. She has gone on her way to Italy. Surely it is not one of her sisters? Yes, Father, it *is* one of them. Pray do not be horrified. She is the middle sister, Konstanze." Unlike Aloysia, she was far from beautiful. But she had two piercing eyes, a trim figure, a good, solid soul. She hardly understood music, but she adored Mozart. To avoid family interference the couple eloped. And as if inspired by the moment, Mozart wrote an opera entitled *The Elopement from the Seraglio.*

And then the things for which he had yearned came quickly within his reach. Recognition, adulation, fame. The public went wild with acclamation over this "opera of the harem." "They're literally daft about it," he wrote to his father. Daft indeed! For Mozart received a wealth of ovations—and no money. There were no royalty laws in those days. The theater manager kept all the profits. Unless a composer was extremely businesslike he was allowed to remain honored and hungry to the end of his days. The world worshiped its gods and refused to feed them. Such was the fate of Mozart, the starving Apollo of the new German opera.

He now followed up the "success" of his first opera with a similar "success." It was *The Marriage of Figaro*, based upon the story of *The Barber of Seville*. In Prague the audience gave the composer an ovation he never forgot. "The people hop about delightedly to the music of my *Figaro* which has been turned into *contra-dances* and *allemands*. Here nothing is talked about except *Figaro;* nothing played, piped, sung or whistled except *Figaro;* no opera is attended except *Figaro*. Always *Figaro*."

And Mozart danced too, but not for pleasure. A friend who called on him one morning found him waltzing madly around the room. "You see," he said with a sheepish smile, "this is an economic way to keep warm. It is bitter cold and we have no fuel."

Poverty was not the only obstacle against which Mozart was obliged to contend. The jealous musicians of Vienna began to bombard him with the poisoned arrows of vituperation. They entered upon a concerted attempt to poison the mind of the emperor against him. "My dear Mozart," said the emperor, "your music has too many notes." Whereupon Mozart retorted, "Just as many notes as are necessary, Your Majesty."

Yet Mozart was too poor a politician and too honest a man to cope successfully with this undercover attack of his enemies. Instead he turned the bitterness of his heart into the tragedy of music. And he wrote his finest opera to date, *Don Giovanni*. It is the story of Don Juan, the young gallant who is the hero of a thousand amorous adventures. And in this one adventure he becomes the villain. In order to facilitate his elopement with a girl he loves he murders her father. Soon he abandons her and seeks for new conquests. But he cannot escape the consequences of his act. The past catches up with him. The man he has murdered stalks out of his grave and summons the adventurer to his doom. Such is the tragedy of a lover. And the composer, too, was a lover who had met tragedy—a man who, though he had inflicted injury upon no one, was yet marching steadily to his doom. His music, always sweet, was never filled with a more tragic sweetness than now. The white purity of sound can be as ghastly as it is gentle. White roses are never so sadly beautiful as when they surround death. *Don Giovanni* is an opera of death and the night. The magic of the moonlight over a cypress grove —such is the haunting spell of this music.

At the production of *Don Giovanni* the orchestra greeted the arrival of the composer with a flourish of trumpets as though he were the emperor himself. The crowd shouted, "Long live Mozart!" He smiled to himself as he acknowledged the applause. "What they really mean to say," he reflected bitterly, "is— 'Long *starve* Mozart!' "

His fame was now at its height. Even the emperor had given way at last before the tremendous success of this opera. He held out the hand of friendship to Mozart and actually offered him a small position at court. But in deference to the wishes of his other musicians he took care that the position entailed neither great responsibility nor much prestige. Nominally Mozart was appointed to the post that Gluck had occupied before his death. Actually he was given a secondary job at one third the regular salary.

His heart was broken. He knew full well that the emperor had adopted him as a charity case in order to save his own face before the public. And Mozart was compelled to swallow his pride and to accept his charity. A few of the finer spirits protested against this outrage. Many miles away, in the little town of Salzburg, an aged man had walked with trembling steps up to Papa Mozart and had whispered with tears in his eyes, "I swear before God, I swear it on my honor, your son is the greatest composer that has ever lived!" But the words of this little man carried no weight in the world. For he was no emperor or wealthy prelate—he was merely Joseph Haydn, a fellow servant with Mozart in the eyes of men.

V

THERE WAS WINTER in Mozart's heart. He was given his meager salary and told to keep his place. His new "position" was a cruel blow. The only thing that kept him going was his self-respect.

Before long, however, he lost even this humiliating post at the court. The emperor died, and Mozart was left once more to his "sonatas and his self-respect."

"I could go around Vienna looking like a tramp," he wrote to his father, "but I must not. My linen is pitiable. No servant has shirts of such coarse stuff as mine—and certainly that is a frightful thing for a man with pride." Well, he can go back to his music lessons. "At present I have only one pupil." He might get several more if he were willing to lower his price. But this would lower his reputation too. He refused to surrender his reputation. "My price is six ducats for twelve lessons; and I make it clear besides that I give the lessons at that price as a favor. You must not throw yourself away—that is the first principle—or you are ruined forever."

He walked around as if in a bad dream. He had a curious way of putting his fingers to his lips to hush everybody who came to his house. For his wife was ill and no one must raise his voice to disturb her from her sleep.

Most of the day he sat by her bedside and composed his music, ever on the alert for the slightest stir. Watching over his wife didn't interrupt the flow of his music. He could compose anywhere. Before he put down a single note he had the completed score mapped out in his head. Had he not transcribed the entire overture of *Don Giovanni* from memory the evening before the production of the opera, writing down the music while his wife told him amusing little fairy tales such as *Aladdin's Lamp* and *Cinderella*. And how many unwritten symphonies and overtures he had created and filed away in his mind for his own pleasure—notes he would never transcribe for a misunderstanding world! Every morning he arose from the side of his ailing wife and went for a short ride on horseback, for his own strength was failing and the doctors had advised this means for taking the air. But before he left he would pin a note to her pillow: "Good morning, dear little wife. I hope you have slept well and have not been disturbed. Take care not to catch cold. . . . I will not be long away; I will be back punctually."

His wife recovered, but she was very weak. He was desperate for money. He begged Leopold, the new emperor, to hire him as the instructor of the royal children, "because of the little fame the world has accorded me for my skill at the piano." He did not even receive the courtesy of an answer. He resorted with new vigor to his music lessons. "I now have two scholars," he wrote to a friend. "I would like to bring the number up to eight." And he added humbly, "Try to spread it abroad that I am giving lessons, will you, please?"

When he heard that the emperor was about to travel to Frankfort for his coronation he determined to make the trip and to play before the crowds "for a few gulden." As only the court musicians were allowed to ride in the emperor's train without charge, Mozart was forced to defray the expenses of the journey by pawning his silverware. The hotel and the food bills exhausted his money, and at the end of his stay in Frankfort he found his purse empty. He mortgaged himself to a money-lender for a thousand florins. From Frankfort he went to Mainz, but he had no better luck. He borrowed more money. He wrote very frankly to his wife about these transactions. ". . . Once more, you see, I am destitute . . . I have wept a good deal while writing you this long letter . . . But now I snap my fingers at sorrow. Hold up your hands, little wife—around your head innumerable kisses are flying." Was it unbusinesslike for him to deliver himself to moneylenders? Years ago his father had upbraided him for his poor business head. "How could I learn to value money? I have never had enough of it in my hands . . . Ah, my best and dearest little wife, you'll see. I'll fool them yet!" What a playful, thoughtful, impractical, tender little child of a husband! "If I were to tell you all the things I do with your portrait, my sweetest wife, you would laugh heartily. For instance, when I take it out of its prison house I say, 'God bless you, Stanzerl, God bless you, little rascal—*Krallerballer*—Sharpnose—little Bagatelle!' And when I put it back I let it slip down slowly . . . and say, 'Nu-Nu-Nu-Nu . . . good night, little mouse, sleep well!' Dear little wife, I have a multitude of requests. First, I beg of you not to be sad; second, that you take care of your health and do not trust the spring air. . . ."

Soon he was back in Vienna. He wrote to the city magistrates requesting them, inasmuch as "my talents as a musician and my works are known abroad and my name is held in certain esteem," to appoint him as the "humble assistant to the Kapellmeister Hoffman of St Stephen's Church." The magistrates were overwhelmed with this modest petition. They appointed Mozart to the post immediately—as an honorary employee without a salary!

He was slowly breaking down. His mind became haunted with somber visions. Thoughts of death obsessed him. "Death is the only worthwhile goal of life. It is a real and devoted friend." He joined the Free Masons not only for their humanitarian ideals of self-sacrifice but also for their unyielding faith in the sanctity of death.

Many of the noblest spirits in Germany had joined the Masons. And a few of the lesser nobility in character had joined also, but for less spiritual reasons. One of these "lesser souls" was a theater manager by the name of Schikaneder. Bankrupt in finances but not in ideas, this man appealed to Mozart in the name of their sacred brotherhood to compose the music to the libretto of a "magic opera" which he had just written. Mozart was dubious. "I have never yet composed a magic opera. If we are unsuccessful in the matter . . ." "Don't worry," beamed the great showman, "we won't be unsuccessful." Schikaneder was the P. T. Barnum of Vienna. His ambition was bounded only by the stars. To make sure that Mozart wouldn't "loaf" on the job he built him a pavilion on the theater lawn and directed that the composer live there until he had finished the score. He filled Mozart's head with wine and stuffed his ears with flattery. "Yes, my friend, you will achieve success at last after a lifetime of patient suffering. This is a fairy opera, *The Magic Flute*, and it deals with the ravishing Queen of the Night. The strange, mystic night that snuffs out the glare of the sunlight and stills the fever of the day. It alights in a soft swirling rain of whispers —whispers and dreams. It lifts the nodding head from the flat pillow of mortality, into the vision of the infinite. No more pain for you, my friend . . . Why tremble at the night? Come, Mozart, you of all people should not fear it. Compose your music for the night. Weave its shadows into your tonal witchery. Come, come, my friend, you *are* the night!"

And Mozart, bewitched by the flattery of Schikaneder and imprisoned in his pavilion, poured out his ebbing strength into the music of *The Magic Flute*.

VI

A STRANGER dressed in somber colors appeared before Mozart and handed him a sealed commission. He was to compose a *Requiem*—a mass for the dead. To whom was he indebted for the commission? This the stranger refused to divulge. As a matter of fact, a wealthy amateur musician, a vainglorious nobleman who was in the habit of ordering great composers to write music which he signed with his own name, had sent this servant to put Mozart to work on a mass for his deceased wife. But he didn't care to disclose his identity. Mozart was curious indeed. For whom was the mass to be written? To this question there was no answer, although the servant in gray appeared periodically and commanded him in deep mysterious tones to get on with this work for the dead. However, Mozart neglected the *Requiem* during the months that he was engaged on the score of *The Magic Flute.*

The opera was finished. It became an instant success. And while Mozart worked at the *Requiem* with a religious fervor, *The Magic Flute* played to crowded houses for two hundred successive performances—a record that far eclipsed anything else in the history of entertainment up to that time. But the receipts of this huge success never came to Mozart. Every cent had found its way into the pockets of the crafty Schikaneder who, as a result of his success in this venture, erected a statue in his own honor and beamed patronizingly upon Mozart who had "merely assisted him" with his music.

But what did it matter? The strength of Mozart had given out. Silent he sat with a cloud in his eye and wrote the notes for his *Requiem.* No longer could he cut his meat at table with his own hand. No longer was he concerned when his wife reminded him that the musical world had finally acknowledged a great composer in their midst and that comfort and security were on the verge of coming his way at last. The nobility of Hungary had sent him an offer of a yearly pension amounting to a thousand florins. Wealthy circles in England had officially requested that he make his home there. A similar offer had come from the people of Holland. But what did all this matter now?

Now he must go, when success was assured him. At last he had learned the identity of the person for whom he was composing his *Requiem.* The answer had come to him in the night. *"I am composing it for myself!"* What need to listen to the applause of the living when already ringing in his ears was the applause of the hosts of the dead? They were cheering him on with ghostly whispers. "Bravo, Maestro! Viva il Maestrino!" They were clapping their skeleton hands and calling for an encore. "Encore!"

He lay pale. It was the paleness not of sorrow but of peace. A fever had extinguished his life at thirty-five. The *Requiem* was unfinished. He left behind him thirty-eight dollars' worth of worldly goods.

A wealthy friend promised to finance the funeral. He was a great admirer of music, this friend, but he wasn't anxious for an expensive burial. Something more modest, a pauper's grave. A handful of people set out to escort the body on its last journey. Blasts of cold wind struck the faces of the little party. Then the heavens burst with rain. One by one the mourners turned up their collars, pulled down their hats and stole off to the warmth of their fireplaces. When the body reached the cemetery gates the gravediggers were the only living people present.

Konstanze had been placed under a doctor's care. A few days after the funeral she stole away to the cemetery. With feeble steps she sought her husband's grave. But she found no sign. She stumbled upon the hut of the caretaker. "Can you tell me, sir," she asked in a trembling voice, "where they have buried my husband? His name was Mozart."

"Mozart?" repeated the caretaker. "I have never heard of him."

BEETHOVEN

Great Compositions by Beethoven

VOCAL:

Mass in C.

Mass in D (*Missa Solemnis*).

10 Cantatas.

Opera, *Fidelio.*

Over 250 Songs, including *An die Hoffnung, An die Ferne Geliebte, Adelaide, In Questa Tomba.*

Oratorio, *Christ on the Mount of Olives.*

INSTRUMENTAL:

9 Symphonies, in the following keys: C, D, E flat (*Eroica*), B flat, C minor, F (*Pastoral*), A, F, D minor (*Choral*, so called because the fourth movement of this *Ninth Symphony* contains a choral passage).

Overtures to *Egmont, Coriolanus, Fidelio, King Stephen, Ruins of Athens, Leonore* (1–4).

5 Concertos for the piano.

Concerto for the violin.

16 Quartets for strings.

Sextet for strings and winds.

13 trios.

About 50 Sonatas and over 100 smaller pieces.

Beethoven

Ludwig Van Beethoven

1770–1827

Bᴀᴄʜ was the mathematician of music; Mozart, the poet; Beethoven, the philosopher. In the garden of the human mind the seed of philosophy is the last to come to full flower.

Beethoven was no child prodigy. Nor was he precocious even as a young man. He made little impression upon his teachers. "Beethoven," said Albrechtsberger, who was trying to teach him composition, "never has learned anything and never will learn anything. As a composer he is hopeless." Even Haydn, who taught Beethoven harmony for a time, was unable to recognize the latent genius of this young Philistine who refused to clip his wings to his master's dainty little flights of lyrical sweetness. Beethoven's imagination dwelt in heights above the vision of his masters. But as yet it had not found a familiar home there. It was not until his thirtieth year (in 1800) that he composed his *First Symphony*.

Yet as a pianist he showed early promise. His short, stubby fingers were able to play magic with the keyboard. His father, the Kapellmeister at the court of the Elector at Bonn, began to teach him both clavier and violin in his fourth year. Shiftless, improvident and poor, Johann van Beethoven was anxious to raise his talented child as an assistant breadwinner. And Ludwig was expert enough to play in public at seven. At thirteen he began to contribute to the family income through his appointment as the assistant court organist. Four years later he spent a short time in Vienna, where he took a few lessons under Mozart. His mother's illness, however, recalled him to Bonn. Shortly after his return his mother died of tuberculosis, and for a time he feared that he, too, was threatened with this disease.

His father in the meantime had given way to drink, and Ludwig was obliged to take upon his shoulders the entire support of the family. In addition to the father there were two younger brothers—Caspar Anton Carl and Nikolaus Johann. It was no easy task for Ludwig to attend to the petty details of the household. For great thoughts were beginning to stir within him. Disgusted with his lot and anxious about his health, he became bitter, sarcastic, morose. He acted toward his friends like a caged young lion—hair disheveled, eyes scowling, lips tightly pressed together, conversation reduced to a growl. Hardly a pleasant companion for the members of the theater orchestra at Bonn, where Beethoven played viola. They called him "the mad Spaniard," because of his swarthy complexion and his black temper. (There may possibly have been a strain of Spanish blood in him, since the Beethovens on the male side were Belgians and the Spaniards had occupied Belgium in the seventeenth century.)

He was subject to wild fits of rage and equally wild outbursts of remorse. "Dearest! Best!" he wrote to his friend Dr Wegeler, after one of his volcanic eruptions. "In what an odious light you have exhibited me to myself! I acknowledge it, I do not deserve your friendship . . . but, thank heaven, it was no intentional or deliberate malice which induced me to act as I did towards you. It was my inexcusable thoughtlessness which prevented me from seeing the matter in its true light. . . . Ah, Wegeler,

[74]

do not reject this hand of reconciliation . . . I am coming to throw myself into your arms. . . . Pray give yourself back to me, your penitent, loving, never-forgetting friend."

He had a knack of making friends in spite of his fiery temper and his caustic tongue. People admired his genuine, untamed, rebellious spirit, his utter disregard of the niceties in the presence of the realities of life. He was strangely out of place in the drawing room, yet he completely dominated it. There was a powerful fascination in his stumpy, uncouth, athletic figure and his stubborn, assertive, uncompromising mind. "I am glad," said a friend after Beethoven's visit to the court, "that you knew the proper etiquette in the presence of the nobility." Whereupon Beethoven retorted, "You ought to be glad that the nobility knew the proper etiquette in the presence of genius."

II

AT THE AGE OF TWENTY-TWO he settled permanently in Vienna. He was now able to stand on his own feet—or, to use a more appropriate metaphor, to lean on his own hands. For those hands of his were blessed with a power and technique possessed by few of his contemporary rivals. His skill at the piano attracted to him the friendship of Prince Carl Lichnowsky, a member of the Austrian aristocracy and a passionate devotee of music. The prince and his wife took Beethoven into their home, they gave him a pension of six hundred florins (about three hundred dollars) a year and they introduced him to the most exclusive social circles of Vienna.

For a time Beethoven tried to assume the role of the gay cavalier. He even permitted himself the luxury of a horse and a carriage. He dressed himself in rich colors, he took dancing lessons and he set out to conquer the fickle hearts of the ladies who showered him with their homage. He became the hub of the social whirl of Vienna. He was invited everywhere. "Come next Wednesday if you can," wrote the Baron von Swieten. "We shall expect you at half-past eight—with your nightcap in your pocket."

But the rapid turning of the wheel of admiration made Beethoven dizzy. His was not a spirit born for play. "Happiness," he said, "is not intended for me; or rather, I am not intended for happiness." His genius needed solitude for its development. Solitude and suffering. "I have been put into the world not to enjoy a pleasant life, but to accomplish a great work." He withdrew from society into the hermit shell of his rebelliousness and his gruffness. His manners often tried the patience of the Prince and the Princess Lichnowsky. But they bore with his caprices. The prince even went so far as to tell his servant that if Beethoven's bell and his own were to ring at the same time he was to attend to Beethoven first. "Art before everything."

Beethoven's temperament was explosive and arrogant—and sad. For he who feels intensely suffers intensely. An instrument attuned to beauty is sensitive to pain. Beethoven was a hypochondriac. The same nervous responsiveness which gave him his genius gave him also his unhappiness. All his life he complained of real or imaginary illness. And the pain is real even when the illness is imaginary.

Added to his physical suffering was his mental distress. Everybody praised him as a player, and nobody recognized him as a composer. His early compositions were regarded as the clever exercises of a musician who could play but who couldn't create. Yet creation was the absorbing passion of his life. Even at Bonn he had made it the sole end of his ambition to become a great composer. But here he was, in his late twenties, and the dreams that kept crowding so powerfully into his mind became dissolved, when he tried to put them on paper, into the tenuous mists of unimportant little trills and trifles.

He longed to be himself. A lady once asked him if he went to see Mozart's operas. "No," he replied, "I do not care to hear the music of others lest I forfeit some of my own originality." Some-day, he told his friends, he would show them. They would hear his music and marvel at the new creative giant that had stalked over the horizon. But his friends looked at his pock-marked face and his stumpy little peasant figure and laughed. This man a creative giant? Preposterous!

Yet Beethoven, in spite of the inability of his friends to recognize the fact, was moving in the right direction. His "unimportant little trills and trifles" were the first auroral flushes of a new sunrise. He took the gay and rollicking minuets of Haydn and transformed them into satirical scherzos of irony and pity—the laughter of the gods at the stupidities of mankind. His *First Symphony*, though still reminiscent of the music of the past, was an instinctive groping toward a different kind of music. It was an old language with a new idiom. A few of his friends understood and waited breathlessly for the further development of this strange and enchanting idiom. Most of the critics, however, merely nodded their heads and snickered at this "bumpkin who called himself a genius." They advised him to stick to the old forms and not to plunge recklessly into waters that were beyond his depth.

Yet plunge he did, and soon he learned to swim about familiarly in these strange waters. His *Second Symphony* was a still further departure from the musical conventions and the advice of his critics. In the second movement of this symphony, the *Larghetto*, he introduced an innovation that almost threw his critics into a fit. This innovation was a musical tête-à-tête between the various instruments of the orchestra—an animated interchange of song gossip in which one group broke in upon another group, only to be interrupted in turn by a third group, so that the audience got the effect of listening to a brilliant and stimulating human conversation. "If Beethoven continues this sort of trash," said one of the scandalized critics, "our orchestras will degenerate into instrumental debating societies."

But Beethoven merely growled at his critics and went right ahead with his experimentations. "A few fly bites," he said, "can not stop a spirited horse." Whereupon his critics insisted that his music was not only conversational but ungrammatical. It was the speech of an uneducated man. "Ah yes," retorted Beethoven, "they are amazed and they put their heads together because they have never found it in any book on thorough bass."

He was impatient of any spur upon his genius. When his critics observed—and this time justly—that some of his musical passages were beyond the capacity of the instruments for which he wrote them, he made the utterly illogical but adequately artistic reply, "Do they believe that I think of a wretched fiddle when the spirit speaks to me?" As well expect a volcano to pour its lava into artificial molds prepared by human hands.

III

IN KEEPING with his ardent temperament, Beethoven was always falling in love with some woman or other. He strictly refrained, however, from poaching upon the preserves of married folk. "It is one of my foremost principles," he said, "never to occupy any other relations than those of friendship with the wife of another man." Perhaps it is true, as some cynics would have us believe, that chastity is largely a question of physical appearance rather than one of spiritual restraint. It is easy for a homely person to remain morally pure. Certainly Beethoven was not the type of man to conquer the female heart. In his youth he made a proposal of marriage to the beautiful opera singer, Magdalena Willmann, but nothing came of the proposal. In later years, when asked why she had refused Beethoven, she laughingly replied, "Because he was so ugly, and half crazy!"

Added to his other physical defects was his increasing deafness, which had begun to press down upon him shortly before the completion of his *First Symphony*. Deafness and romance have never yet been on speaking terms. Tender words of affection are meant to be whispered, not shouted. The women of Beethoven's circle admired him, pitied him, at times even adored him; but they never loved him. They showered him with invitations to give concerts at their homes. So busy was he at times with these concerts that he was obliged to begin some of them as early as six o'clock in the morning. And he always drew audiences to fill "the capacity of the house." It was an age of musical virtuosity. "In Vienna," remarked the famous pianist Hümmel, "there are a hundred ladies who can play the piano better than I." And these ladies were anxious to hear and to applaud Beethoven. But not to flirt with him. One does not flirt with a god—especially when he is homely and deaf.

Beethoven's deafness was almost more than he could bear. For it not only isolated him from society but it removed him from the sound of his own music. "This affliction," he wrote, "is more difficult for the artist than for any other man . . . It was impossible for me to say to my friends, 'Speak louder, shout, for I am deaf.' Ah, was it possible for me to proclaim a deficiency in that one sense which in my case ought to have been more perfect than in all others? . . . For me there can be no recreation in human society, refined conversation, mutual exchange of thoughts and feelings . . . I must live like an exile . . . A little more and I should have put an end to my life."

But he soon gave up the thought of death. He had something to live for—his art. "Art alone has detained me . . . I have emptied the cup of bitter suffering . . . It shall be transformed into beauty in my soul . . ." Suffering, and patience, and work. "I owe it to myself, to mankind and to the Almighty . . . I must write my music . . . to the eternal glory of God."

To sing to the eternal glory of God and to the brotherhood of man—*this*, henceforth, was to be the chief purpose of Beethoven's life. He renounced the world in order to attain salvation—

salvation through music. And on the battlefields of Europe at that moment there was another man who, like Beethoven, seemed to be aiming at salvation—salvation through conquest. Beethoven had a great admiration for Napoleon, whom he regarded as the arch-enemy of imperialism and the savior of mankind. He dedicated his *Third Symphony* to him. But just as he was preparing to send the work to Paris he received the news that Napoleon had betrayed his principles and declared himself emperor. In a rage he tore off the title page bearing the dedication. "So Napoleon is nothing but an ordinary man!" he cried. "Like all the other tyrants he is trampling on the human heart!" He renamed the symphony the *Eroica*, "in memory of a great man"—a man whose body was still alive but whose soul was dead.

IV

BEETHOVEN'S CYNICISM grew with the years. To many of his contemporaries he was not a genius but a crank. He fumed at his friends and threw books at his servants and insulted his patrons even to their face. One evening, as he arrived at the Silesian castle of Prince Lichnowsky, he found there a number of French officers who had been quartered at that estate. For Napoleon had overrun Silesia, and his soldiers were living off the land that they had conquered. When Beethoven saw Napoleon's officers at his patron's house he scowled, and when they asked him to play for them, he flatly refused. He knew that he was regarded merely as a curiosity, like a juggler or dancer or sleight-of-hand magician. But the prince, who was playing host to the Frenchmen, insisted that Beethoven should accede to the officers' request. "Either you play for us," he said by way of a jest, "or you will be confined in the castle as a prisoner of war." Whereupon Beethoven, without another word, stormed out of the castle and walked three miles to the next village through a pelting rain. Here, while waiting for the post chaise, he wrote the following letter to Prince Lichnowsky:

"Prince! What you are you owe to chance and birth. What I am, I am through myself. There have been and there will be thousands of princes. But there is only one Beethoven."

His biting sarcasm extended to his pupils. "You will have to practice long and faithfully," he said to one of them, "before you realize that you cannot play." Not even in the presence of his female students was he able to curb his temper. "Wild? Impetuous? Ah yes," writes his famous pupil, the Baroness Ertmann. "But it was the wildness and fire of a volcano, the great forces of Nature herself, for in him a Titan sat. At my lessons he would tear the music into bits and stamp on it on the floor."

Yet his outward bluster concealed a gentle heart. "When my child died," continues the Baroness Ertmann, "it was Beethoven's gentleness and tenderness that consoled me most." In his more serene moments he was the very spirit of generosity. He had no conception of the value of money save as a convenient thing to give to a friend in distress. And when a friend asked him for money and he had none he would give him one of his compositions and tell him to turn it into cash.

His friendships, however, were but an incident in his life. His one passion was music. Creation in solitude. "The artist," he said, "carries his happiness within him . . . I live alone, but I do not regret it. For I know that God is nearer to me than to the others."

Beethoven calling to God—and a new music is born. With the *Third Symphony* he had finished his apprenticeship. From now on he was his own master. The years following the first approach of his deafness were years of prolific creation. A Niagara of music poured forth from his heart—dramatic music in *Fidelio*, tragic music in the *Appassionata Sonata*, tranquil music in the *Fourth Symphony*—and in every case music with a unique, original

[*81*]

and divine stamp, minted out of the pure metal of Beethoven's fantasy. The music of Beethoven, interpreting the ideas of God.

And then came the *Fifth Symphony*. It is useless to add any further words to the library of praise that has already been written about this work. Suffice it to say that the *Fifth Symphony* is the first full utterance of Beethoven's mature genius, the New Testament in the religion of music—the story of the struggle of Man against Fate and the victory of Man under the guidance of Heaven. It is the epic of Man's pilgrimage from suffering to wisdom, from wisdom to courage, from courage to hope and from hope to eternal life.

V

ONE OF THE GREAT EVENTS in Beethoven's life was his meeting with Goethe. He had suffered a nervous breakdown and had gone for a cure, upon the advice of his physician, to the Bohemian baths of Teplitz. It was here that the tone-poet made the acquaintance of the word-poet. Goethe, who was already advanced in years, made a profound impression upon his younger fellow artist. "He is the most precious jewel of our nation," observed Beethoven. "The appearance of such a man is, in my opinion, the greatest thing that can happen in any epoch." As for Goethe's attitude toward Beethoven, he regarded this "young man"—although Beethoven was forty-two at the time—as an "entirely untamed personality, but the sincerest artist I ever saw."

The two men saw a good deal of each other during their summer vacation at Teplitz. They entered into few discussions, for conversation was difficult owing to Beethoven's deafness. But they took long walks together, each absorbed in his own ideas—two supreme artists translating the mystery of the world into diverse languages. At times their ideas of the world came to a violent clash—as, for example, on the following occasion: Goethe and Beethoven were walking through the streets of Teplitz when they met the entire royal family, including the Empress of Austria and the various archdukes. Goethe stepped aside, removed his hat and bowed low. Beethoven, however, walked straight through the party with his arms folded and his hat firmly planted on his head. Goethe was scandalized at this "ill-mannered rudeness" of Beethoven, and not a few of Beethoven's biographers are in agreement with Goethe on this point. Yet isn't this a one-sided view of the matter? Was it more rude of genius to show its contempt for kings than of kings to show their contempt for genius? Was it a sign of good breeding for a noble-man to kick a musician downstairs and ill breeding for a mu-sician to stand up proudly before a nobleman? It would seem rather that the philosophy of Goethe was that of the slave and the philosophy of Beethoven that of a free man. And the sub-mission of slavery is no better sign of good breeding than the assertion of freedom. The difference between the attitude of Goethe and that of Beethoven lay far beneath the mere surface artificialities of good or ill breeding. It was a difference in principles, a profound disagreement as to the real values of life. To Goethe royalty was more important than genius. To Beetho-ven genius was more important than royalty.

And before we dismiss this incident let us not forget the cour-age of Beethoven. His livelihood depended almost entirely upon the good will of his royal and his other aristocratic patrons. Indeed, three of his patrons, the Archduke Rudolph, Prince Lobkowitz and Prince Ferdinand Kinsky, had agreed to pro-vide him with a yearly pension of four thousand florins (about two thousand dollars). But for one reason or another this pension was hardly ever paid in full. Financially Beethoven was com-pelled to struggle for the greater part of his life. Goethe's sub-missiveness, if not the more ideal, was certainly the more practi-cal philosophy. He took care never to offend his royal patrons at Weimar. And he always received his pensions promptly.

VI

TOWARD HIS RELATIVES Beethoven presented the same personality that he did toward the rest of the world—a surly demeanor and a tender heart. One of his younger brothers, Johann, had prospered in the drug business; but Beethoven showed him none the greater respect for all his prosperity. Naïvely proud of his success, Johann boasted about it on every occasion. He was especially anxious to advertise the fact that he had bought a sumptuous country estate at Gneixendorf. One New Year's Day, as Beethoven was sitting down to dinner, a card was brought in:

> Johann van Beethoven
> *Gutsbesitzer* (Landowner)

Beethoven took the card and wrote on the back of it:

> Ludwig van Beethoven
> *Hirnsbesitzer* (Brainowner)

To his brother Caspar, however, Beethoven showed an entirely different disposition. For a time he employed him as his secretary, and when Caspar died Beethoven undertook the guardianship of his little son Carl, who was nine years old at the time.

When he offered to take care of his little nephew, Beethoven brought upon himself a burden that was to plague him for the rest of his days. Carl's mother, who was the daughter of a rich upholsterer, contested Beethoven's right to the possession of her child and instituted legal proceedings against her brother-in-law. The litigation lasted for several years, the courts ruling now in favor of the one and now in favor of the other. The responsibility of the boy's care, and the lawsuits attendant upon it, proved to be a drain upon Beethoven's purse as well as upon his health. Yet he managed to lay aside a sum of money for

Carl's future, frequently undergoing privation himself as a result.

Beethoven had laid ambitious plans for his nephew, hoping that the child might grow up into a great musician or scholar. But in this hope he was doomed to disappointment. Carl was an unmanageable child whose tastes ran to the billiard room rather than the classroom. As he grew older he got into undesirable company and ran up debts that were far beyond his weekly allowance. And once, when Beethoven refused to pay these debts, the boy made an attempt at suicide. The attempt was frustrated, but it left Beethoven a broken man.

It is interesting to note, in passing, that Carl grew up to be a respectable citizen, fond of his music and devoted to the memory of his uncle. But Beethoven did not live to see this transformation in Carl's character. He knew his adopted child only in the turmoil of his adolescence but not in the placidity of his manhood.

And it was through those years of turmoil that Beethoven was obliged to steer the final course of his own destiny. His productiveness had slowed down considerably under the burden of his worries and his ill health. He had written his first eight symphonies before 1815, the year in which he adopted Carl. His *Ninth Symphony* was not completed until 1824. Nine years of sorrow, resulting in a final outburst of joy. Professor Santayana once remarked that God created the world in order that the *Ninth Symphony* might be written. And Wagner had this to say of the *Ninth Symphony:* "We stand today before it as before the landmark of an entirely new period in the history of universal art, for through it there came into the world a phenomenon not even remotely approached by anything the art of any age or any people has to show us." It has been suggested that Beethoven wrote this symphony as a musical counterpart to Goethe's *Faust* —the poem of the soul's adventure from Earth through Hell to Heaven. This is to an extent true of all his other *Symphonies,* especially the *Fifth*. Yet nowhere is Beethoven's philosophy of life so completely and so satisfactorily summarized as in the five instrumental and seven vocal movements of the *Ninth Symphony*. Let the critics quarrel about the propriety or the impropriety of introducing choral passages into symphonic structures. All such discussions are petty and irrelevant in the presence of this music. In the Song of Creation the Lord united a multitude of sounds into a single harmony—man and beast, wind and wave, ripple and roar, the crash of the thunder and the still small voice of the growing plant; all these are blended into one concordant hymn to the glory of life. And in the *Ninth Symphony* Beethoven has caught an authentic echo of this hymn. Beethoven's deafness was no accident and it was no tragedy. It was the preparation of the soil for the flowering of his genius. The sounds of the earth were stilled for him, that in the silence he might catch the harmonies of heaven.

And what is the secret and the meaning of these harmonies? The oneness of all, the unity of mankind into a brotherhood of love. "Universal love alone can transform and redeem the world." It is the teaching of all the great poets, all the great artists, all the great saviors of mankind. It is the doctrine of Jesus, of Buddha, of Zoroaster, of Plato, of Spinoza—the dreamers of the East, the thinkers of the West. And it is the doctrine, expressed in music instead of words, that Beethoven sings to us triumphantly in his *Ninth* and *Last Symphony*. The Testament of Love. *Seid umschlungen, Millionen! Diesen Kuss der ganzen Welt.* "Be embraced in love, ye millions! Here's a kiss for all the world."

This, then, is the substance of Beethoven's *Ninth Symphony*. In spite of our defeats and our doubts the heart of the world is sound, the plan of God is good and the destiny of Man is joy.

For the keynote of life is Love.

VII

BEETHOVEN lay on his deathbed. He had been ill for several months. The final death struggle had lasted forty-eight hours. He was unconscious now. Outdoors a terrific storm was raging. A sudden flash of lightning. The dying musician opened his eyes and raised his clenched fist into the air. Then he fell back dead.

The spirit of Man, unconquerable to the end!

SCHUBERT

Great Compositions by Schubert

VOCAL:

Over 650 Songs, including *Erlkönig, Gretchen am Spinnrade, Der Wanderer, Heidenröslein,* etc.

Several Song Cycles, including *Die Winterreise, Die Schöne Müllerin, Ossian, Schwannengesang.*

Several Masses.

2 Cantatas.

Oratorio.

INSTRUMENTAL:

8 Symphonies, including the *Unfinished Symphony.*

Overture to *Rosamunde,* and 6 other Overtures.

About 15 Quartets for strings.

24 Sonatas for the piano.

Dances, Marches, Impromptus, *Moments Musicales,* etc.

Schubert

Franz Schubert

1797–1828

IN 1805 the French army under Napoleon stormed the gates of
Vienna. The half a million Viennese, accustomed to the laughter
and gaiety of peace, were thrown into a panic. The bombardment was terrific. The shells burst everywhere. The older boys
from the university flocked to the colors and marched to fight
against the legions of the Corsican. The little boys in the paro-
chial schools huddled together in their bedrooms in terror and
stuffed cotton into their ears to lessen the noise. A shell hit the
Jesuit Grammar School. It fell in the middle of the stone-flagged
corridors and tore the high windows apart. One of the students,
an eight-year-old tubby-faced little fellow with steel-rimmed
glasses, was in his room playing the piano. He jumped up in
confusion. His small eyes widened with horror. He fell to the
floor and hid his face.

"Schubert, Franz Schubert!" called the schoolmaster. He was
counting the heads of his young pupils to see if anyone had been
hit. "Are you all right?" The round friendly face came into view.
"We can't afford to lose the choirboy with the best voice in the

school," added the schoolmaster in a tone of relief. "Who would do the singing on Sundays?"

Franz Schubert was a shy, obscure little lad who spent all his spare time in his bedroom keeping his own counsel and his own silence. One of the few things that distinguished him among his fellow pupils was his beautiful soprano voice. But this distinction soon failed him. A note written in a scrawling hand over the flyleaf of his schoolbook informs us that "Franz Schubert has crowed for the last time, Sunday, July 26, 18—." From now on he would talk in low, manly tones. The school must look for its sopranos elsewhere. Franz Schubert had become a man.

II

HE PLAYED VIOLIN in the school orchestra. And he did a fine job of it. He took upon himself the task of looking after the instruments, to see that they were properly tuned; he gave out the parts and placed them on the music stand. He attended to the tallow-candle illuminations. Clumsy as he was in his movements and ungraceful in his speech, he nevertheless had about him a quiet charm that went straight to everybody's heart. He was saturated with music; he talked of nothing but music; and he got the thrill of his young life when a Viennese aristocrat asked the school orchestra to play at his home when the great Beethoven was an invited guest. To be sure, when someone suggested that the boys play one of Beethoven's symphonies the composer begged them to desist, explaining that he was rather particular about listening to his own music. This rebuke somewhat daunted Franz. For the rest of his life he never got over his fear of the old musician.

Schubert's father believed that Franz was spending too much time on his music. He wanted to know why the boy had failed in mathematics. It was a severe question put by a severe man, a phlegmatic schoolteacher whose horizon was bounded by the

[*92*]

classroom and whose ambition was to turn his sons into peda-
gogues like himself. For schoolteachers were at least certain of a
regular wage—Schubert's father was earning two hundred
dollars a year. Compared to the musicians, the teachers were
the aristocrats of the starving fraternity. If teaching meant a
dead living, music meant a living death. And so Franz had
better stick to his mathematics and forget his silly compositions.

In answer to his father Schubert composed a poem on the
wisdom of God and the foolishness of man—and then he went
on with his music. He was fifteen now and as much of a recluse
as ever behind the barrier of his steel-rimmed spectacles. He was
incredibly nearsighted. His schoolmates jestingly remarked that
he kept his glasses on his head even when he slept. The masters
thought that he was too serious for his own good. But they
recognized that here was a boy with extraordinary talent and a
deep imagination—though the Lord alone knew the source from
which it had sprung. Certainly not from Papa Schubert.

Young Schubert's allowance was as skimpy as his knowledge
of mathematics. Occasionally he wrote to his older brother,
Ferdinand, for money. We have one of these rather naïve letters.
"Let me bring out at once what is on my mind," writes Franz,
"so that I may come to the point and not just meander coyly
around it. . . . The few groschen that my father allows me are all
spent—the devil knows how—in the first few days. What am I
to do, then, for the rest of the time? 'They who put their trust in
Thee shall not be confounded.' *Matthew, Chap. 3. verse 4.* I think
so myself. . . . How would it be if you were to let me have a few
kreutzers each month? You would not really feel it, while I
should consider myself so lucky, and be quite satisfied in my
cloistered retreat. As I said before, I rely on the words of the
Apostle Matthew where he says: 'He that hath two coats let
him give one to the poor . . .' "

All this time he was composing quietly in his room. He wrote
a fantasia, a duet for the piano in twelve movements, an over-

[93]

ture, two string quartets and a sonata. He rarely used a piano for his composition; he said that it interrupted his train of thoughts. Sometimes he drummed his fingers on his desk, as if trying out a musical passage. He wrote easily and rapidly and made few corrections. A handful of his intimate school friends read his compositions. Music was his best medium of communication with these friends, since he was frequently at a loss for words. When the pupils went out for their daily walk Schubert kept apart from the others, head bent to the ground and hands behind his back with the fingers constantly moving as if they were playing the keys. He had a mobile face. It expressed many moods. Conversation with him was unnecessary. When he did speak it was briefly and to the point. Although he rarely laughed, he had an abundance of quiet humor.

The following year, his sixteenth, brought no change in his situation. He was the first violinist of the Jesuit orchestra, and he composed incessantly in all his spare time. His only formal training as a composer came from the school's musical director, Salieri, who gave him lessons in thorough bass and counterpoint. He still failed regularly in his mathematics. This inability of Schubert's to do his sums was a source of deep chagrin to his mother as well as to his father. Mama Schubert, a cook before her marriage, was a simple and practical soul who regarded her poor Frantzl as a stupid and idle good-for-nothing.

In this opinion she died when Schubert was seventeen years old.

III

FRANZ'S FATHER had his way at last. Shortly after the death of Mama Schubert, Franz entered the Normal School of St Anna to begin his training as a schoolteacher. When he came up for compulsory military service he was rejected. For he was anemic, undersized and "blind as a bat." Three times he was called up for a physical examination, and each time he failed to pass the test. Poor material for killing. He was allowed to remain at the Normal School and to prepare himself for living.

Yet Schubert was unhappy. Teaching was as distasteful to him as soldiering. The classroom was a prison house. He felt completely out of his element. To escape from the monotony of the academic life he began to court the company of a young lady whose passion, like his own, was music. She had a charming soprano voice. Franz fell in love with her and under her influence composed nearly a hundred and fifty songs. Yet he was too shy to express his love in words. "It's strange," he wrote in his diary, "how some people try to picture their feelings in plain, moving language, only to turn themselves into a laughing stock. To speak easily is a gift of nature." Schubert lacked this; he possessed only the gift of melody. And it was in this language of melody that he tried to convey his sentiments to Theresa Grob. But the gods are ironical. Theresa Grob spurned the arms of the master musician and became the wife of a master baker. She preferred the realism of fresh buns to the romanticism of inspired song.

But if unlucky in love, Schubert was lucky in his friendships. Like himself, his friends were interested in music and the arts. Whenever a new person was brought into his company Franz would always turn to a comrade and whisper, "Can he do something?"

These friends formed a small but appreciative audience for his songs. They would discuss his compositions with a fanatical enthusiasm. Franz alone did not join in the discussions. He allowed his music to express all his moods. His music, and his pipe. He was an incessant smoker.

His development as a musician was incredible. Within two years he composed two hundred and fifty songs. At last he definitely decided to give up his job as a teacher and to starve as a musician. He secured an introduction to the foremost singer in Germany, Johann Michael Vogel, a giant of a man

[95]

with a gigantic reputation—a huge Greek god with a monocle. This favorite of society examined a number of Schubert's songs. One of them especially caught his attention. He hummed it over to himself and then tried it on the piano. "Not bad," he murmured. It was a setting to one of Goethe's most touching poems, the *Erl-King*. A father on horseback is carrying his little son through the night and the wind. The child is terrified. "Look, Father, look, the Erl-King. See where he stands!" The father sees nothing. "My child, it is only the mist and the rain." But the voice of the Erl-King whispers seductively into the ear of the child. "Come along with me back to my home, you lovely child. . . . There you will find flowers to pick and fine clothes to wear . . . and many a pretty toy to play with." "Father, oh, Father, do you hear what he sings?" "There, there now, my child. There is nothing to mind. It is only the leaves that are tossed by the wind." "Come down, pretty child, come down to the deep. . . . My maidens will rock you and sing you to sleep." And then the voice becomes more menacing. "Come, come, now, I'll seat you a-top of my horse. . . . If you come not yourself, I will take you by force!" "Father, dear Father, *he won't let me go. The Erl-King is hurting me, hurting me—so!*" The father shudders and hurries desperately home. But when he arrives there, in anguish and dread, the child in his arms lies quiet . . . and dead.

The simple nobility of Schubert's setting to this poem made a deep impression upon many people. Johann Vogel, who was considerably older than Schubert, became his sworn friend. Yet curiously enough, when Schubert sent this song to Goethe, the poet did not even deign to acknowledge the present from the unheralded young musician. He did not find the music outstanding. It was not until several years later, when Goethe attended a concert at which the song was sung, that the glory of the melody burst upon him for the first time. Tears rushed to his eyes as he applauded. But it was too late to make amends to Schubert. For the composer had been dead two years.

But to return to our living Schubert. Although by the time he was twenty he had completed six symphonies in addition to his numerous songs, he possessed no financial resources whatsoever. Not a single work of his—and by this time there were several hundred—had been either published or publicly performed. Clearly music was not a profitable profession for the young man.

But he had good friends. They worshiped him. Most of the time he was kept at the house of one or another of these people rent free. *Schwämmerl* (Fatty), his companions affectionately called him. Through one of them he received an introduction to the Count Esterhazy and a position as musical instructor to his children. But he despised the unimaginative spirit of the ducal family, none of whom manifested a sincere devotion to the art. It was a great relief for him to retire into the sanctuary of his room, alone with his beloved pianoforte and his scribbled sheets of music piled untidily from floor to ceiling. There, away from the tables of the rich and the petty talk of the titled, he was free to proclaim: "I give to the world what I feel in my heart."

IV

ONE OF THE GREAT IRONIES of Schubert's life was that he never fully realized where the strength of his true genius lay. That he was the writer of the purest songs in the world was a matter of indifference to him. Melody was so much a question of second nature, and he composed his songs with such rapid facility, that he thrust most of the sheets into abandoned drawers and dusty corners without giving the music a thought once he had written it down. It was his life's ambition to write successful operas. He looked enviously upon Rossini, whose genius for melody had brought him wealth and fame. He determined to try his hand at the opera. But in this field he was destined never to achieve success, financial or artistic. He wrote a comic opera entitled *The Twins*, which ran for six performances and then closed.

Neither the public nor the press had taken warmly to it. The critics had observed that some of the purely lyrical passages of the opera possessed moments of great beauty but that the music as a whole lacked the dramatic quality necessary for the stage. This should have been a strong hint to Schubert. But instead of taking the hint he tried his hand at a serious opera, *The Magic Harp*. Again the criticism was in the same vein. "Herr Schubert needs a closer knowledge of the stage. Until then his attempts are bound to fail." Schubert was heartbroken and poured out his disappointment in scores of songs that only his friends heard in the quiet of his room—heard and worshiped.

Once he had written in his diary: "The world resembles a stage on which every man is playing a part. . . . The manager is to be blamed if he distributes to his players such parts as they are unable to act." As he sat in the tavern of the *Schwarze Katze* and sipped his Bavarian beer he felt that he was most strangely miscast in this role of life—he and the friends who flocked to him. Their diet consisted of beer and song and sorrow.

But they were young and their sorrow sat lightly upon their shoulders. They met for their meals in the upper room of the tavern—painters, poets, musicians, actors, Bohemians all. The city of Vienna was a Bagdad of intrigue and adventure and nocturnal pageantry. To Schubert's overworked brain and tired heart the society of these pagan young radicals came as a great relaxation.

And yet Schubert's moods were decidedly religious. The music of Bach and of Handel stirred him profoundly. When he listened to the works of these great composers he folded his hands in emotion and pressed them to his mouth. At such moments he was not ashamed of his failure or embittered about his poverty. Revelry and religion—these were the two props that upheld his drooping spirits. Schubert was a pagan with a Christian prayer in his heart.

When he submitted the *Erl-King* to the publishers they rejected it. He tried to sell them his other songs, but with the same negative results. Thereupon several of his friends interested a number of people to print for private subscription a hundred copies of one volume of his songs. This private edition sold rapidly—so rapidly in fact that several music publishers in Vienna offered to republish the volume. They persuaded the unbusinesslike composer to sell them the complete rights to the songs, including the plates, for three hundred and fifty dollars. He was so anxious to get a little money into his pockets that he forgot about the prospect of royalties. Probably, too, he was unprepared for the great wave of popularity that his songs were about to arouse. In two years his publishers realized fifteen thousand dollars on one song alone—*The Wanderers*. And Schubert remained as poor as ever. His publishers systematically swindled him.

Once he had a strange dream. He dreamt that his father struck him in the face and told him to leave the house. And then he wandered off to distant lands, dejected and solitary and silent —silent but for his songs. Through the long years he sang his songs. "But when I wished to sing of love, it turned to sorrow." Such had been the love songs he had dedicated to Theresa Grob and to the world. He had offered them love and for his trouble they had requited him with sorrow. He took more strongly to the wine cup and wandered into the forbidden haunts of meretricious pleasure. In 1823, his twenty-sixth year, he contracted a horrible disease. He was sent to the General Hospital in Vienna, where a long and painful treatment stilled his fever and checked the acute form of the malady. But the doctors could not cure him permanently. Throughout the remainder of his life he was subject to frequent attacks which gradually weakened his resistance and brought him to the verge of despair.

And now, having been repaid for his love with sorrow, he transmuted his sorrow once more into love. Out of the soil of his suffering blossomed his epic love song, the *Unfinished Symphony*.

V

IT WAS in the following frame of mind that Schubert wrote his *Unfinished Symphony:* "Picture to yourself," he said, "a man who will never recover his health . . . whose brilliant hopes have come to nothing." The symphony, a lyric poem in an epic form, consists of two movements. Though Schubert made sketches of a third movement, the Scherzo, and actually scored a page or two, he evidently found no ending that pleased him sufficiently; and so he left the music unfinished—or rather a completely finished fragment, like the life of a beautiful character—his own life—cut off in its youth.

It is not clear that Schubert realized the significance of the symphony: for, as usual, he was concentrating all his efforts on another stage piece. He completely neglected the symphony that was destined to give him undying fame for the score of an opera that brought him nothing but obscurity and defeat. He never heard the *Unfinished Symphony* performed by an orchestra. He had plucked it like a flower from the exuberant garden of his genius and flung it carelessly to an unheeding world. It was found, many years after his death, in the desk of a friend.

During his entire life Schubert drew a total income of less than three thousand dollars for his compositions. At no time more than a step ahead of starvation, he began to lose faith in his ability to compose. The older he grew, the less he received for his work. The reason for this was that his publishers, well aware of his poverty and his desperation and his debts, offered him smaller sums for each new composition. Schubert was one of the greatest geniuses and one of the worst businessmen in the nineteenth century.

Added to his insufficient business ability, or rather included as a constituent part of this inability, was a stubbornness that made it impossible for Schubert to get along with practical people. He couldn't stoop to conquer. On one occasion there was a vacancy at the Imperial Opera House of Vienna. Schubert had a good chance for the appointment. He possessed all the necessary qualifications for the job. He had powerful friends and admirers who interceded for him and persuaded the trustees to give him a trial. Rehearsals were started on a libretto to which Schubert wrote some musical sketches. But when the soprano of the company complained that some of the notes in the arias assigned to her were too high Schubert refused to modify them. During the final rehearsal, at which the directors of the opera were present, the prima donna struggled bravely with the troublesome passages; but her voice broke and she was too exhausted to continue. The directors conversed in low tones with the singer and then walked over to the conductor's stand. "We shall postpone the rehearsals for a few days, Herr Schubert," said their spokesman. "In the meantime we beg of you to make the alterations which Fräulein Schechner desires." Schubert grew purple in the face. "I will not change a single note!" he shouted, slammed down the score and marched angrily out of the auditorium and out of his job.

On another occasion his friends suggested that he give a concert of his own works. "Your name is on everybody's tongue," they told him, "and every new song of yours is an event." The public, they assured him, would fight for the tickets and he would become a "veritable Croesus." Schubert agreed. The concert was arranged and the hall was filled to the last seat. On this single evening he made over a hundred and fifty dollars— to Schubert a fabulous sum. The public clamored for a second concert. But the peculiar stubbornness in the composer would not let him comply with the popular demand. He didn't care for the mob, he said, and he wanted none of its patronage.

At about this time he neglected another opportunity to enrich his purse. The publishers asked him to supply them with songs that would be less difficult technically. And they promised to buy his work in large quantities. But the composer refused to write music that would please them. He insisted, fortunately for the music lovers of subsequent generations, to write only those songs which would meet his own high and sometimes difficult standards. He had become increasingly impatient at the standards of the world.

Yet, after all, the world was not to blame if it sometimes failed to understand the idiosyncrasies of his temperament. Those who knew him catered to him and treated him with a kindness accorded to few men. And even those who did not know him intimately, apart from a few unscrupulous publishers who deliberately took advantage of him, were not hostile to him. In fact, they were quite receptive. But Schubert, worn out with disease and continual disappointments, had developed an acid attitude which frightened the public away from him.

He vented his bitterness not only against the public but sometimes even against his fellow musicians. Once a few well-meaning but mediocre musicians espied Schubert sipping his beer in the *Gasthaus*. They rushed over to him and begged him to write them some compositions for their instruments. Franz drew himself to his full height. "For you," he shouted, his face flushed with the contents of the cup, "for you I shall write nothing!"

"And why not, Herr Schubert?"

"You think you are artists," continued Franz. "Tootlers and fiddlers—that's what you are. I am an artist—I, Franz Schubert. I have written great and noble works, the most beautiful symphonies, cantatas, operas and quartets. Yet they call me nothing but a singer of trifles, and they call you artists—you creeping, gnawing worms whom I disdain even to crush under my heel. For whilst you are wriggling and rotting in the dust, I have learned to walk among the stars!"

VI

SCHUBERT continued his solitary dreams among the stars. Poverty, disillusionment, disease could not still his music. Many a time he had declared that he would never write another song. He was tired of scattering his treasures to the fickle winds. But he never stopped. Sitting at the tavern amidst the clatter of ninepins and the laughter of the drinkers, he would suddenly snatch up a menu and dash off upon the back of it a melody that bubbled like wine out of his overflowing heart.

One day a friend asked him to set to music the words of a little poem he had composed for a young lady's birthday. Schubert, who knew nothing of the young lady, scribbled down a handful of notes and gave them to his friend with an apology. "Sorry, but I haven't the time for anything more serious just now." His friend took the music home and tried it on the piano. He was so delighted with it that he made arrangements to have Schubert play it at the home of a mutual friend before a select circle of music lovers.

At the appointed hour everybody was there—except Schubert. The composer was nowhere to be found. The hostess was beside herself. She sent one of Schubert's companions to search all the beer taverns in town, certain that he would be found in some isolated corner, sipping his beverage and shaping his dreams. She was right. Schubert was discovered in one of his favorite haunts. Dragged unceremoniously to the drawing room, he confessed that he had forgotten all about the appointment. He sat down and played the song he had scribbled for his friend in such a hurry. When he had finished playing the tears came into his eyes. "I hadn't realized it was so beautiful," he said.

The name of this song? Schubert's *Serenade*.

Schubert composed this serenade toward the end of the brief summer of his life. The winter was at hand—a premature winter, for Schubert was scarcely thirty. As if aware of his approaching death, he composed a hymn to the Virgin, *Ave Maria*. For, as he remarked, "in order to have understanding, one must have faith." People said of him, as he played the piano during this last year of his life, that the keys were transformed into "singing voices." The voices sang from every fiber of his being—an anthem of faith in his own ultimate destiny far from the squabbles of publishers and the noises of men. Once during a trip through southern Germany he had written in a note of exaltation to his father: "Why do men fear death? If only they could see these marvelous mountains and lakes whose giant contours are waiting at every moment to absorb us, they would become less enamoured of the tiny span of human life. They would be eager to give their bodies to the earth that they may be quickened by its forces into new life."

And in preparation for this new life, the dawning of the unknown spring, he composed his last *Symphony* (in C major) and a farewell series of songs—*Winterreise* (Winter Journeys). "In the dark and hallowed hours of his final days," observed his friend Bauernfeld, "he wrote the most sadly beautiful of his songs." His friends were amazed and frightened at the morbid melody of these winter songs. But Schubert reassured them. "Someday this music will comfort you as it comforts me. For in it you will hear the rustling of the wings of the angel who is calling me home."

In March 1827 he attended the funeral of Beethoven. After the burial he went with several of his friends to a tavern and raised the wine to his lips with the words, "To him we have just buried." Then he refilled his glass with the salute, "To him who will be next." It was a toast to himself he was drinking. Just nineteen months later (November 19, 1828) he was laid in his own grave, only a few yards away from the tomb of the great master.

MENDELSSOHN

Great Compositions by Mendelssohn

VOCAL:

3 Oratorios, including *Elijah*.

Cantata, *Lobgesang*.

Opera, *Lorelei* (unfinished).

About 80 Songs.

INSTRUMENTAL:

4 Symphonies, in the following keys: C minor, A minor (*Scotch*), A major (*Italian*), D major (*Reformation*).

Overture to *A Midsummer Night's Dream*.

Overtures to *Ruy Blas, Hebrides, Fingal's Cave*.

Concertos for piano and for violin.

Songs without Words (Books 1–8).

7 String Quartets.

Variations Serieuses, etc.

Mendelssohn

Felix Mendelssohn

1809–1847

He BEGAN to compose at ten. At eleven he had written a trio
for piano and strings, a sonata for piano and violin, four pieces
for the organ, a comic operetta in three scenes and a cantata.
At twelve he composed five quartets for strings, nine fugues,
several piano pieces and two more operettas. At thirteen he
played his own piano concerto in public. On his fifteenth birthday his opera, *The Two Nephews*, was rehearsed for the first time
with orchestra. The same year saw the completion of his
thirteenth symphony. And at seventeen he conducted his own
overture to *A Midsummer Night's Dream*.

His literary talent was as precocious as his musical genius.
On November 6, 1821, he was taken on a visit to Goethe. And
here is the letter that the little twelve-year-old "man of the
world" wrote to his mother about the Sage of Weimar: "It does
not strike me that the old gentleman's figure is imposing. He is
not much taller than father; but his look, his language, his name
—*they* are imposing. His hair is not yet white, his step is firm, his
manner is mild. But the amount of sound in his voice is wonderful, and he can shout like ten thousand warriors."

Felix Mendelssohn inherited his intellectual equipment from his grandfather, Moses Mendelssohn, the humpbacked little "Jewish Socrates" whose pungent wisdom had seasoned the intellectual banquet at the court of Frederick the Great. For a generation the Mendelssohn genius had lain fallow. Abraham Mendelssohn, the son of Moses and the father of Felix, had jestingly alluded to himself as a mere hyphen between two inspired syllables. But he was more than that. He was the chosen instrument through which the seed of philosophy was to be transmuted into the flower of music.

Felix was not the only musical member of the Mendelssohn family. His sister Fanny, too, was born—to use their mother's expression—with "Bach fugue fingers." The musical training of the two children began almost from their infancy, and their mother was their first teacher. The easy circumstances of the family—Abraham Mendelssohn was a prosperous banker—enabled the children to receive a general as well as a musical education. They were supplied with the best available teachers in Latin, Greek, history, drawing, harmony, piano and violin, and they were kept at their lessons from five o'clock in the morning until late in the afternoon. It was in the Mendelssohn blood, this incessant and restless activity. Felix's grandfather, Moses, had won two things (he said) from his devoted application to his studies: a wise head and a crooked back. Though Felix's back remained straight, his health was undermined. Unwittingly he was laying the foundation for a precocious career and an early death.

Yet as a child he was athletic and handsome as a young prince out of the Old Testament. His slender figure, his black curls, his fiery dark eyes and his fetching smile endeared him to everybody as much as his talent. Goethe lovingly referred to him as "my little David who plays to me, his grouchy old Saul, whenever I am weary with the world."

Felix possessed the charm of David, and his pride. One eve-

ning, during his visit to Goethe at Weimar, he was summoned
to play before the grand duchess at the court circle. When he
arrived he was ushered into a small cloakroom and ordered to
wait. For half an hour he chafed impatiently, and then he seized
his hat and rushed out. A flunky tried to stop him. "Don't go," he
cautioned. "You will offend Her Ladyship with your rudeness."

"Really?" flung back Mendelssohn. "Well, tell Her Ladyship
that I am offended with *her* rudeness."

II

MENDELSSOHN'S FATHER had decided to bring up his family in
the Christian faith. And it was a fortunate thing. For the way of
the Jew in the Germany of the nineteenth century was perilous
and steep. The few drops of water at the baptismal font had
performed a miracle for Felix. They had straightened out a pre-
cipitous path into an easy road. Through the mere transference
of the day of his worship from Satu ay to Sunday, he could
stand up before the world as a genius instead of a Jew. He had
no difficulty in matriculating at the University of Berlin. The
family had adopted the Christian name of Bartholdy as an addition to their Jewish name of Mendelssohn, and this Christian
name served Felix as an open sesame to the doors of the educa-
tional and social world of Germany.

And the Mendelssohn home itself had become the social and
the musical center of Berlin. Number 3 Leipzigerstrasse—an
estate fit for a king. In the back of the main structure stretched
a seven-acre garden which had originally served as a part of
Frederick the Great's hunting preserve. In the middle of the
garden, where the sunlight descended like a benediction, there
was a fresco-painted portico capable of seating several hundred
guests. Open in the summer and enclosed within glass walls in
the winter, it was converted into a concert hall and theater.
Here young Felix, the boy who "had been born on a lucky day,"

dreamed his musical dreams and translated them into beauty in the presence of some of the most gifted men of Germany— Alexander von Humboldt, Hegel, Heyse, Klingemann, Zelter, Moscheles, Weber, Schleiermacher and Rietz. To Mendelssohn this spot was the Garden of Eden, and many a charming daughter of Eve came here to beguile him with her adoration and her flirtation.

But life couldn't go on like this forever. Mendelssohn was growing up and, in spite of his father's wealth, he must begin to think of a career for himself. His father thought that a trip to England might be a good beginning for such a career. "It will give you an opportunity," he said, "to make your talents known in other lands." To be sure, the English had a reputation for swallowing, like ostriches, "pebbles of dissonance and sweetmeats of music" with equal relish. But they did show a genuine desire to welcome the composer of *A Midsummer Night's Dream* into their midst. They begged him to come for a visit. "As one of the directors of the London Philharmonic," wrote Sir George Smart, "I assure you, your debut will be made under the most proper auspices."

He reached England in the spring of 1829. The city of London made a profound impression upon the sensitive young musician of twenty. "It is fearful!" he wrote to his parents. "It is maddening! I am quite giddy and confused. London is the grandest and most complicated monster on the face of the earth."

And this "grand and complicated monster" took him to its heart and whirled him along in a vortex of adulation. "By Jove," he confided to his parents, "I play better here than in Berlin. And why is that? Because the people here exhibit more pleasure in listening to me."

The Philharmonic played his *Symphony in C minor*, and Mendelssohn conducted. When he was introduced to the players at the rehearsal, "some of them," he wrote, "looked rather amused to see this little fellow with his white baton in place of their regular powdered and bewigged conductor." When they were through with the rehearsal, however, their amusement had turned to amazement. The success of the rehearsal was repeated at the concert. The reviewers as well as the rest of the audience were carried away into extravaganzas of enthusiasm. They forgot the imperfections of his music in watching the perfection of his motions. What a strange phenomenon, this young composer-conductor—in body little more than a child, in talent little less than a god!

Five days after his debut as conductor he made his initial appearance as pianist. Once more his audience listened and looked on in astonishment, for he played the entire score of Weber's *Concertstück* from memory. So crowded was the hall that many of the ladies, we are told, "might be seen among the double basses, between the bassoons and double horns, and one seated on a kettledrum!"

But if Mendelssohn was the observed of all, he was also the observer of all. As he sat playing at the piano his eyes were as busy as his fingers. After the concert he recorded his impressions of the audience. "It amused me to see the ladies' bonnets agitated at every little cadenza, which to me and to many critics brought to mind the simile of the wind and the tulip bed. I noticed that some of the ladies on the stage were very handsome, and that Sir George, on whom I cast a fleeting glance, took a pinch of snuff."

And now, having captivated the ears and the hearts of London, he extended his triumphal tour to Scotland. This country of "highland forests and enchanted caverns" inspired him to write some of his most delightful music—*Sonate Ecossaise*, the (Scotch) *Symphony in A minor*, and the *Hebrides Overture*, better known as the *Isles of Fingal*. The magic of the Scottish landscapes awakened not only his musical but his poetical fancy: "When God Himself takes to panorama painting," he wrote in a letter from Scotland, "He turns out strangely beautiful pictures."

From Scotland he returned to London. Here he busied himself with two works of unusual interest—an organ piece for his sister Fanny's wedding to the painter, Wilhelm Hensel, and an operetta for the silver wedding of his parents. He was in a feverish haste to finish these pieces so that he might bring them home in time for the double ceremony. But an accident upset all his plans. He was riding in a carriage which suddenly turned over and fell upon his leg. When he was extricated from the wreckage he was found to have suffered a severe injury in the knee. Instead of playing at his sister's nuptials he was obliged to send her a congratulatory letter from his sickbed.

He was confined to his bed for two months—a period of restless impatience, hot poultices, nauseating odors and painful bloodletting, "during which he felt all his creative energy trickling drop by drop into the basin."

And then recovery and the resumption of his travels. Wherever he went—Munich, Vienna, Venice, Bologna, Florence, Rome—he was "the darling of every house, the center of every circle"—the pampered yet generous child of fortune. "To his friends he was truly devoted," writes his biographer Devrient. "It was indeed felicity to be beloved by Felix." And to love Felix. Everybody tried to spoil him. "It remains a marvel that egotism did not prevail more than it did over his inborn nobility." Fortunately he possessed a sense of humor, an ability to realize the littleness of man in the greatness of the universe. Like the rest of the Mendelssohns, he had schooled himself to a philosophic outlook upon life. He saw his hopes, his ambitions, his affections and his talents *sub specie aeternitatis*, in the framework of eternity. As he stood beside the tombs of Beethoven and of Schubert in Vienna he observed: "The grave is the end of all endeavor. Genius must relinquish its labors to the world, and then crawl into a corner to die."

His thoughts for the most part, however, were far from death. For a perpetual spring song bubbled in the gaiety of his heart.

[*112*]

Music in the morning, visits to the picture galleries in the afternoon and dancing in the evening—such was the daily round of his activities in Italy. In the ballroom, with his elegant figure, his long white trousers, his blue dress coat and his gaily colored waistcoat, he was the central light around which fluttered the most gorgeous butterflies of Italian society, begging to be singed by the fire of his kisses and his smiles. And of these he was not sparing. "Yes, children," he wrote in one of his effervescent letters, "I do nothing but flirt." He was always falling in love; yet, unlike Liszt, he never stole the love of another. "No breath of scandal," as his biographer Stephen S. Stratton reminds us, "ever bedimmed the brightness of his character." His presence amidst the intrigues of the artistic and social circles of Rome was like a breath of fresh air circulating through a stuffy drawing room.

It was with reluctance that he left Rome to return to Berlin. For this was the end of his holiday. From now on his real work must begin.

III

ON NOVEMBER 5, 1832, Mendelssohn received a commission from the London Philharmonic Society to write for it a symphony, an overture and a vocal composition. The following May he was invited to conduct at the Düsseldorf Festival. As a result of his success on this occasion, he was offered the post of "director of all the public and private musical establishments of the town for a period of three years, with a salary of six hundred thalers." Herr Felix—for so he was generally called—was now professionally launched upon his musical career. His father, who was present in Düsseldorf when Mendelssohn received this flattering if not lucrative offer, wrote home about it in his usual vein of humor: "One thing I especially like about Felix's position here is, that whilst so many others have titles without an office, he will have an office without a title."

From Düsseldorf he was invited to conduct at Leipzig. In his letter of acknowledgment he showed the generosity of his character. "Before I give a decided answer to your proposal, I must beg you to inform me whether . . . by my acceptance I would injure any other musician?" It was only after he had been reassured on this point that he accepted the offer.

Shortly after his arrival in Leipzig he experienced the first great sorrow of his life—the death of his father. A heart attack. This sudden type of heart attack was to become an all-too-frequent visitor in the Mendelssohn family.

His anguish at the loss of his father found solace in the company of Schumann, the composer-critic who was consumed by a threefold passion—wine, music and friendship. His admiration for Mendelssohn knew no bounds. "The leading light of musical Germany," he wrote of him. "Not a day passes without his producing at least a few thoughts that ought to be straightway engraved in gold."

For a time the two friends became inseparable—Mendelssohn the recognized and Schumann the unrecognized genius. And Schumann generously swallowed his disappointment at his own obscurity and helped to spread the fame of Mendelssohn. He wrote glowing articles about Mendelssohn's compositions. He rejoiced when the University of Leipzig bestowed upon Mendelssohn the honorary degree of Doctor of Philosophy for "extraordinary merit in music." And he was one of the first to congratulate Mendelssohn on the occasion of his betrothal to Cécile Jeanrenaud, daughter of the pastor of the French Reformed Church at Frankfort.

IV

WHEN Mendelssohn married Cécile Jeanrenaud he was twenty-seven and she seventeen. Cécile was neither exceptionally brilliant nor exceptionally accomplished. But she was exceptionally beautiful and as gentle as she was beautiful. "Her serene and cheerful disposition," he wrote, "is like a cooling drink to my restless spirit." Mendelssohn's sister, who visited the young couple shortly after their wedding, corroborated Felix's high opinion of Cécile. "You are most fortunate in your choice," she said. "This child, with her lovely eyes and her tranquil disposition, will most likely cure your fits of irritability altogether."

And Mendelssohn's sister was right. Under Cécile's tender care he settled down to the most significant period of his life. He transformed the rather mediocre orchestra at Leipzig into the leading musical organization in Europe. His name became a legend in musical circles everywhere. Players and composers from every part of the world made pilgrimages to see the young maestro and to drink the words of wisdom from his lips. And hundreds of eyes looked on with unconcealed admiration whenever Herr Felix, wrapped in his Spanish cloak, strolled along the boulevard with his lovely Madame Cécile on his arm.

And then—a family of five golden-haired cherubs, and their happiness was complete. Mendelssohn was now in his early thirties. A lifetime of glory had been crowded into this short space of time. The fates had produced a human masterpiece. But it was a *brief* masterpiece, lyric rather than epic in length. The last line was about to be written. The day of Mendelssohn's glory was drawing to an end.

But before the end a few more hours of dazzling brightness. His work was not yet completed. Feverishly, as if conscious of the fact that he had but a short time to live, he threw himself into several projects at once. Without relinquishing his position at Leipzig he accepted an offer to direct the department of music at the Berlin Academy of Arts. He composed symphonies, concertos, overtures, sonatas and songs. He organized a movement to raise a monument to Bach, and he worked slavishly in his effort to collect the necessary funds. He opened an Academy of Music at Leipzig. And he conducted and played at concerts,

[*115*]

many of them for purposes of charity, until he was ready to drop from fatigue. His audiences were literally killing him with their kindness. At one of the concerts a throng of three thousand admirers almost suffocated him in their effort to get close to him and to shake his hand. On another occasion a delirious audience called for encore after encore until at last he implored to be excused, as he had not an ounce of strength left. Delegations, speeches, serenades—glory heaped upon glory, torture following upon torture. The price of a too great success. The poisoned apple of excessive fame. His health broke down under the strain.

He begged for a leave of absence. A brief rest, and then he was obliged to return to the nightmare of his greatness. Not an hour to himself, for his genius had become a public trust. The adoration of the public demanded the continual presence of their god. A smiling but exhausted god, ready to lay aside his outworn mortal garment.

V

A FINAL VISIT TO ENGLAND. Concerts in Manchester, Birmingham, London. Radiant days. Sleepless nights. He was invited to play before Queen Victoria and Prince Albert at Buckingham Palace. The queen offered to sing one of Mendelssohn's songs. "She sang simply and charmingly," wrote Mendelssohn. "Only in the phrase where the music goes down to D . . . she sang D sharp each time. And as I ventured to correct her the first two times, the last time she sang D where it should have been D sharp."

As he was about to leave, the queen inquired if there was anything she could do to give "Doctor Mendelssohn" pleasure.

"Yes," replied Mendelssohn. "A visit to the royal nursery would give me the greatest pleasure."

Delighted at the request, Victoria led the way. And soon the queen and the musician had forgotten their artificial distinction in their common parenthood. For half an hour they chatted freely and pleasantly about their children. Mother Victoria, Father Felix—two enchanted creatures standing in wonder before the miracle of the human flower in the unfolding.

And before long Mendelssohn was to stand in equal wonder before the miracle of the human flower in the plucking. The miracle and the bitter mystery. His sister Fanny had just died. That Mendelssohn scourge, the sudden heart attack.

The shock of Fanny's death brought about the rupture of a blood vessel in his head. He recovered temporarily and tried to resume his work. He did a little composing, he attended a concert or two, and once he sat down at the organ and played with the old-time skill but no longer with the old-time fire. "When I heard this organ playing," remarked his friend Henry F. Chorley, "I felt as if I had taken leave of the greatest music forever."

Before his final relapse he succeeded in writing one more song —*Nachtlied*. "Departed is the light of day." Mendelssohn was now only in his thirty-ninth year.

When the end was near crowds of people waited anxiously before the door. Bulletins about his condition were issued every hour. Seven o'clock in the evening—"Herr Mendelssohn is sinking rapidly." The children were called in. Eight o'clock—"No hope." Cécile was kneeling at his pillow. Nine o'clock—"It is almost over." Mendelssohn was unconscious. The din of a passing carnival burst into the sickroom. Suddenly the master raised his head and threw it back in a gesture well known to the bystanders. It was his characteristic movement when he gave his orchestra the signal to begin. The maestro had been summoned to conduct his first concert in the beyond.

CHOPIN

Great Compositions by Chopin

VOCAL:
Several Songs.

INSTRUMENTAL:
Sonata for piano and cello.
Etudes for Piano, Series I (1–12).
Etudes for Piano, Series II (1–12).

19 Nocturnes.
4 Ballades.
11 Polonaises.
24 Preludes.
13 Waltzes.
4 Fantasies.
54 Mazurkas.
17 Polish Songs.

Chopin

Frederic François Chopin

1809–1849

HE WAS THE SON of a Frenchman and a Polish woman. His father had come to Poland in 1787 and had entered the tobacco business with a friend of his. But his tobacco fortune went up in smoke, and he accepted a position as tutor in a family of Polish patriots. In his social hours he met the aristocratic young girl who became his wife. In the town of Zela-zowa-Wola, six miles from Warsaw, their son Frederic François was born. A tender, delicate little creature, this fourth child of theirs. The other three children were girls, but in some respects the fourth was the most girlish of them all. The family moved to Warsaw, where Nicholas Chopin was appointed to a professorship at the university. The children began to take piano lessons, and Frederic showed his unusual talents at once. He was a "moonstruck, pale, sentimental little calf," with a musical instinct almost as keen as that of Mozart, an ability for mimicry that would have secured him a job as an actor and a predisposition to lung trouble that meant an early death. Such were nature's indiscriminate gifts to one of her chosen sons.

His delicate constitution was a source of anxiety to his relatives. "Wrap your coat tightly around you, Frederic," they would caution him whenever he prepared to leave the house. And as he grew in years he was forced to wrap the cloak even more tightly—a futile gesture. Within the coat a slow process of disintegration was taking place. And Frederic knew it only too well.

He was sickly, yet proud and aristocratic and vain. As he grew to adolescence he developed a profound contempt for the sensual dissipations of the average young man. It made him sick to smell the smoke of a cigarette. A glass of wine was far too dangerous for his head. He was expensively feminine in his dress. There was only one class of people that he really cared to please. "My manner of playing delights the ladies so much," he admitted proudly. His person, like his music, was an elegant poem. And this was a source of great satisfaction to him. He boasted about it to his friends. "I believe I did it yesterday," he remarked concerning a concert he had given. Did what? "I bowed with a real grace, for Brandt has taught me how to do it properly."

Such was his vanity. And it was a vanity born out of his physical infirmity. It has been said that every mortal man has been a million times a woman. And there was much mortality to this strange fellow. When he appeared on the concert stage to play his own music—of which he had composed a great deal before his twentieth year—one old lady remarked, "What a pity the young man doesn't make a sturdier appearance!" So under-sized was he, and effeminate, a delicate creature of the night. Sorrow is a hard word to apply to a young man of twenty. Yet sorrow was his talisman, with which he desperately strove to ward off the pains of his joy. He was an inspired believer in melancholy—a bundle of overexcited, tired nerves, a shattered tubercular wreck at twenty.

His sadness, however, was not the vivid sadness of experience. It was rather a vague sort of sadness such as one encounters in a dream. And with it was the pleasure of hopelessness that only an imaginative consumptive can feel. Aware of his early death, he tried to live a lifetime in his few allotted years. Thus far—at the age of twenty—his experiences had been limited to one dispassionate love affair and one passionate friendship. His love for the young soprano, Constantia Gladkowska, was transitory. His friendship for his boyhood chum, Titus Woyciechowsky, was lifelong. For the strong limbs and the masculine mind of this young giant were a necessary complement to Chopin's fragile body and sensitive soul.

And now there came into his life a new experience—indeed, a major crisis. The Poles, patriots to the core, were chafing under the Russian rule to which they had been committed under the terms of the Treaty of Vienna after the Napoleonic Wars. It was evident that they would make a desperate attempt to throw off the Russian yoke. All the young Polish students were fired with the cause of freedom. A period of insurrection and social upheaval was imminent. Clearly Poland was no place for an artist who must work in quiet. Chopin was urged by his friends to leave for other parts of Europe. But all these companions of his were ready to take up arms; why, then, shouldn't he do likewise? His conscience tortured him. It was a moment of national hysteria. People had forgotten the humanities, the arts, the sciences, the peace of contemplation and creation. It was a time for action. Chopin wrestled with the problem for many months. Could he bear to leave his parents and his friends? "How terrible it must be to die among strangers, in a foreign land!" However, he finally persuaded himself to take the step. "Nothing remains but to strap my trunk. My outfit is ready; my orchestrations are recopied; my handkerchiefs hemmed; my new trousers fitted." And still he hesitated! They knew what he was thinking. He was a coward not to stay. Even if he couldn't bear arms in the supreme struggle, he could help somehow. His physical insignificance, especially at a time when true manhood was needed—

this hurt him deeply. Of what use was he? Why had he been wrapped in such a shabby garment of flesh? Others could fight and sweat and die in the glory of their efforts, and he—why his very soul was hunchbacked.

His friends, however, would not listen to him. On the morning set for his departure they visited him in a group. Probably they would never see him again. Perhaps by the time Frederic reached Paris, Poland would be a heap of ashes. Well, never mind! Part of Poland, regardless of the outcome of the battle, would live forever in the music of the young lad of twenty whom they were sending away.

They presented him with a cup of Polish soil, a little remembrance of the happy days. But in the days of our sorrow, as Dante has observed, no pain is so bitter as the memory of our past joys. Chopin was unhappy in his exile. But he had a solemn duty to perform—a duty greater than that of any soldier. A friend of the family had sent him a letter: "Keep always in view the idea of nationality, nationality, and again nationality. . . . Yes, there is a national melody just as there is a national climate. Our mountains, our forests, our waters and our prairies all speak our Polish language and sing our Polish songs. . . ."

He traveled to Vienna. In his notebook next to his heart was a sketch of Warsaw in the moonlight. But a storm had gathered in Poland. The news reached him that the Russians had crushed the revolution and captured Warsaw. His family, his friends, what had become of them? "The suburbs have been reduced to ashes." John Willy probably dead in battle; Marcel wounded; Sowinski in the hands of those imperial scoundrels; his family, like all the other unhappy families of Poland, adrift on the waters of an uncertain future. Civilization seemed to be dying around him. An age of barbarism was descending upon the earth. "And here am I with empty hands, pouring out my despair in tinkling notes while Moscow rules the world."

II

AFTER A WHILE his extreme mental anguish released its hold.
He journeyed to Paris where he hoped, amidst the brilliant
society and the sunny surroundings, to strengthen his frame and
to hearten his thoughts. France, hit hard by the scourge of
Napoleon and the frightful loss of blood in her interminable
battles, was like a wounded Amazonian warrior returned to her
family—new and hopeful generations of children who adored
her and built a legend around her and gave her fresh strength.
These children were the French romanticists—Alfred de Musset,
Hector Berlioz, Victor Hugo, Baudelaire, Balzac. These children
of the romantic movement were visited by their foster brothers
from across the Rhine—Heinrich Heine, Franz Liszt, Hiller,
Mickiewicz and Mendelssohn.

Into this society of magnificent dreamers, artists who had
the audacity to envisage a better world, walked the sad and
sickly Pole. He sat down at the piano and entranced them all
with his poetry. He was in his early twenties and he felt that he
still had much to learn about his craft. Accordingly he visited
the pompous dictator of the pianists, the unimaginative Kalkbrenner, with a view to receiving his advice. "Take lessons from
me for three years and I will make a musician out of you," was
the pedantic recommendation of the self-satisfied professor. But
Chopin saw through the imposing exterior to the essential
shallowness of the man. Just as Heine did. "Kalkbrenner," said
Heine in one of those cruel epigrams of his, "is like a chocolate
fallen in the mud. There is nothing the matter with it, but everybody leaves it where it lies." Chopin realized that he had nothing to learn from the "muddy sweetness" of Kalkbrenner's
music.

Among the first to recognize the genius of Chopin was Franz
Liszt, the greatest pianist of his day. Liszt was present at a con-

cert given by the newcomer in Paris, and by his side sat that other music-magician, Felix Mendelssohn. When Chopin commenced to play both realized that God was speaking through that young man's fingers. At the conclusion of the concert both of them applauded enthusiastically. Liszt had, as a matter of fact, entertained some misgivings that this sallow-faced rival might eclipse his own genius. But in the discovery of a new planet all thoughts of individual proprietorship are banished. Liszt and Chopin became lifelong friends.

Unlike Liszt, Chopin was somewhat of a recluse. Undemocratic by instinct, he had no love for mankind in the mass. He was afraid of crowds. But he felt no hesitation in entering the salons of the aristocrats, and whenever he played for them he "peopled the dark with a conclave of fairies." Prosperity had begun to smile upon him. Money from concerts, money from music lessons rolled in. He installed himself in a luxurious apartment and sniffed the perfume of violets in his solitude. He became deeply attached to a number of women. They pitied him, adored him, mothered him. A child himself, he developed a fondness for children. They understood and appreciated the handwriting of his genius, he maintained. He would submit his piano compositions to the judgment of a child rather than to all the legions of professional critics.

His love for women, as for children, was devoid of passion. He was forced by virtue of his fragile body to lead the life of an ascetic. But as a recompense for the enforced sobriety of his physical life he endowed his music with a psychic intoxication beyond compare.

Under thirty, writing exclusively for the piano, spitting blood from his ruined lungs, adored for his music, laughed at for his woman's soul! He needed some new, powerful, masculine attachment or he could not go on. For his heart was not virile. And who can write strong music when the heart is weak? His moods were always somber. "Though I see the green even in winter I see only through the head. In the heart, on the other hand, it is always dreary and cold." He needed a strong, active love to awaken the slow feminine fires. He wanted the right touch to put the stream of life into his sickly fingers.

In Paris at this time lived Aurore Dudevant, a woman of letters and vice and wisdom, known to the world as George Sand. An insatiable writer of books and mistress of men. Short, dumpy and voluptuous, she had the fine frank eyes and the high forehead of a philosopher. Politically she was a feminist; psychologically, a man. As in the case of Chopin, nature had given her a body entirely uncongenial to her soul. Just as Chopin was a woman born in the guise of a man, George Sand was a man created in the form of a woman. She drank strong drinks and smoked black cigars and swore like a trooper and loved like a prince.

In 1838, the year in which she met Chopin, she had just concluded the final chapter of an *affaire de coeur* with the poet, Alfred de Musset. She was thirty-four, the mother of two legitimate children and the guardian of a thousand illegitimate memories. She was still searching for that absorbing passion that would quench desire and let her be. But none of her lovers was as powerful as herself. No one could subdue her. At best she was a mother to her lovers—their mistress but not their slave. In seeking new conquests she longed to be conquered. "If Prosper Mérimée," she wrote concerning one of her typical lovers, "had understood me, he might perhaps have loved me; and if he had loved me, he might have vanquished me; and if I had been able to submit to a man, I should have been saved because my liberty devours and kills me."

Balzac had met her and judged her correctly. "She is a bachelor, she is an artist, she is big, generous, loyal, chaste. . . . Morally she is a man of twenty. . . . She dresses her little daughter Solange as a little boy, and that is not right."

It was tragic that Chopin should fall in love with such a

woman. And yet perhaps it was inevitable. For she too, like Chopin's friend Titus, was the exact complement to him. As Chopin was the principle of death, George Sand was the principle of life. And when life looked out at the artist from her large frank eyes it whispered, "*Je vous adore.*"

III

GEORGE SAND transferred her two children and herself to Chopin's custody. She solemnly promised that she would dedicate her life to his recovery. In the winter of 1839–40 they traveled to the island of Majorca for his health. It was a dismal honeymoon. Doctors hovered around him, inspecting his sputum, examining his lungs and shaking their heads. "They treated me like an animal," he complained in his letters. "One said I would die, the second said I was about to die, the third said I was already dead." When they were finally settled in a villa the medical authorities of the island ordered Chopin from the town and repapered the entire house at his expense. The lovers were forced to retreat to the confines of a Carthusian monastery for the remainder of their vacation. It was an old ruined building of Gothic masonry with hollow stone corridors and silent cells overlooking a cypress-laden cemetery. Here dwelt the ghosts of the fifteenth century and on the roof fell the monotonous tapping of the rain.

Valdemosa, as the monastery was called, was a most congenial home for the monkish soul of Chopin. Though his strength ebbed fast, the mighty flare of his genius took hold of him and stirred him to a fury of creation. He sat at his piano and lost himself in music. "He does not know on what planet he exists," remarked George Sand. The winds came, and the snow and the rain; the monks went about their solemn, pious tasks in the interests of infinity—and Chopin, buried in his music, was oblivious to it all.

[*128*]

CHOPIN

As he sat at the piano he launched "a terrible declaration of war against a whole musical past." He broke away from the traditional pianoforte sonata with its allegro, adagio and finale. He didn't write like Beethoven or Bach. But Heine didn't write like Shakespeare. Chopin, like Heine, was an inspired tone-poet. He refused to express the truth in long, involved, periodic sentences. He preferred the simple, whispered phrase. His musical language was couched in fragments of beauty. He gave himself entirely to his piano, leaving the great works of orchestration to other more pretentious musicians. People castigated him for his decision. Friends urged him to write in the operatic and symphonic forms in order that he might "prove his talent to a doubting world." But he shrugged his shoulders with a smile. "Whoever could read his face was able to see how often he felt convinced that among all the well-dressed gentlemen, among all the perfumed ladies at his concerts there was not one who really understood his purpose."

And this purpose was—to spiritualize the timbre of the keyboard, to give the piano a soul. For this instrument of inspired tone had been sadly neglected. Few of the musicians who played it and composed for it had been able to touch it into real life. A handful, indeed, had succeeded—Mozart, Beethoven, one or two others. But Mozart had treated it with a brilliant and patronizing carelessness, like an older brother humoring an immature child. Beethoven, too, had disdained it, but in a more savage manner. He had chastised it and forced fire and pain and bitterness from its soul. As for the rest of the world, they couldn't compare the "drabness" of the piano with the "splendor" of the orchestra. They regarded it as a sickly, undersized invalid, just as they regarded the young composer who so clearly understood the essence of its music.

And Chopin sat in his cell and conversed with his piano and watched his life ebbing away. "I drink neither coffee nor beer, only milk. I keep warm, feverishly warm, and compose my music." In the chapel of the monastery knelt a small company of friars. Around them everything was a blanket of silence so intense that it was almost like a song. No beginning and no end—a gray sea of undulating silence washing no shore, anchoring no ship. The piano too is a sanctuary of tone, a monastery of strings, a chapel of praying monks, a vast silent sea awaiting the arrival of the storm. "I will wake it into sound."

"It was a wonderful sight to see Chopin's small hands expand and cover the keyboard." Each one of his fingers "was a delicately differentiated voice." He sat at the piano and transformed it into life. Sad life, like himself, like his country. He remembered the words of his friends who had sent him off into the world with a bit of Polish soil in his pocket. "Write waltzes and embody the dances of the Polish peasants. Describe the stately pomp of the Polish court in the measures of the polonaise. Sing a dirge for the lost pageantry of a glorious day. Do not be afraid of sorrow. Teach the world to dance mazurkas to tunes in minor keys. Are you not the offspring of a nation doomed to suffering?"

Doomed to suffering, like his nation. He was failing day by day. "My dear corpse," George Sand addressed him lovingly. His life was dissolving into music. Hardly any body. But a gigantic mind. A mind full of visions and music and sorrow. The room he worked in was shaped like a coffin. Indeed, he felt more at home in the coffin than in the nuptial bed. His thoughts were almost always centered on death. George Sand left him alone with his work and took long walks through the countryside. On her return one evening, in the midst of a storm, she found him at his piano. The lights were low. He was playing arpeggios. There were tears in his eyes. The notes were like the whips of a sleet storm lashing across the room. As George entered he looked at her with a start. "I dreamt you were dead," he said. On another occasion he shrieked in terror as a chord had set loose a host of demons in the room—a marching army of devils dressed in medieval armor. He sprang up from the piano and fled to his couch. He could stand Majorca no longer. He had awakened the monster in the piano and it was darting shafts of melancholy into his heart.

They returned to France, he and the mistress with the motherly heart. They played man and wife in an expensive salon with oriental hangings and soft green couches. In a corner of the room, against the background of the white walls, stood an ebony piano. Bunches of violets—his favorite flower—were scattered in vases all over the room. He sniffed their fragrance and bathed his temples in eau de cologne. He took opium in a little water. Faint perfume. Perfumed music. Twilight songs of fragrant sadness.

IV

HE BECAME an almost legendary figure. He wore white gloves and grew side whiskers on the half of his face that met the audience at his concerts. He was dressed as immaculately as a corpse in its burial clothes. There was a faint smell of the grave about him, people said—and, added his critics, about his compositions too. They disliked their sad, morbid loveliness—"tombstones buried in the fragrance of flowers." There was a putrescence to the fragrance, they maintained. Something was not quite right. A voice with no body, the sound of a river flowing in underground caverns, a haunting wistfulness that drove the listener to distraction. They doubted whether there was solid flesh underneath those immaculate evening clothes. Confound those delicate perfumes with which he surrounded himself! He was a phantom with a pair of nostrils and nothing more. And his music was just as elegant and unsubstantial. Shadows of sound without substance. Like his *Funeral March*, for example—that cadence of muffled footsteps in the eternal parade of the dead.

And not all his critics were strangers. Expostulation, weariness, disgust came from closer home. George Sand grew unbearably tired of her unequal love affair. His music began to pall

[*131*]

upon her. His coughing maddened her. She looked anxiously for an opportunity to leave him. Nine years of life with a man condemned to die. Her children were growing up. She herself was getting old. Her hold on life was beginning to relax. She needed a final, strong, healthy love affair to restore her faith in life. Chopin had nothing more to offer her. She had long since discounted his body and lived in marital intimacy with his soul. And she had exhausted her curiosity and her lust. She was forever turning her experiences into books, and now she had completed her most ambitious novel. This novel, *Lucretia Floriani*, is an amazing work of self-revelation, or rather of self-deception. It tells the story of a middle-aged woman, an artist of great fame, who renounces everything to return the love of an invalid. By forcing herself to live with this man at the sacrifice of her own interests, she inspires him with new strength and new ambition. But Charles repays her love with contempt. He tortures her with his petty jealousy, separates her from her art and regains health by forcing her into illness. This fiction ends with the death of Lucretia and with a glowing tribute to her martyrdom. By a curious whim of subtle brutality George gave the proofs of the novel to Chopin for correction. He said never a word to her about it. Not even when the world smacked its lips and wagged its tongue over the spicy tidbit of the "Chopin family scandal."

She left him, and there was nothing now to keep him from the arms of his next mistress—Death. He lived only two years after his separation from George Sand. Only once during these last two years did he see her again. They met by accident in the house of a mutual friend. She pressed his hand. It was ice. He withdrew it quickly and fled. "I do not believe any longer in tears," he murmured. "It is because I saw her crying."

V

A LONELY, strange figure in Paris, this flickering candle in the city of lights. More than once his death had been reported in the newspapers. His friends, he smilingly observed, were so anxious to pay tribute to his immortality that they wished him already dead. "It embarrasses them to tolerate me any longer as a living person." His body moved like a shadow through the concert halls of Paris. His brain and his fingers alone were alive. His delicate music still trembled like a flame in the wind. Strange, melancholy music in minor keys, songs of the wind and the stars and the mysteries of the night. The critics cast their heavy stones at this music; but poets understood it, and lovers and children. Once a group of children had stopped in their play to listen enraptured to a mazurka of Chopin. "Heaven lies about us in our infancy." The children must have recognized the familiar echoes of a music they had known in a previous world. "Let the critics laugh!" Someday they, too, would understand. Someday after sunset. Their souls, like Chopin's, would become attuned to the music of the night. For the night is but a prelude to another day.

To the very end of his life Chopin believed, with the intensity of a child, in this other day that was to come after the night. "When I am gone"—these were his last words (and he was only forty at the time)—"play me some music, and I know that I will hear you from beyond."

SCHUMANN

Great Compositions by Schumann

VOCAL:
Chorale, *Paradise and the Peri.*
Faust.
Requiem for Mignon.
Opera, *Genoveva.*
2 Masses.
Several Cantatas.
Numerous Songs.

INSTRUMENTAL:
4 Symphonies, in the following keys: B flat (*Spring*), C major, E flat (*Rhenish*), D minor.

Concerto in A minor, for piano and orchestra.
Concertos for cello, for violin, etc.
Music to Byron's *Manfred.*
Overtures: *Hermann und Dorothea, Die Braut von Messina, Julius Caesar, Festouverture.*
Numerous pieces for piano, including *Papillon, Carnaval, Abegg Variations, Toccata, Davidsbündlertänze, Kinderscenen, Etudes Symphoniques, Fantasiestücke, Noveletten* (4 books), etc.

Schumann

Robert Schumann

1810–1856

ROBERT SCHUMANN was born in Zwickau, Saxony, toward the
end of the Napoleonic Wars. His father, a bookseller, was an
uninspired intellectual who dabbled in writing. He translated
the thoughts of others into his own words. He attempted several
novels whose qualities have consigned them to oblivion. He was
a fine example of frustrated talent, possessing the desire but not
the capacity for original work. His only creativeness consisted in
a better than average ability to produce children.

Robert, one of five, was the favorite child. His boyhood was
happy though unexciting. Zwickau was a town of quiet, slow-
moving and slow-thinking Saxons. Their pattern of life, simple
and homespun, was tangled only momentarily through the
topsy-turvy sequence of events set into motion by Napoleon.
Yet the rumble of the cannon, heard beyond the horizon, could
not knock their evening pipes from their mouths. Nor could the
turmoil of the battle disturb the crimson sunsets of their little
town. And when peace had come to Europe and the Industrial
Revolution had begun to blacken the city skies with its smoke,

the little town of Zwickau remained still serene, unclouded, undisturbed.

It was in this atmosphere that Robert spent his childhood. A twofold talent had awakened early in him—a gift for literature and a gift for music. During his adolescence his literary impulse was the stronger. When he was seventeen he had already devoured the Latin and the Greek classics and had acquired an intimate friendship with the works of the romantic poet, Jean Paul Richter. This poet's adolescent exuberance and unbridled imagination had produced a powerful influence upon Schumann's sensitive soul. Richter was intoxicated with the love of nature. And the young Schumann became intoxicated with the nature of love. While still in his teens he had lost his heart to "the Moon Goddess of Saxony"—a simple little country lass by the name of Liddy. He had caught the glance of his beloved in a lunar rainbow and he fancied he could hear her laughter in the breeze as it danced over a mountain pool. "At that moment I grasped the sublime idea of the Godhead," he jotted down in his notebook during his seventeenth year. "I could see my beloved . . . standing in ecstasy before me and smiling kindly upon me. . . ." On another occasion, as he was holding a tryst with his "young goddess—behold, rapid as a flash a black cloud arose in the East, and then more of them flocked and piled themselves up on high, and I seized Liddy's hand and said, 'Ach, my beloved, even such is life!' "

No average lad of seventeen could speak in this hyperbole. The pen was a necessary and eloquent friend to Robert Schumann.

But it was not his only friend. He had struck up a comradeship with the piano. Since his earliest childhood he had delighted in the songs of Franz Schubert. This "maker of sad melody" seemed to him to be the musical counterpart of Richter. Often Robert turned to the keyboard when his head burst with sentiments that lay too deep for tears—and words.

[*138*]

At eighteen he left high school. While he wavered in his choice between music and poetry for his life's work his mother thrust him into the profession of law.

II

"Now," said Schumann's mother, "the man within you must come forth and show what stuff he's made of." But Schumann was bound to disappoint. He was thoroughly unhappy at the Leipzig law school. For a time he tried to submit to his mother's will—his father had gone to his rest—but the final outcome of this struggle between mother and son was never in doubt. Robert was strong-willed. He was self-centered. He was a poet, not a barrister. Law was too prosaic a companion for him. A musical career would be more in keeping with his lavish taste for friendship and champagne and pretty women. He believed devoutly in the adage,

> Who knows not women, wine, and song,
> Remains a fool his whole life long.

Cooped up as he was in his academic atmosphere, Schumann longed for freedom. And he knew that music alone could free him. He was subject to intense fits of melancholy. He wrote to his mother about his unhappiness in a style calculated to wring her heart. "If only I had someone here who understood me rightly and sympathetically and who did everything for my sake out of a pure and unselfish love for me!"

Evidently there were some people who understood him "rightly and sympathetically." His letters are full of references to his love affairs. Ladies of various classes and manners and morals. He was a dreamy, voluptuous, romantic and not altogether unattractive young man. To judge from his correspondence, he was literally "besieged by all the young ladies" of Germany. "I am too softhearted," he complained.

[*139*]

He was a spendthrift. His allowance prohibited his enjoyment of life's extravagances and he was continually pleading with his mother for more money. He wrote home that he could afford meat only once a week, that most of the time he ate "plain potatoes," that he was abused by the landlord because he couldn't pay his rent, that he was unable to buy postage stamps, or to have his piano tuned, or to purchase clothes—that he was, in short, down to his last pfennig. "I cannot even shoot myself in my despair because I lack the necessary cash to buy a pistol." These and similar complaints. Finally he came out with the bold statement that he would quit his legal studies. He had been taking piano lessons from a teacher by the name of Frederick Wieck. He was bursting with the impulse to compose. His legal studies had frustrated him. Moreover, there was now a new magnet that drew him away from his Pandects of Justinian. This new magnet was Clara Wieck, the lovely and talented daughter of his music teacher. The three conspirators, Frederick Wieck, his daughter Clara and Schumann, began to play upon the sympathies of Robert's mother. At last she yielded and Robert gave up his lawbooks. He was twenty at the time.

And now he was confronted with the serious problem of supporting himself. The life of a composer offered but a dreary prospect to one who loved to live. At best it was precarious. At anything less than best it meant obscurity, privation, rebuffs. He wanted to compose but he also wanted to eat. Accordingly he decided to give piano lessons as an insurance against that "protracted period of unrecognition." Long he labored to perfect his playing technique. But he did not neglect his composition during this period. His days were a series of moods that fluctuated violently between ecstasy and despair. He worshiped greatness and burned with an overwhelming desire to produce something great himself. He bubbled over with a profusion of musical ideas. But from the very first he found technical obstacles in his way. He hadn't begun his formal training as a composer until he was relatively advanced in life. Furthermore, he had divided his time between music and poetry. He expressed himself equally well with the piano and with the pen. And this was a source of weakness in a sense. For he was like a man who is confused with the choice of sitting down upon one of two stools and ends by landing between them. As he himself declared, "If only my talent for poetry and music were concentrated upon one point, the light would not be so greatly broken up. . . ."

He realized with sadness that he would never be able to take a seat with the very greatest. And yet he could never give up the attempt. "I cannot reconcile myself to the thought of dying a Philistine."

For a while he entertained the hope of earning his living as a piano virtuoso. But the idea was rudely eliminated from his mind when he strained one of his fingers from constant practice. From now on—he was only twenty-two—his hands were useless for heavy exertion on the keyboard. Fate had made up his mind for him. He must now devote all his time to teaching and composing.

III

HIS SOCIAL LIFE was centered at the Wieck house. Here he entertained the fourteen-year-old daughter of his music teacher. He played the part of an older brother amusing his sister. She had been a pretty, precocious little girl of thirteen when Schumann had first met her. She revered him with the guileless devotion of the young. She listened to his tales of ghosts and goblins and applauded his charades. Whenever she left Leipzig on a concert tour they corresponded with each other. To Robert she was a lovable child, and more than that—a fellow subject in the enchanted kingdom of his music. He adored her genius just as she adored his. In the friendship of genius the meat of familiarity is seasoned with the salt of respect. "I often think of you, Clara," he told her, "not as a friend thinks of his friend, but as a pilgrim

[*141*]

thinks of the distant altarpiece." But for all that, she was still a little girl. And for grown-up love he looked elsewhere.

One young lady of plump figure and complacent disposition had exchanged understanding glances with him. She was a fellow pupil of his at the house of Frederick Wieck. Her name was Ernestine von Fricken. Schumann, with the flaxen hair and the sensuous eye, could not fail to attract her. The attraction soon developed into fondness. Ernestine was mentally on a much lower level than Schumann, but she was abundantly blessed with the external graces of her sex. Moreover, Schumann had heard that she was the daughter of a Bohemian baron and he was not the one to balk at social connections. The two young lovers began to spend much time in each other's company, and they enlisted the services of little Clara Wieck to guard them against unfriendly intrusion and to carry their secret notes to each other.

Clara was terribly jealous, as she confided to Schumann years later. "You talked only to her . . . With me you merely played all sorts of games. This hurt me a good deal, but I consoled myself with the thought that it was simply because you had me always with you. Besides, Ernestine was older than I. Strange feelings stirred my heart . . ."

But the affair with Ernestine was abruptly terminated. Schumann had discovered that he had made a mistake about Ernestine's lineage. She was only the illegitimate daughter of Baron von Fricken. More important than that, Schumann had learned that she was nothing but a pauper in her own right. He had little taste for fleshly portraits unless they were surrounded with a frame of gold.

Sooner or later it was inevitable that he would turn to Clara, who was now ripening into adolescent beauty and who still worshiped him from afar. "There is nobody I love so much as Robert," she had confided to a friend, "and he has not so much as looked at me." But Clara was mistaken. Robert had looked at her, and suddenly he had beheld something new. "I saw you for the first time. You seemed taller and stranger. You were no longer a child with whom I should have liked to play and laugh. . . . You spoke so sensibly, and in your eyes I saw a deep, secret gleam of love."

But at this juncture Clara's father stepped in. He was anxious to keep his daughter single. Marriage would jeopardize her musical career. And what sort of future could this poor, drifting composer offer her? He sent Clara away from Leipzig and forbade any further communication between the lovers. When he discovered that in spite of his orders Schumann had contrived to meet her in secret he sent the young man a letter full of abuse. Clara's mail was thoroughly censored. All her movements were checked. "My stars are in great confusion," Schumann told his companions. "Things have come to such a pass that either I shall never be able to speak to Clara again, or she must become entirely mine." Herr Wieck was more determined than ever to keep the lovers apart. He threatened to kill Schumann if the latter continued to "persecute" Clara. To add confusion to vexation, Schumann heard that Clara had become engaged to another man. The young lover plunged into his work to forget. He wrote for the piano a sonata in F minor—a desperate cry of passion. He threw himself into the arms of his friends, the most understanding of whom was Felix Mendelssohn. He turned to women of pleasure. And Clara received garbled reports of Schumann's infidelity. The estrangement grew deeper. Their pride would not allow them to heal the breach. Night after night Schumann prayed to Heaven, "Only let this one night pass by without the loss of my reason!"

And then there came a reconciliation. Clara gave a concert at Leipzig. Schumann attended it. She played his *Sonata in F minor*, for she knew no other way of proving the intensity of her feeling for him. She was unable to communicate with him in secret, and so she did it in public. "Do you think my heart was

not trembling? . . . I was unspeakably miserable. . . . Afterwards
I went for a walk, but I saw neither trees, nor meadows, nor
flowers; I saw only you."

It was all the encouragement Robert needed. He met her;
made Clara promise to hand her father a letter from him on her
birthday. In this letter he would ask Herr Wieck for Clara's
hand. What could the answer be but *Yes?* "Can God intend to
make your eighteenth birthday a day of grief?" But Clara's
father remained firm. Schumann tried to follow the letter with
an interview, but he was driven from the house. The old gentleman just wouldn't listen to reason. "If he doesn't grant his consent within two years, we shall have to assert our rights . . . And
then the authorities will marry us."

But Clara weakened. She couldn't bring herself to enter into
any plan of rebellion against her father. Brokenhearted as she
was, she yet pitied him in his loneliness.

At this point Schumann broke down. All his life he had been
obsessed with the notion that he was losing his reason. At the
death of his sister-in-law, a woman to whom he had been deeply
attached, he had suffered a mental breakdown. And now when
it seemed to him that he was about to lose Clara he wrote her a
strange letter. He referred to the "dark side" of his life and
stated that he desired someday to divulge the secret of a "grave
psychical malady" from which he had suffered "in earlier days."
Did she wonder at the emotional unbalance he had so often displayed? One day she would have the "key" to all his actions,
"to the whole of my strange nature."

He was writing music that was unappreciated. The musical
idiom was somewhat strange to him. The critics frowned upon
what they called the "formlessness" of his works. They conceded
that he could write songs of profound beauty. "But a lyrical
talent alone will not make a great composer." A song writer
may have the talent to express himself in a series of detached
episodes. But music consists of sustained inspiration. "Can

young Schumann construct a cathedral of musical ideas? So far he has only proved himself capable of building one-story hovels."

Schumann was unhappy over his slow progress. Not only the critics but even Clara seemed to have lost faith in him. He took a bold step; he would force a decision in the matter of his determination to marry her. He drafted a legal appeal urging the court to compel her father to give his consent. Wieck replied by charging before the court that Schumann was a habitual drunkard and therefore unfit to take a wife. This slander crushed Schumann's sensitive nature. But his friends, with Mendelssohn in the vanguard, rose to a man and cleared him of the charge. On top of this vindication the University of Jena awarded him a doctorate, so that Wieck was further discredited. On August 1, 1840, the court awarded the marriage decree. Schumann had won his bride after a struggle of four years.

IV

THEY LIVED TOGETHER fourteen years—on the whole, happy years. It was necessary for two such strong-willed individuals to make delicate adjustments. Clara was a famous musician; Robert was humble and obscure. He didn't fancy the idea of being regarded as "Mr Clara Wieck," and yet he was constrained to suffer innumerable insults to his pride. Again and again his friends disparaged his own "mediocre talents" as compared with his wife's "surpassing genius." Once, at a concert in the palace of the German prince, Clara played with her usual brilliance. The prince, upon learning that Robert also was a musician, turned to him and asked naïvely, "And what instrument do *you* play?" Whereupon Schumann left the palace in a rage.

Clara, too, had her difficulties. She was never allowed to practice on the piano while her husband was at work, since he demanded absolute silence. Furthermore, her exacting duties as a Hausfrau interfered with her musical progress. Schumann was not easy to get along with. In many respects he was an overgrown adolescent. He was absent-minded, unconventional, impetuous, indecisive and fitful as the wind. Generous to a fault and clumsy as a bear. Prone to melancholy, he believed that his marriage would cure him of his periodic spells of gloom. And his marriage, even if it did not cure him completely, proved to be indeed a blessing. Repeatedly he wrote of his good fortune in possessing "a wife to whom I am bound by art, mental affinity, the habit of many years' friendship and the deepest, holiest love. . . . My life is filled with joy and activity." And Clara in return worshiped him. "My respect for Robert's genius, intelligence and gifts as a composer increases with every one of his works." As for Clara's father, he made overtures for a reconciliation as soon as the pair were united. And so there was no longer any villain in the happy drama of their life.

Schumann divided his time between his composition and his literary activity. He published a musical review, the *Neue Zeitschrift*, a fresh challenge to the hidebound musical criticism of the Germans who extolled the third-rate composers above Schubert, who passed over the quartets of Mozart and Beethoven as "worthless trash" and who called Chopin's works a "school of errors."

He expressed his musical credo through the dialogues of two fictitious characters, Eusebius and Florestan, two different types of music lovers—the one gentle and receptive with little discriminatory taste, the other proud and idealistic, a fighter for all noble and progressive ideas. The progressive fighter, needless to say, was Schumann himself.

Schumann was bitter toward the Philistines but generous to his fellow artists. Yet Schumann's fellow artists were not always generous to him. Mendelssohn, for example, looked down upon Schumann's musical work, insisting that a man who was so thorough a critic must be suspect as a creative artist. Himself an impeccable musician, hailed everywhere as the Mozart of the nineteenth century, he sneered at the clumsiness of Schumann's craftsmanship. "It is remarkable," he once observed, "that a man who has conceived such beautiful ideas should allow himself to be so awkward in their execution." Whereupon Schumann remarked with true insight, "If I had grown up in circumstances like Mendelssohn's, destined to music from earliest childhood, I should have outsoared you one and all."

Gossip tried to create a breach in the friendship of the two composers. But while Schumann might have lost faith in Mendelssohn the man, he never wavered in his loyalty to the music that was Mendelssohn. Some years after Mendelssohn's death the musical arbiter of his generation, Franz Liszt, paid a visit to Schumann. In the course of the conversation Liszt remarked that Myerbeer was a far better composer than Mendelssohn. Schumann furiously retorted that compared to Mendelssohn Myerbeer was a pygmy, that Myerbeer had written for a little group in Leipzig but that Mendelssohn had composed for the entire world. So saying, he grasped Liszt by the shoulders, shook him violently and flung out of the room. Whether in anger or in love, Schumann never did anything by halves.

V

FOUR YEARS after his marriage Schumann handed over his job as editor of the *Neue Zeitschrift* to a colleague and thereafter devoted himself entirely to his composition. He left Leipzig and settled down in Dresden. An aristocrat by virtue of his genius, he remained a proletarian in his family life. He became the proud though harassed father of three daughters and three sons. He suffered continually from melancholy spells and traveled frequently to the country for his health. Frightful nightmares about insane asylums disturbed his sleep. An inexorable doom was hanging over him, he said. His sanity, he feared, was giving way.

He entered into a race against time and plunged desperately into his work. Sonatas for the piano, quartets for strings, symphonies, songs, a glittering assortment of jewels cascaded from the reservoir of his mind that was so soon to break down. With his nerves tensed to the breaking point, he was afraid of death and afraid of life. When the rebellion of 1848 broke out and the citizens' committee passed a decree compelling all able-bodied men to bear arms in the revolutionary cause, Schumann fled from the city in the dead of the night together with his wife and his children. He did not return until the revolution was put down by the royalist soldiers.

Added to his mental distress was the burden of his poverty. For years he had hoped in vain to get an appointment as the conductor of an orchestra. He had been deeply hurt when Mendelssohn had resigned from his position as Kapellmeister and had recommended another man to the vacancy. In 1849, however, his wish was finally realized. The townspeople of Düsseldorf-on-the-Rhine offered him the post of civic concert director. The income was small. Düsseldorf was not one of the musical centers of Germany. But to Schumann it meant a temporary escape from the shackles of despair. He accepted the offer.

The position proved to be indeed temporary. He was not a success as a conductor. Even the good-natured burghers of Düsseldorf, who were not particularly severe in their musical judgments, began to clamor for his dismissal. His interpretation of the music, they said, was not as clear as it might have been. "He is struggling with forces beyond his control." The Catholic Rhinelanders had an additional grievance. They found Schumann "an aristocrat and a snob." They were nettled at this "Protestant of the North who shunned society." For Schumann was aloof from most of his fellows. He was a man with mighty emotions and a defective tongue. "When my thoughts are most eloquent," he complained, "I find myself speechless."

The concert committee at Düsseldorf took steps to get rid of him. This was a heavy blow for the composer. Too much genius, too little talent. Such was the paradox of the man. He was suffering from the nervous excitability of an overfertile brain. And this nervous excitability brought him the burden of sorrow in one hand and the gift of song in the other. During the months of his greatest humiliation—his resignation from the Düsseldorf concert society—he was writing his noble *Fourth Symphony in D minor*. It sang continually in his ear. And so did the strains of his *Spring* and his *Rhenish Symphonies*—the sweet music of his failures. His music would not let him rest. He suffered from auditory hallucinations. He felt that his strength was giving out. And just then there came a great blessing to him—a new strong hand to carry the torch of his genius onward and upward. A youthful admirer had visited him and had become very friendly with him. This young man had played him some of his own compositions. When Schumann heard the first notes a voice cried out within him, "You have found a son!" A new meteor had blazed across the heavens. His name was Johannes Brahms.

VI

SCHUMANN celebrated his fourteenth wedding anniversary in an atmosphere of comparative peace. He played for his wife a group of songs he had dedicated to her when they were very young. Clara confided her happiness on this day to her diary. "Perhaps it sounds presumptuous to say so, but is it not true that I am the most fortunate woman on earth?" Yet the stage was all set for the great tragedy. Schumann had written to one of his friends a letter in which appeared the following ominous words: "Music is silent . . . Night is beginning to fall . . ." An acquaintance of Schumann's was visiting him. Suddenly the composer looked up from a book and asked in an excited voice, "Do you know anything about table rapping?" And then he added mysteriously, "The tables know everything!" Frequently now he would shut himself up in his room and talk coaxingly to his table. "Come now, my table, how do the first bars of Beethoven's *Fifth Symphony* go?" And when he fancied he heard an answer he would say, "But the tempo is quicker, quicker!"

His friends grew seriously alarmed. He complained to Clara that a musical chord kept pounding in his ear. It wouldn't let him rest. Soon the note was split up into a thousand sounds. A thousand majestic tones. It was no longer painful for him to hear. It was wonderful. His eyes shone with visions of heaven. All noises had become transformed into music for his ears. And such splendid music—the like of it had never been heard on earth. "I suffer *wonderfully*."

One morning he rushed from bed crying that the angels were singing him a theme which he must copy down. "You will believe, dear Clara, that I am not telling you an untruth?"

And then he rushed from the house and hurled himself into the Rhine. He was rescued and sent to an insane asylum—that dreadful place the visions of which had made him shudder all his life. Perhaps there had been premonitions . . .

Such was the tragedy of his mind. The supersensitive artist had lived a life of mental frustration. It couldn't end happily, this story of a genius so powerful with so limited an opportunity for expression, this active volcano of music choked up with the ashes of an unheeding world. It was bound to explode.

For two years he lingered on amidst this living death. Except for a few lucid intervals he forgot his wife, forgot his children. He lived in a world of heavenly music—those celestial harmonies that wouldn't let him rest. Just before the end his wife came to the asylum and saw him for the first time since the day of his confinement. He was only forty-six. But he was already the ghost of a man. He seemed to recognize her for one brief flickering moment. "He smiled at me . . . He put his arms around me. But it was with great difficulty, for he had almost completely lost control of his limbs. . . ." The light of the sun is but a mocking memory in the darkness of the storm. She tried to forget the fourteen years of their happiness. "I couldn't bear the thought of it as I sat in the presence of his sorrow." But just as she got up to leave he kissed her. It was the instinctive, trustful and helpless kiss of a little child. "Never shall I forget that moment. I wouldn't give up that kiss for all the treasures in the world."

LISZT

Great Compositions by Liszt

Symphonic Poems: *Les Préludes, Von der Wiege bis zum Grabe, Hamlet.*

Symphonies: *Faust, Prometheus, Dante, Orpheus.*

15 Hungarian Rhapsodies.

Etude, *La Campanella.*

Liebesträume.

Frühlingsnacht.

Funérailles.

Lorelei.

Soirée de Vienne.

St Francis Walking on the Water.

Todtentanz (Dance of Death).

Valse Oubliée (Forgotten Waltz).

Piano Concerto No. 1, in E flat.

Piano Concerto No. 2, in A major.

About 60 songs for the piano.

Liszt

Franz Liszt

1811–1886

H<small>E WAS</small> a sickly, ethereal, passionate little body, almost too delicate for a mortal child. Once he had been seized with a cramp, and his father, certain that he was going to die, had ordered a coffin from the village carpenter. But Franz—they called him Putzi at home—recovered from the illness, although a younger brother had succumbed to the same disease.

He was full of music and mischief. His father, an amateur pianist who had been compelled to give up a precarious musical career for a steady job as the overseer of the duke's cattle at the Hungarian village of Doborjan, was determined that his son should succeed where he had failed. Accordingly he made Franz practice on the piano from sunrise to noon every day. And to the little child of seven this practice was no hardship, but fun. Once, when he tried an exercise by Ries, he was non-plused to find that there was an interval of ten notes in the bass. How in the world could he negotiate this big stretch with his tiny hand? But immediately he thought of a way out of the difficulty. He struck one note with his finger and the other with his nose. Every day he prayed that his hands might grow bigger overnight, so that he would be able to strike the octave without any trouble. Once he even thought of making cuts between his fingers with his father's razor. Fortunately his father was able to prevent this experiment in time.

There was another experiment, however, which his father was not able to prevent in time. And this experiment had nothing to do with his music. His father kept a bag of gunpowder in the big chest under the window of the living room. Franz was always curious as to what might happen if he put a light to some of that powder. And one day he decided to put his curiosity to the test. As luck would have it, Franz was dressed in his best Hungarian suit on that day; for the duke was to pass by the house in his carriage, and Papa Liszt was anxious to show off his infant prodigy to His Highness.

But little Franz, unaware of the momentous occasion, was interested only in his experiment. Taking a handful of the gunpowder out of the bag, he threw it into the stove, touched it with a lighted twig and then rushed back to the door to watch the fireworks.

A terrific explosion, and little Franz was tumbled head over heels. When his parents rushed screaming into the room they found him as black as a chimney sweep. Fortunately he was more frightened than hurt. His father tried his fingers. They were as flexible as ever. Thank God, his child would yet be a great musician.

It was to this end, the musical greatness of his child, that his father dedicated his entire life. He succeeded in arranging an audience before the duke—the same patron who had encouraged the genius of Haydn. On the night of the concert young Franz and Papa Liszt were obliged, like obedient lackeys, to come into the palace through the back stairs. And when he played in the drawing room his mother was compelled to wait outside, among the servants. But the concert was a success. The ladies fondled him, the duke patted him on the head and Fuchs, the conductor of the ducal orchestra, undertook to pave the way for the child's further study at Vienna. Thanks to the interposition of Fuchs, Papa Liszt obtained a year's leave of absence from the duke's service. He sold his furniture and his watch, scraped together his pennies and recklessly embarked with his family upon the sea of certain poverty and uncertain hope.

II

WHEN the Liszts arrived at the Austrian capital (in 1821) Franz was only ten years old. But he already played with the technique and the emotion of a full-grown virtuoso. His father was determined to get him the best teacher in Vienna, and so he took him without delay to Czerny's studio.

But Czerny already had more pupils than he could handle. He was sick of listening to the succession of "infant prodigies" that were constantly being paraded before him. "I am sorry," he said to Papa Liszt, "but you are wasting your time. I can't take on any more pupils at present——"

Suddenly Czerny stopped short. Franz had slipped over to the piano and had begun to play the most difficult of Czerny's études. He listened in silence until the boy was through. And then . . .

"Amazing! I haven't heard such talent since Schubert."

Right then and there he agreed to take Franz as a pupil—at only two florins a lesson, a mere fraction of his customary fee.

The Liszt family moved into a tiny room at the Green Hedgehog, about an hour's distance from Czerny's studio. Three times a week the boy walked to the studio and back, regardless of the weather. At night he slept on the floor underneath the piano. Indeed, the piano became the very center of his life. It was his playmate, his chapel, his altar, his prayer desk. He had learned, he told his parents after a few lessons with Czerny, that it was possible "to pray at the piano." He was deeply religious.

Music to him was a devout service, a hymn of thanksgiving to the Lord for the joyous life that was his.

And his life, in spite of his cramped quarters and his insufficient food, was joyous in the extreme. For the news of his talent had been spread abroad. He was recognized not only as an outstanding virtuoso but as a genuine composer. He was now studying composition with Salieri, and his teacher had promised to publish his first piece—a *tantum ergo* written for four voices with organ accompaniment. Soon, very soon, he would be rich and famous. He would be able to repay his parents for all their sacrifices, all their hardships.

But for the present, work—and more and more work. No time for general education. No time for play. His father was planning a concert for him. Practice, study, memorize, from sunrise to sunset. "You ought to thank your lucky stars," said Czerny. "I have never come across such a gift for memorizing in all my life." And now there is a rehearsal for the concert. With the entire orchestra. The players are tuning up. A sudden idea strikes the head of the little maestro. "See what I can do!" he cries and turns a perfect cartwheel on the platform.

The musicians smile indulgently. After all, he is nothing but a child. But his father is furious. "Do you realize that you might have sprained your fingers with this crazy somersault?" A genius can't afford the playful pastimes of other children. But then there are compensations. So on with the rehearsal and away with childish games!

He sits down at the piano. The members of the orchestra look on in astonishment. "Incredible!" cries a gray-haired viola player. "Why, this child is every bit as good as Mozart!"

And "every bit as good as Mozart" was the verdict of the amazed audience at the concert. And there were mighty men at this concert—Metternich, Rossini, even Beethoven. It was a great surprise to everybody to see Beethoven here. When he had received the ticket to the concert he had thrown it aside. "I am

[*158*]

sick of infant prodigies," he had growled. But here he was, sitting motionless in his chair, with his lips pressed tightly together. He couldn't hear a single note, of course, for by this time his deafness was practically complete. But he kept looking at the child, impassive, frowning, aloof like a god. When the concert was over he made his way to the platform, took Franz into his bearlike arms and kissed him on the forehead. "My child," he said, "you will be a real musician someday."

This praise from Beethoven was among the dearest recollections of his childhood. Beethoven's praise and Caroline Unger's smiles. Caroline, a beautiful singer, was almost twice as old as himself. She had performed at the same concert with him, and she too had been a huge success. After the concert she had squeezed his hand. Such warm, thrilling fingers, such fiery, thrilling eyes.

The next day she left Vienna to study music at Milan. But her memory remained like a fragrance for many months. Already in his childhood he felt that the smile of a beautiful woman was, next to his music, the most irresistible thing in the world.

III

MORE CONCERTS in Vienna, in Pressburg and in Budapest, invitations to the houses of the aristocracy, adulation, caresses, trinkets, purses of gold—and finally a trip to Paris. For Czerny had told him that he had nothing more to teach him. "There are in Europe today," he said to his eleven-year-old pupil, "only three pianists better than yourself—Moscheles, Hümmel and Mendelssohn. And a few years' study at the Conservatoire will make you the greatest of them all."

But when the Liszts arrived in Paris Franz was unable to obtain admission to the Conservatoire. For only French students were allowed to study there. He did, however, succeed in becoming a pupil of Paer, and under him he continued his meteoric progress to the pinnacle of contemporary virtuosity. One evening he was invited to play at the palace of the Princess de Berry. The entire royal family was present at the concert. The princess had her two baby children with her. One of the children was playing with an enormous Pierrot doll. Little Franz almost lost his footing as he walked over the slippery polished floor to the piano. But the moment his hands touched the keyboard he was transformed. It was not a child playing, but the Spirit of Music incarnate. He played Hümmel's *Concerto*, but Hümmel himself couldn't have rendered it more skillfully.

When he got through playing even the tired old king applauded. Princess de Berry took him into her arms. "Ask me for anything you like, and you shall have it."

Franz's eyes glittered. "Do you really mean it, Your Highness?"

"Yes, I do. Anything you like."

The little virtuoso pointed to the Pierrot doll. "I would like—that."

IV

PAPA LISZT'S STRUGGLES were now at an end. For Franz's magic fingers turned music into gold. From Paris his father took him to London, where they found the music lovers waiting hungrily for the arrival of "le petit Liszt." He played at a concert and made his usual success. "This Hungarian boy," said Clementi, "is without a doubt the greatest pianist now living."

He was invited to play before King George IV. He tried several Czerny variations, improvising as he went on from theme to theme. When he was through with this improvisation the king turned to him. "My child, I think you are better than Moscheles."

He then asked him to continue, and Franz played Hümmel, Rossini, Mozart, Ries, Beethoven. It was late when the concert was over, and the king asked Franz and his father to stay overnight at Windsor Castle.

"Imagine," whispered his father as they were shown into the guest room. "The cattle hand of Doborjan sleeping in the palace of the English king!"

But Franz merely yawned. He was too tired to reply.

Always at work like a full-grown and able-bodied man was this delicate child of twelve. He celebrated his thirteenth birthday by completing his first opera. Never was a child so blessed with genius. Never was a child so hungry for play.

But his father wouldn't let him play. More work, more concerts, more fame. There was no time to rest. They traveled all over Europe and never saw any of its sights. From coach to hotel room, from hotel room to concert hall, from concert hall to the next coach.

At last, however, he had to take a forced vacation. The doctors ordered him to Boulogne. As he stood timidly on the beach in his bathing drawers the sun-tanned children looked contemptuously at his white skin and his spindly legs. His father told him to go and play with the other youngsters. For a few minutes he tried to do so and then he ran back to Papa Liszt. "I can't play with the children. I don't know what to say to them."

After a couple of weeks in the unfamiliar sunlight he returned to the familiar artificial lights of the concert hall. Here he felt once more at home. His opera had been accepted for production in Paris. Another round of rehearsals, concerts, triumphs and everlasting weariness. But in spite of his delicate appearance he had a constitution of iron. The first to give out as a result of the continual strain was not himself but his father. They were again at Boulogne when his father complained of a fever. Franz was inclined to laugh it off, for Adam Liszt always complained of something or other. But the fever grew worse, and on August 24, 1827, Franz sent a letter to his mother in Paris,

[*161*]

urging her to come before it was too late. Adam Liszt died before she arrived. With his last breath he whispered to his son a word of advice and of warning: "Stick to your music, my boy . . . and beware of women."

V

WHEN ADAM LISZT DIED Franz promptly forgot his warning. He fell in love with a girl above his station. Liline Saint-Cricq was the daughter of the French minister of commerce. Franz was engaged as her music teacher; and her mother, the Countess Saint-Cricq, attended the lessons as her chaperon. The countess had no objection to their love affair; indeed, she did everything in her power to forward it. But the countess died, and the count put an end to their impossible dream. One night, as Liszt came to the Hôtel Saint-Cricq, the porter shut the door in his face. A few days later he heard that Liline was engaged to be married to the Count d'Artigaux, a man of her own class. To all his entreaties that he might be able to see Liline again, if but for a single moment, her father returned a curt refusal. The affair was at an end.

Attempts at suicide. Thoughts of the priesthood. Readings in the bitterness of Byron and Voltaire. A long and critical illness. And then Liszt emerged as a fascinating, brilliant, reckless, cynical and irresistible darling of the French salons. Apollo, the God of Music. Bacchus, the Spirit of Intrigue. The seducer and the seduced of the most beautiful young matrons of Paris. Camilla Pleyel, the Countess Plater, the Countess Laprunarède, the Princess Duras, George Sand, the Princess Belgiojoso—one after another he gathered them into his arms like a bouquet of flowers whose fragrance intoxicated him. The handsomest man in Paris as well as the greatest pianist in the world, he was painted and modeled and eulogized by the leading artists and sculptors and poets. When he walked on the boulevards everybody pointed and whispered, "This is the great Liszt." He was fully aware of this adulation and drank it in like a rich champagne. "Look how charming I am!" he exclaimed to his mother, pointing to one of his pictures.

"You're a spoiled child, my boy."

"I know it," he smiled. "But how can I help it after ten years' adoration as an infant prodigy?"

The adoration of the public had spoiled his morals but not his music. The orchid of his genius expanded in the sunlight of his applause. And it was an orchid of gorgeous beauty such as the world had rarely seen. His artistic and mental virtuosity attracted not only the most attractive women but the most brilliant men of Paris—Heine, Hiller, Berlioz, Hugo, Mendelssohn, Chopin. It was a glorious company, where music flowed like wine and conversation was the gossip of the gods. A restless young god, this musician ever seeking for new triumphs, this lover ever on the quest for new adventures.

And at last there came an adventure which brought him a cup of multiflavored vintage—excitement, romance, passion, joyousness, disillusion, pain. But no peace. It was not within the stormy character of Franz Liszt ever to experience the blessings of peace.

One evening he was playing at the house of the Marquise La Valette. Among those present was the Countess d'Agoult, the most charming as well as the most exclusive of the younger social set of Paris. Only the nobility were invited to her house. Liszt looked at her golden hair, her eyes of ultramarine blue, her soft skin, her elegant slender figure, and decided upon her conquest right then and there. Heine had told him that such a conquest would be impossible, since her heart was encased in several inches of ice. But now as he talked to her and watched her reaction Liszt wondered whether that external covering of ice didn't conceal a volcano of fire.

He was soon to find out. She invited him to her home. She

confided to him that she was unhappily married. Boldly he suggested an elopement. But she recoiled in horror. She was the mother of two children. Besides, she had a position to uphold. What would the world say if she, the proud Countess d'Agoult, ran away with another man like an ordinary cocotte of the Parisian gutters?

Liszt swallowed his disappointment and bided his time. He knew that he would win in the end. Again and again he returned to the subject, and each time he succeeded in melting away a part of her reserve. One of her children died, and the mother poured out her grief in a letter to Liszt: "I seek a hand to comfort me. That hand is yours. . . . May God forgive me the sin I have committed in loving you with all my heart." To which confession Liszt replied: "How proud you have made me! . . . But this is not the time. . . . Listen to the words of your daughter who blesses you from heaven and comforts you."

After a brief period of mourning he returned to the siege until Marie at last, "saying she would ne'er consent, consented." They left for Switzerland and settled in Geneva.

And so they were unmarried and lived unhappily ever after. Three children came of this unhallowed union, and Liszt was destined to receive the joy of none of them. During their childhood and their adolescence he scarcely ever saw them, for the demands upon his genius kept him constantly a-gypsying from one end of Europe to the other. And with every concert his fame grew—and his discontent. The fire of his passion for Marie had smoldered away into the ashes of a bitter disillusionment. Their love had turned into hatred. The children were now living with Liszt's mother. When he came to see them after an absence of several years they treated him with the distant respect due to a great man but with none of the spontaneous affection for which his heart ached. The older they grew the more distant they became. Yet even from a distance he was fated to hear nothing but sad news about them. Daniel, his son, was an early prey to consumption. Blandine, his oldest daughter, died in childbirth. And Cosima, his other daughter, followed in his own evil footsteps. Leaving her husband, Hans von Bülow, she eloped with another man—Richard Wagner.

VI

THE ELOPEMENT OF COSIMA with Wagner was the bitterest blow of Liszt's life. For to him it was a double betrayal. He had begged not only Cosima but Wagner to spare him this tragedy. Both of them had promised to mind him and had broken their promise. And this, after all he had done for Wagner. Year after year he had sacrificed his own future in order to insure the future of Wagner. Having been appointed as the musical director at Weimar, he had every opportunity to cement his own fame through the composition of symphonies and oratorios and operas. But again and again he neglected this opportunity. To be sure, he beguiled his leisure moments with compositions of secondary importance—gypsy songs, sonatas, Hungarian rhapsodies, a few light symphonies and the like. But for the bigger dreams of his imagination he had no time to spare. For he spent it all on Wagner, the obscure Titan whose visions were beyond the comprehension of the multitude. To make the public hear and understand and acclaim the music of Wagner—to this end he had dedicated the theater at Weimar and his own life. And this was his reward. Wagner had stolen his daughter away from her family.

Ah well, time to forget Cosima and Wagner and to return to his own music. The most dazzling if not the most profound music of his day. Drown your troubles in the wine of the public applause. And in the arms of the beautiful women of Paris, of London, of Vienna, of St Petersburg, of Munich, of Budapest. Once more he played before the picked audiences of Europe and was everywhere greeted as the unquestioned master of them all. There was a new note in his playing now—the note of suffering, of defiance, of rebellion against the hollow pomposities of the world. He trusted nobody, and he bowed the knee to nobody, not even to the crowned heads of Europe. One evening he played at the Russian court. In the middle of the concert he was disturbed by the sound of low conversation. He looked up. The czar was speaking to his adjutant and paying no attention to the music. Liszt stopped suddenly, in the middle of a bar, and put his hands on his knees. It was some time before the czar noticed that the music had ceased. "What is the trouble?" he asked.

"When the Czar is speaking," answered Liszt sarcastically, "it is the musician's duty to be silent."

The czar glared for a moment but then nodded for Liszt to go on.

The next day one of the czar's generals took up his imperial master's quarrel. Rudely and deliberately he tried to insult Liszt. "Tell me," he said, "have you ever been a soldier?"

"No," replied Liszt. "Have you ever given a concert?"

After this sally the general left him severely alone. But not the czar. For Nicholas had found a convenient tool with which to torture Liszt. This tool was the pending divorce of the Princess Sayn-Wittgenstein. She was the last of Franz's lovers. His lover but not his mistress. For she was a woman possessed of the deepest religious scruples. The daughter of a Polish landowner and the wife of an officer in the service of the czar, the Princess Caroline Sayn-Wittgenstein entertained a mystical rather than physical love for Liszt. She had three passions—literature, music and religion. She longed with all her heart to be united to Liszt, but only in holy wedlock. With this in view, she tried to win her freedom from her husband. The prince, a man with a thirst for wine and an eye for other women, was perfectly willing to release her. But the czar interfered. He had an old score to settle with Liszt, and here was his opportunity to have his revenge. To the czar it was a long-drawn-out and sweet revenge. Again and again the divorce was on the point of being granted, and again and again he held up the final decree. He played with Liszt's feelings as a cat plays with a mouse.

Year after year they waited for their opportunity to marry. But the opportunity never came. Caroline's mysticism had become soured into a narrow superstition, and the slender suppleness of her figure had degenerated into the sharp and brittle angles of old age. And she had developed a lashing tongue with which she scourged Liszt incessantly and unmercifully. But Liszt endured it all in patience. It was a fitting punishment, he said, for his past sins. He had been cursed with too handsome a face and too fickle a heart. It had been his evil destiny to break up the homes of other people. And now, in retaliation, he was unable to establish a home for himself.

Vanity of vanities! Love, luxury, fame, music, wealth—all these were nothing but the shadow of a dream. In all the ephemeral adventurings of human life there was only one thing of enduring value—faith in God. Away with the world and its counterfeit pleasures! Happiness could be found in only one place. The cloister.

More and more his attention became focused upon the Church. He rejected all earthly honors. He refused a patent of nobility granted him by the Emperor Franz Josef. He took to reading the Bible as he walked through the streets. Finally his decision was made. He went to Rome and offered himself as a prisoner of God. He became a Catholic priest.

Five days before his consecration he gave his final secular concert. For the last time he put on his dress clothes and his decorations—a gay farewell gesture to his former glory. And then, with the echo of the applause still ringing in his ears, he donned his silk cassock and shut himself up in the monastery. L'Abbé François Liszt.

[*167*]

VII

WAGNER WAS DEAD. Liszt wired his condolences to Cosima, asking whether he might come to the funeral. But Cosima was unforgiving, even in her grief. Instead of answering herself, she ordered her daughter Daniela to send the following reply: "Mama begs you not to come. Please remain at home."

A year later. The musical world was preparing for a production of Wagner's *Parsifal* at Bayreuth. Liszt wrote a letter to Cosima—this time not to ask her whether he might come but to tell her that he was coming. Again he received a reply from Daniela. "Mama has asked me to inform you that our home will be an uncomfortable place for guests, since she will be so busy with the preparations for *Parsifal*. . . . However, she has arranged for a lodging nearby where you will be made comfortable."

He arrived in Bayreuth. His grandchildren came to see him, but not Cosima. Their mother, they said, was too busy to pay him a visit.

On the morning before the performance of *Parsifal* Daniela appeared to tell him that the family box at the theater would be occupied by strangers from abroad but that a stall had been reserved for him.

Liszt shook his head and smiled. When Daniela was gone he packed his belongings and left Bayreuth. He was a nuisance to his grandchildren, to his daughter, to himself. A foolish old man who wept like a child, an ugly old wreck of a once magnificent body. His gums were toothless, the skin on his neck was shriveled, his shoulders were hunched with the weight of his seventy-three years and his nose poked forward like the beak of an owl between his blinking red eyes. Nothing to do but to wait patiently for the night.

Two years later, and a ray of light broke through the cloudy sunset of his life. His granddaughter Daniela was to be married, and he received an invitation to the wedding. It was midsummer when he arrived in Bayreuth, but the chill of winter was in his blood. On the day of the wedding he awoke with a severe pain in his chest. But he insisted upon attending the ceremony.

After the wedding he felt worse, but still he refused to take to his bed. The Wagner festival was on again. Throughout the performance of *Parsifal* he held his handkerchief to his mouth. When he returned home he was seized with a fit of coughing. The doctor was summoned. It was too late. Liszt was suffering from double pneumonia.

He was dying. But things were not so bad after all. For Cosima was holding his hand as he closed his eyes.

WAGNER

Great Compositions by Wagner

OPERAS:
Rienzi, Der Fliegende Holländer, Tannhäuser, Lohengrin, Tristan und Isolde, Die Meistersinger von Nürnberg, Der Ring das Nibelungen (Das Rheingold, Die Valküre, Siegfried, Götterdämmerung), Parsifal.

ORCHESTRAL MUSIC:
Siegfried Idyll. Overtures to the various operas. Several Marches, including *Kaisermarsch, Huldigungsmarsch,* etc.

Wagner

Wilhelm Richard Wagner

1813–1883

THE PORTRAIT of Richard Wagner, if depicted with a realistic and unbiased brush, presents a study in violent contrasts. It tells the story of an ugly personality that produced beautiful music. From earliest childhood he displayed an unbounded belief in himself, an utter disregard for others and an amazing talent for poetry and music. At thirteen he translated, in his spare moments, the first twelve books of the *Odyssey*. He read Shakespeare in German translations, and he knew Weber's opera, *Der Freischütz*, by heart. The youngest of seven children, he lorded it over his brothers and his sisters whose sole reason for existence, he thought, was to dance attendance upon him. His mother and his stepfather—his father had died seven months after Richard's birth and his mother had married the actor, Ludwig Geyer—were scarcely less indulgent toward their beloved little tyrant. But when his stepfather died (in 1821) and the last restraining hand was removed from his undisciplined shoulders he became a source of real anxiety to his relatives. While still in his teens he began to associate with strolling players and musicians, and he became a not infrequent visitor to the smaller gambling dens of Leipzig. Once he staked his mother's entire pension on a single bet. Fortunately for his mother, he won the bet.

He borrowed money recklessly and as recklessly squandered it. "I must have money," he wrote again and again to his friends, "or else I shall go mad." And his friends were generally ready with their purse. For his supreme confidence in his own ability had become contagious. Though self-taught in his music, he felt certain of his ability to astonish and to conquer the world. He would write a German opera—he said—then another, and then still another. And after that he would go to Italy, where he would write Italian operas. And from Italy he would go to France, and there he would write French operas. And everywhere, he assured his friends, an enthusiastic public would shower him with honors and with cash. But in the meantime, "I must have more money or I shall go mad."

He had his moments of depression, to be sure, especially when his friends were a little slow in pouring their funds into the perpetual sieve of his extravagances. But he had a surprising knack for quick recovery. "His temperament," writes Pecht, one of the companions of his youth, "was like a watch spring, easily compressed, but always flying back with redoubled energy."

At twenty this energetic, reckless, yet extremely likable young braggadocio secured, through the theatrical connections of the Geyer family, his first important job on the stage. He became the chorus master of the small operatic company at Würzburg. Here (in 1833) he wrote his earliest opera, *The Fairies*, an exuberant and effervescent outpouring of his untamed youth. The next year he wrote another opera, *The Ban upon Love*, and then promptly disregarded his own ban by falling in love with the actress, Minna Planer. They were married on November 24, 1836—a day that Minna was to remember as the anniversary

[*174*]

of her misfortune. Unhappy are they whose destiny ties them to the fiery wheel of genius.

II

THE FIRST YEARS of their married life were years of privations and disappointments and—on the part of Wagner, at least— undying faith in the ultimate triumph of his genius. In order to bring this genius to the attention of the public he wrote four more operas—*Rienzi, The Flying Dutchman, Tannhäuser* and *Lohengrin.* But the public paid little respect to them. For here was a wild and exotic and new kind of music language. And old ears are slow to catch new cadences. Wagner offered beauty to the world, and the world repaid him with contempt. He traveled everywhere seeking for recognition, and everywhere he met with the same rebuffs. And when his wife complained he silenced her with the words, "Your suffering will ultimately be rewarded by my fame."

"Your suffering . . . my fame." This was the keynote of his life. Let others wear the crown of thorns so that he might receive the reward of glory. Again and again he reduced her to shameful appeals for charity in order that he might be released from the inconvenience of making a living. "I am now fulfilling an unpleasant but, I believe, holy duty," she writes to Wagner's friend, Theodor Apel. "You say in your letter to Richard that it is impossible for you to do more for him than you have already done. . . . Let me, however, without any desire to boast, tell you what I did as a girl for my brother. . . . I undertook to pay for his studies at Leipzig at a time when I had not even four groschen for my dinner. I pawned my earrings and such things, sent the money to my brother and kept only three pfennigs for a piece of bread. . . . I appeal to you, can you make no possible further sacrifice for Richard? In him there is a fine talent to be rescued. If we fail him, this talent will be brought nigh to ruin."

And Richard accepted his charities and nursed his talent and tortured his wife. Minna, he complained, could give him only *material* assistance, but she was incapable of giving him *spiritual* assistance. A man of his inner excitability, he said, needed "mental tending"—soul mates who understood his music and who could inspire him to his "supremest efforts." Perhaps he was artistically justified in this cruel attitude. It is possible that he needed this nectar of passion to feed the fires of his creation. But if this sort of food was life to Wagner, it was gall and worm-wood to Minna. Time and again he formed a liaison with another woman and flaunted it in the face of his wife. And always to the injury of his unfaithfulness he added the insult of his excuse that he preferred his new mistress because of her intellectual superiority to Minna. Once, when he attached him-self to Frau Mathilde Wesendonck, he assured both his own wife and Frau Wesendonck's husband that his heart bled for their misery but that the fates had decreed the sacrifice of their happiness to his genius. Glorious music for the world; cold consolation for the victims of this glorious music.

His unconventional views about music and love extended also to his politics. As soon as he finished *Lohengrin*, in 1848, he threw himself into the revolutionary agitation which at that time was sweeping over Germany. A warrant having been issued for his arrest, he fled to Switzerland—and took along with him into his exile the heart of another young woman, Madame Jessie Laussot.

Jessie Laussot was the English wife of the French wine mer-chant, Eugène Laussot. Wagner had met her in Dresden, and this rather fascinating young woman had expressed her admi-ration for him "in a way," he tells us, "that brought quite a new experience into my life." They began a regular correspondence, and in the early spring of 1850 Wagner received an invitation to the Laussot home. He accepted the invitation with alacrity, excusing himself to Minna on the ground that Monsieur Laussot had promised him an annuity that would free him "from the vulgar necessity of business to the noble cultivation of my art."

When Wagner arrived at the Laussots' he paid his respects to Eugène and then promptly deceived him behind his back. "I soon discovered," he writes in *Mein Leben,* "what a great gulf separated me as well as Jessie from her mother and her husband. While that handsome young man was attending to his business . . . and the mother's deafness excluded her from our conversation, Jessie and I exchanged our ideas upon many important subjects . . . And this soon led to a great bond of sympathy between us."

Together they planned to "flee from the ugly world," somewhere to Greece or to Asia Minor. To his wife he wrote that for *her* sake he thought it best to leave her. "For how can I otherwise ever make you happy? . . . I presume and hope that you are, if perhaps surprised, at any rate not alarmed by my decision."

In the meantime, however, Jessie's husband had got wind of the matter. He threatened to put a bullet through Wagner, and Wagner's enthusiasm for the "spiritual elopement" cooled off. He wrote a letter to Jessie, expressing his "contempt for the conduct of her husband"; and to his friend Karl Ritter, to whom he had confided his plans for the elopement, he wrote another letter, informing him that "nothing can be done with that mad Englishwoman (Jessie Laussot)."

Out of this whole sordid affair only one person—according to Wagner—came out unimpeachable, noble and pure. And that person was Richard Wagner himself. Laussot, said Wagner, had proved himself an arrant scoundrel; Jessie, a fickle jade; and Minna, a jealous fool. "Whoever has observed me closely," he wrote, "must have been surprised at my patience and kindness. . . . If those superficial judges have condemned me, I have fortunately become insensitive to their opinion. . . . As for Minna, she doesn't even understand what true love is, and her rage runs away with her. . . . She really is unfortunate—she would have been happier with a lesser man."

III

FOR TWELVE YEARS Wagner remained in exile, wandering from city to city and from love to love, always insistent upon his own comforts, always forgetful of the comforts of others—"a pocket edition of a man, a folio of vanity, heartlessness and egoism." His attachments for women were not always, as he would have us believe (and probably believed himself), motivated by purely spiritual factors. In the midst of a passionate affair with a young girl he found time for a brief interlude with an old lady. This old lady, a widow with a substantial fortune, had offered to give him "the not inconsiderable sum necessary to maintain me in independence for some time to come." Meeting with the objections of her relatives, however, she withdrew her offer; and Wagner, with a sarcastic fling at "the weakness of her not very independent character," returned to his young love.

And all this time he kept sponging on his friends. It was their duty, he said, to provide him with a living. How else, he asked, could he be free to give his best music to the world? Work like other people? Not he! "The director of the Zurich Theater," wrote Minna to a friend, "has offered Wagner two hundred francs a month if he will accept the post of Kapellmeister. But he thinks it beneath his dignity to earn money and prefers to live on charity." To Wagner, however, this was not charity but tribute—a tribute to his art. "I am different from other men," he said. "The world ought to give me what I need."

He not only *petitioned* his friends for charity, he *demanded* it of them in a tone of arrogance—as if he were the benefactor and they the recipients. And indeed this was exactly the idea he conveyed to them. He gave them, he said, much more than they gave him—the golden coin of his brain for the baser metal of their pockets. He demanded not only money but hospitality. "Dear Hornstein," he writes to one of his "contributing" friends.

[*178*]

"I hear that you have become rich. . . . In order to lift myself above the most distressing obligations that rob me of all freedom of mind, I want an immediate loan of ten thousand francs. . . . Now let me see whether you are the right sort of man! If you prove to be this right sort of man . . . the assistance will bring you into very close touch with me—and next summer you must be pleased to let me come to you for three months at one of your estates, preferably to the Rhine district. I will say no more just now."

Though he had helped him repeatedly in the past, the Baron von Hornstein was for once staggered by the sheer audacity of Wagner's letter. "Yet I must confess," he said, "that the very tone of the letter and the size of the sum made a refusal easier to me. What made it still easier was the knowledge that I was dealing with a bottomless cask. . . . My ten thousand francs would be simply a drop of water falling on a hot stone." His reply to Wagner was polite but sharp. "Dear Herr Wagner," he wrote, "you seem to have a false idea of my riches. I have just a fair income which enables my wife, my child and myself to live in a simple and decent manner. You must therefore turn to your really rich patrons, of whom you have so many all over Europe. . . . As for your offer to pay a long visit to 'one of my estates,' I am sorry that just now I can make no arrangements for such a visit. . . . If I can do so later, I will let you know. . . . Greetings to you and to your wife."

Wagner's reaction to this letter is an interesting study in the impudence of genius. "Dear Herr von Hornstein," he writes, "it would be wrong of me to let your answer pass without the censure that it deserves. It is quite probable that a man of my caliber will not again appeal to a person like you; yet I must point out to you, for your own good, the utter impropriety of your letter. . . . It is not for you to advise me as to who are my 'really rich' patrons—it is for me to decide. . . . If you refuse to have me at one of your estates now, it is offensive of you to tell

[179]

me that you will have me at some future time. In this case, too, it is for me and not for you to choose. . . . Let this end the matter."

In all his quarrels—and he had many of them—Wagner felt convinced that he was absolutely in the right and that everybody else was absolutely in the wrong. He regarded himself, to quote the apt phrase of Ernest Newman, as "the central sun of his universe." The sun must blaze, and all the world must bow down in worshipful service. Wagner believed—and he had the right to believe—that he had been born into the world for the sake of producing sublime music. To that end he was ready to sacrifice everybody, including himself if need be. Suffering, poverty, sickness—nothing could ever swerve him from his self-appointed task. If his ethical vision was somewhat blurred, his artistic ideal was steadfast and clear. And this ideal was, to give always of his best. Perhaps it would not be an exaggeration to say that he was anxious to secure a congenial background for the creation of his music rather than to provide a comfortable life for the recreation of his person. His egoism, if we may so express it, was probably more objective than subjective. Objective beauty through subjective suffering. If others had to suffer along with him, or even without him and because of him —why, it was their bad luck. At whatever cost, the fire must be kept burning on the altar of his art.

IV

WAGNER'S ART, for which he was willing to sacrifice his friends, was something new under the sun. Beethoven, he maintained, had said the last word in instrumental music. The next step would be "music fertilized by poetry." This is the sort of music poetry, or music drama, that Wagner set out to give to the world. "Words alone," said Wagner, "cannot express the highest kind of poetry. The words are the roots, and the music is the flower." To enjoy the perfect plant at the moment of its greatest beauty, you must get the harmonious combination of the two—roots filled with life sap, flowers bursting into color.

Yet the flower to Wagner was more important than the root. For he was primarily, like Beethoven, an instrumental composer. He carried over the idea of Beethoven's *Ninth Symphony* into the opera. He produced, especially in his later works, an orchestral stream of melody with vocal accompaniments and poetical word fantasies to round out the whole. Beethoven's *Ninth*, with its triumphant choral in the Fourth Movement, is a dramatic symphony. Wagner's operas, if we may coin the expression, are symphonic dramas.

All the elements in the symphonic dramas of Wagner—the orchestration, the vocal accompaniment, the words, the scenery, the plot—are woven into an integral and definite pattern. And the design in this pattern, the thread unit which binds the various parts into a compact whole, is what Wagner calls the *leitmotif*. These leitmotifs, varicolored little strands of melody, run throughout his operas like the repeated figures in a tapestry. They identify the characters in the operas, they feature the landscapes and they endow the music with a concrete and recognizable personality.

The leitmotif was not an invention of Wagner's. Other composers before him had made use of this musical label. But in the work of most of the earlier composers it had remained a lifeless identification tag—a mere repetition of the selfsame notes in the selfsame mood. Wagner took this rigid and lifeless formula and transformed it into the plastic features of a living organism. Like the face of a human being, the leitmotif of a Wagnerian opera reflects not only the changing emotions of the character but the sunlight and shadows cast upon the character by the development of the plot.

The leitmotif became more and more a prominent feature of Wagner's music as his art advanced. In his earlier operas he adopted the traditional form of the motif as a melodic symbol.

[*181*]

It was not until the operas of the *Nibelungen Ring*—*The Rhinegold, The Valkyrie, Siegfried* and *The Twilight of the Gods*—that he turned this abstract symbol into a concrete form of musical portraiture. With the perfection of the leitmotif it may be said that Wagner introduced a new instrument into orchestral music.

For his genius, let us repeat, was primarily orchestral. The voice in a Wagnerian opera is but a part of the orchestra. This is true not only of the *Ring* but of the other operas of his later period—*Tristan and Isolde, The Mastersingers* and *Parsifal.* As in the paintings of Leonardo, the human characters of Wagner form but a part of the intricate web of nature which he puts upon the canvas of his theater. And in this respect both Leonardo and Wagner followed the technique of the Great Artist Musician. In the music drama of the universe the life of man forms but a single note.

V

IT WAS A NEW CONCEPT of music and a new philosophy of life that Wagner tried to create in his operas. And the world was slow to recognize this fact. At the age of fifty-one he was still comparatively obscure and desperately poor. Fortunately, at that time he found a patron who stood by him for the rest of his life. This patron was the eighteen-year-old King Ludwig II who had just inherited the crown of Bavaria. Ludwig invited Wagner to Munich, where his operas began to be regularly produced and his fame became firmly established. But the spirit of Wagner remained as restless as ever. He had met and fallen in love with Cosima, the daughter of Liszt and the wife of his friend and musical colleague, Hans von Bülow. While still married to Bülow, Cosima had borne Wagner two children. Finally, when the story of their love had become a public scandal, Wagner and Cosima decided to flaunt the conventions in the face of their friends and to elope. For some years they lived openly together; and then, Minna having died and Cosima having been divorced from Bülow, the two lovers were at last able to legalize their union. They were married on August 25, 1870. Wagner was fifty-seven years old and Cosima thirty-three.

Their marriage was happy. For they had a common interest— both of them adored Richard Wagner.

The Indian summer of his life was pleasant but not always serene. Occasionally he marred the sunlight of his last days with the scowl of his Jovian anger and the thunder of his controversy. He despised everybody, and he insisted that everybody must love him. Toward the end of his life he became a vegetarian, and from that day on all the world must become vegetarian. If a flesh diet was necessary for the people of Northern Europe, then let the people of Northern Europe migrate to the South.

He was an amazing character—a man who was possessed of much genius and not a little madness. Like the ideal philosopher of Emerson, he was a bundle of contradictions—a Christian and a pagan, a patriot and an internationalist, an ascetic and a voluptuary. He praised the virtues of the poor and surrounded himself with every sort of luxury. He dressed himself in silk trousers and a silk jacket—heavily padded, for he was suscepti- ble to drafts. His living room at Munich was decorated with "white tulle . . . rose-colored silks . . . yellow satins. . . . The ceil- ing was entirely covered with richly festooned white satin. . . . The ground was spread with a soft Smyrna carpet. . . . The couches were upholstered in a white flowered mohair. . . . The windows, the mirrors and the pictures were draped in silks and satins of various hues." And in the midst of all this sat the frown- ing little god in his crimson trousers and sang about the virtues of renunciation. For this doctrine of renunciation was the central theme of his music dramas.

Thoughtless as a rule toward others, he was astonished that anyone should ever be thoughtless toward him. On occasion, to be sure, he could display a great deal of charm; but it was the charm of a despot who gloried in his power over his slaves.

[*183*]

He patronized people, he tyrannized over them, at times he even smiled upon them—but he never befriended them. The world, as he saw it, consisted of millions of ciphers that followed a single unit—himself. "He treats us all," writes Cornelius, who adored Wagner, "like so many pieces of spiritual furniture. . . . Wagner never for a moment thinks of anyone but himself."

VI

SUCH was the musical dictator of Germany when, in 1872, he laid the cornerstone for the dream theater of his life—the *Festspielhaus* (Festival Playhouse) at Bayreuth. This was to be the lasting monument to his genius—the temple in which the two arts, poetry and music, were to be joined in holy wedlock. Four years after the laying of the foundation stone the *Festspielhaus* was ready for the first production of the *Nibelungen Ring*. The opening night of the performance, August 13, 1876, marked an epoch in the history of music.

He lived five and a half years longer—a flaming little Vesuvius of a man, always extolling his own work, always condemning the work of others, a "protean nature" who would "leap like a tiger"—we are quoting his friend, Edouard Schuré —"pace the room like a caged lion, roar like a stag. When he was excited his words came out like screams; his speech lashed about at random. He seemed at these times like some elemental force unchained. . . . The least little contradiction provoked him to incredible fury." In his moments of joy he was no less demonstrative than in his periods of rage. "When I came to visit him," writes Liszt, "he wept, laughed and ranted out of sheer rapture for at least a quarter of an hour." And when some visitor rendered one of his own pieces with exceptional skill, "he would spring up"—Sebastian Röckl is our authority for this quotation—"embrace or kiss the singer warmly, or out of pure joy stand on his head on the sofa, creep under the piano, jump up onto it or run into the garden and scramble joyously up a tree."

None of his friends could escape the magnetism of this man. Yet none could remain for any length of time in the highly charged field of this magnetism. One by one they came to him, laid their hearts at the shrine of his genius and then fell silently away. During the last days of his life he was practically alone.

But when he dropped dead (of a heart attack) on February 13, 1883, a unique personality had passed out of the world—a mischief-making child who had learned to converse with the gods.

VERDI

Great Compositions by Verdi

OPERAS:
Ernani, Macbeth, Rigoletto, Il Trovatore, La Traviata, Simone Boccanegra, Don Carlos, Aïda, Otello, Falstaff, I Lombardi, Nabucco, Giovanna d'Arco (Joan of Arc), Jerusalem, Stiffelio, Un Ballo in Maschera (A Masked Ball).

OTHER COMPOSITIONS:
String Quartet.
Pater Noster.
Ave Maria.
Stabat Mater.
Songs in Praise of the Virgin.
Requiem.

Verdi

Giuseppe Verdi

1813–1901

As a result of the Napoleonic conquests the Italian village of Le Roncole, in the province of Piacenza, was French territory. And it was in the French language that the young storekeeper, Carlo Verdi, recorded the birth of his son Giuseppe on October 10, 1813.

A few months later the Russian and the Austrian soldiers invaded the territory of Piacenza and, to vent their spite against Napoleon, massacred many of the inhabitants of that province —women and children as well as men. In Le Roncole a number of the women fled for refuge to the village church. But the soldiers pursued them and slaughtered them in the midst of their prayers. One of the women, however, was lucky enough to hide herself, together with her infant son, in the belfry. And this is how Giuseppe Verdi was saved from the sword that he might enrich the world with his song.

II

Though his parents neither sang nor played, their strange and silent child was passionately fond of music. His happiest hours were on Sunday, when he heard the organ at the parish church. At the age of seven he became an acolyte in the church. One day he was so enraptured with the playing of the organist that he forgot to hand the water to the priest. Whereupon the saintly man lost his temper and kicked him down the altar steps. When the child reached home, bruised and bleeding, his parents asked him what was the matter. His only reply was, "Please, I want to learn music."

Some years later the priest was struck by lightning, and the superstitious villagers saw in this tragedy a judgment from heaven for his ill-treatment of young Giuseppe.

But if heaven had seen fit to punish the poor fellow's outburst of temper, Giuseppe had long forgotten it. For his parents had bought him an old spinet, and this was more than a sufficient reward for his suffering. The village organist, Baistrocci, became his first instructor; but he was not nearly so hard a taskmaster to the young pupil as was Giuseppe himself. One day, when he was unable to strike a desired chord on the spinet, he became so enraged that he hit the instrument with a hammer. A piano tuner from the neighboring town of Busseto was called in to repair the instrument. He refused to take payment for his work. Instead he pasted inside the spinet a piece of paper with the following words: "I, Stephen Cavalletti, have repaired these jacks and put on the pedals, of all of which I make him a present, seeing how eager the young Giuseppe Verdi is to learn to play this instrument. His devotion to music is payment enough for my labor."

Within a short period Giuseppe's devotion to music had carried him beyond the capacity of his teacher. And so his parents sent him to Busseto for his further training. Compared to Le Roncole, the town of Busseto with its two thousand inhabitants was a very metropolis of art and culture. For it boasted a Philharmonic Society and a brass band. Thither the young musician of twelve repaired to seek his inspiration and his fortune. He took lodgings with a shoemaker, at five cents a day, and walked back to Le Roncole every Sunday for the church services. For he was now the assistant organist at the parish church—a job for which he received the munificent salary of forty lire (about eight dollars) a year.

The Sunday pilgrimages between Busseto and Le Roncole were not always pleasant. For he had to make them every week, rain or shine, winter as well as summer. One stormy Christmas Eve he fell into a ditch and was unable to get out until he was rescued by a passer-by. This life of all work and no play made Giuseppe a melancholy though by no means a dull boy. From earliest childhood he had never known what it meant to be care-free. Often he went hungry. If life was a beautiful song, it was also a tragic song. The future composer of the music of pity was receiving a thorough education in the school of suffering.

Fortunately, however, he soon found a patron in the person of Antonio Barezzi, a kindhearted and prosperous wholesale merchant from whom Carlo Verdi purchased the supplies for his store. Giuseppe had frequently visited Barezzi's warehouse on errands from his father. Barezzi took a fancy to the youngster; for he too, like Giuseppe, was an ardent lover of music. He played the flute and the clarinet, and he was the president of the Philharmonic Society.

It was with great joy, therefore, that young Verdi accepted an offer of apprenticeship in the warehouse of "Signor Antonio." He was to help Barezzi not only in his business but also in transcribing and arranging new music for the Society. In return for these services his patron gave him his board and his lodging and supplied him with teachers in Latin and in music. In short, young "Beppino" became an intimate member of the Barezzi household.

And the lover of Barezzi's daughter Margherita. The two youngsters played duets on the new piano which Barezzi had bought especially for them. Together they lived in their music and dreamed about their future marriage—a marriage which was to bring Verdi his greatest happiness and his greatest sorrow.

For the present, however, it was too early to plan for their marriage. For Verdi was still but a boy, and his musical education had just begun. A charitable society at Busseto made him a grant of three hundred lire a year, to which sum Barezzi added an allowance of his own, and Verdi went to Milan for the entrance examination to the Conservatorio.

He failed in the examination. But let us not blame the examiners for his failure. There were two definite and legitimate reasons for their rejection of Verdi—his excessive age and his insufficient knowledge. It was a rule of the institution that entering pupils must be under fourteen years of age and that they must show an adequate mastery of the piano. That the eighteen-year-old candidate showed a mediocre skill at the piano was a reflection not on the talent of Verdi but on the ability of his teachers. Indeed, the examiners praised his talent and recommended him to a private teacher, the composer Lavigna.

This, in spite of Verdi's bitter disappointment, turned out to be a lucky thing for him. For Lavigna was the cembalist in the orchestra of the Scala Theater, and it was through him that Verdi was able to become familiar with operatic music. Thus the failure of Verdi was but a step to success, a detour from the highways of academic erudition to the byways of independent creation. Verdi was born to be a writer of opera, and it was into this channel that a wise Providence had guided his steps.

For two years he studied under Lavigna, and then he began to make a name for himself. The conductor of the Milan Philharmonic Society had been planning to produce Haydn's *Creation*. At the last moment, however, he took fright. He complained that his chorus had been insufficiently rehearsed, and he suggested that Verdi take his place as the conductor. Verdi agreed to do this and turned an expected fiasco into a brilliant success.

As a result of this success the conductor of the Philharmonic urged him to write an opera and sent him a libretto. The title of this libretto was *Oberto, Conte di San Bonifacio*. The young musician of Le Roncole was now launched upon an operatic career that was to extend over a period of sixty years.

But before he wrote his first opera he returned to Busseto and married his boyhood sweetheart, Margherita Barezzi. Two years later, when he came once more to Milan, he was rich in the possession of a beautiful wife, a completed opera and two little bambini, a boy and a girl.

III

Oberto was produced at the Scala Theater in the fall of 1839. Its success, to quote Verdi himself, was "not very great, but good enough." Good enough to secure for him a commission to write two more operas.

The first of these operas was to be on a serious subject. But no sooner had Verdi started on it than Merelli, the director of the Scala Theater, changed his mind. The financial condition of the theater, he said, necessitated the production of a comic opera. Accordingly he sent Verdi a new libretto, *Un Giorno di Regno* (A Day of Dominion), and told him to set it to music at his "funniest best."

But at this time Verdi was in no mood for "funny" music. For misfortune had begun to accumulate upon his head. He had become a prey to a series of heart attacks—due possibly to a constitution weakened by frequent hunger in his childhood days. Unable to work and overwhelmed by an accumulation of debts, he asked Merelli for an advance on his contract, only to be met with a refusal. In order to pay the overdue rent his wife was obliged to pawn her jewelry.

"This," wrote Verdi in later years, "was only the beginning of my troubles. In April (1840) my little boy fell ill; and before the doctors were able to diagnose the sickness, the poor little fellow died in the arms of his distracted mother. As if this were not enough, a few days afterwards my little girl fell ill in her turn, and she too died. And, as if even this were not full measure, my poor wife was seized with a violent inflammation of the brain, and on the 3rd of June a third coffin left my house. . . . And in the midst of these terrible griefs I had to write a comic opera!"

The opera, as might have been expected, was a complete failure. He took this failure all the more keenly to heart because he looked upon it as insult added to injury. The public, he complained, had no business "thus to maltreat the work of a poor sick young man, worried by the shortness of time, and with his heart bruised by his awful misfortunes." Apparently the audience had not been silent in its disapproval, and this especially had cut him to the quick. "Had the audience, I will not say applauded, but just received the opera in silence, I could not have found words enough to express my thanks."

As a result of "the punishment of the gods and the pitilessness of his fellow men," Verdi was tempted for a time to yield to his despair. "I was alone, alone, alone! . . . With my soul tortured by my domestic misfortunes, and chagrined by the callousness of the public, I felt certain that it was hopeless to look to art for consolation, and I decided I would compose no more."

But one night he met Merelli, and his resolution to compose no more was broken down. Merelli had handed him a libretto on the subject of Nebuchadnezzar. "Take it home," he said, "and read it. Not that I expect you to set it to music. I merely want you to tell me what you think of it."

Verdi took the manuscript home, read it and decided to write the opera. For it breathed a spirit of rebellion akin to his own. It told the story of a suffering, oppressed race. His own race,

too, was suffering under the oppressive heel of Austria. Verdi
was a rebel. His heart was aflame with Italy's battle for freedom.
He would write music that would be a bugle call to this battle—
harmonies that would give "sustenance and strength" to his
fallen people, that would enable them to raise their heads, to
square their shoulders and to throw off the fetters of their
slavery.

It was in this mood that he wrote *Nabucco* (Nebuchadnezzar).
And the people, sensing the mood and catching the rebellious
spirit of the music, hailed Verdi as their national prophet composer, the Mazzini of the Italian opera. So deeply stirred was
the audience on the opening night that at the end of each act
the entire house rose in a united shout of acclamation. The
most successful number in the opera was a chorus of the captive
Hebrews—"Fly, my hope, on golden wings." This chorus was
taken up by the Italian people and was flung like a hymn of
defiance into the faces of the Austrian soldiers.

Verdi had returned from his solitude and had once more
taken his place in the world. And this regeneration of his drooping spirits was due not only to the devotion of the public but to
the affection of Giuseppina Strepponi. This talented young
actress had sung the soprano part in *Nabucco*. Indeed, it was her
ardent admiration for the music of this opera that had fired the
entire cast into a supreme effort. Her admiration for the music
was soon translated into admiration for the musician. Admiration ripened into love, and love opened the way to an intimate
relationship between the two. For some years, however, this
relationship remained unsanctioned by the legality of marriage,
and people began to wag their tongues. Verdi, who was conventional neither in his music nor in his character, paid no attention to the idle gossip of the public. But when his former
patron, Antonio Barezzi, added his own voice to the chorus of
disapproval Verdi felt constrained to write him a letter of re-
monstrance. "After so long a silence," complained Verdi, "I

did not expect to receive from you so formal a letter containing expressions which, if I interpret them correctly, have caused me great pain. If it were not signed by my benefactor, I should answer it very curtly, or not at all. But since it bears a name which it is my duty ever to respect, I must try to convince you that I do not deserve your censure. . . .

"I do not believe you would have written the letter if you had been following the dictates of your own heart. But you live among people who suffer from the habit of prying into the affairs of their neighbors and of condemning any action which does not conform to their own standards. It is my custom not to interfere with others, and I expect others not to interfere with me. . . .

". . . I have not the slightest objection to raising the curtain which hides the mystery of four walls . . . I have nothing to hide. In my house there lives a lady, free, independent, like myself a lover of the country, the possessor of a private income which raises her beyond the need of patronage. Neither of us is obliged to account for our actions to anybody. Our relationship is our own affair. What justification has the public to ferret out the claims that either of us may have upon the other? Whose business is it whether she is my wife or not? . . . Who has a right to ostracize us? . . . And let me say this: in my house she is entitled to the respect due to myself—nay, more; and on no consideration whatever must this be forgotten. Her conduct and her character give her a special claim to the consideration which she, on her part, has never failed to show to others."

It was not until 1859—seventeen years after their first meeting —that they were married. Their union, both before and after the marriage, was happy, though their characters were in some respects incompatible. They differed especially in their views about religion. Giuseppina was a pious Catholic, and Verdi was an agnostic. But both of them, whether believer or not, possessed the divine grace of tolerance. Giuseppina felt sorry for Verdi's skepticism, but she respected it. "My *brigand*," she writes playfully in one of her letters to her physician Cesare Vigna, "professes, with a calm obstinacy which makes me furious, to be, I will not say an atheist, but a very doubtful believer." But even a "doubtful believer" or a downright unbeliever, she admits in another of her letters (written to her friend Clarina Maffei), may be blessed with the grace of a good character. "Verdi is a noble soul, and may God give him many years of happiness! . . . There are some virtuous natures for whom a belief in God is a necessity; others, equally perfect, are happier believing nothing. Manzoni the believer, and Verdi the unbeliever—these two great men give me food for thought."

As for Verdi's attitude toward Giuseppina, he looked upon her piety as a necessary prop for those who are not strong enough to stand alone; but he loved her for what he regarded as her weakness as well as for what he recognized as her strength. She was the conformist, and he the revolutionist. And Verdi as well as Giuseppina realized that the perfect union consisted in the harmonious blending of the two opposite characters. No, not opposite, but supplementary. In the dangerous voyage of life there are two things of equal importance—a steady hand to guide the tiller, and a fearless mind to chart the course.

Yet Giuseppina and Verdi, though different in their attitude toward the Church, were alike in three essential respects—their devotion to charity, their love for the solitude of the country and their passion for music.

Charity was the one subject that was never discussed between the two. Each of them took the other's generosity for granted, and neither of them ever asked the other for an accounting of that generosity. "When we come to figure up our expenses," writes Giuseppina, "a conspicuous sum is always missing. And Verdi never offers an explanation—he doesn't have to. Every cent of that missing money has gone to help some poor devil in distress." Verdi, on his part, was equally tactful about the sums missing from Giuseppina's accounts owing to her own generosity. At times they collaborated in their charity—especially on those occasions when their fellow musicians were in need of help. Their spacious country home was always a haven for their less fortunate friends.

This country home of the Verdis, on the lake of Sant' Agata, had started with a small cottage and had gradually developed into a magnificent estate. For Verdi was a practical businessman and natural farmer. "I am and always will be a Roncole peasant," he said. He spent perhaps as much time on the cultivation of his land as he did on the writing of his music. He even assisted in the building of the various houses on the estate. "Verdi," confides Giuseppina to her friend Clarina Maffei, "has turned architect. . . . He is directing a legion of workmen at Sant' Agata. . . . I cannot tell you how often during the building operations beds, wardrobes and furniture danced from room to room. . . ." Once, when distinguished visitors came to the Verdis in the midst of their seemingly interminable process of building, "they had the honor of dining in a sort of anteroom, or rather corridor adorned with birds' nests where swallows flew in and out carrying food for their young." And Verdi was obliged to throw off his working clothes and to dress himself "respectably" in order to receive his guests. For Verdi was "always at work around the estate; and I assure you"—observes Giuseppina—"that he does his part as well as, and perhaps better than, a real architect."

Verdi was interested not only in the building but in the management of the estate. "My 'brigand' earns his daily bread as foreman at Sant' Agata." On market days he attended personally to the selling of his livestock. On his trips away from home he kept fully informed about the management of his estate and the movements of his hired help. "You say nothing of the servants," he writes during one of his absences to his caretaker. "Are they all dead? . . . How is the groom? What is he doing? . . . I understand that you do not give Milord (one of his horses) enough exercise and that you haven't as yet broken in the foal. This will not do. Horses will not keep fit and are likely to get fat and lazy if they are not exercised. And, I insist, the horses must be fed on our own hay." The gentleman farmer of Sant' Agata was a meticulous and exacting manager.

And in between the thousand and one duties pertaining to the management of his estate he wrote those "operatic experiments" which were gradually to bring him into the front rank of European composers. Thirteen operas in eight years: *I Lombardi*, *Ernani* (based on the poetic drama by Victor Hugo), *I due Foscari*, *Giovanna d'Arco* (Joan of Arc), *Alzira*, *Attila*, *Macbeth*, *I Masnadieri*, *Jerusalem*, *Il Corsaro*, *La Battaglia di Legnano*, *Luisa Miller* and *Stiffelio*.

Verdi was not a dreamer whose spirit floated above the realities of life. His feet were planted firmly upon the ground. He had acquired, especially under the tuition of Giuseppina, the very practical art of translating his genius into hard cash. When he was invited to write *I Lombardi* he asked Giuseppina what price he ought to demand for it. She advised him to get as much as he could but not to go too far. Taking her advice he asked, and received, fifteen hundred dollars for this opera. From that time on his prices kept going up all the way from twenty-five hundred dollars for *Luisa Miller* to thirty thousand dollars for *Aïda*.

Verdi was that rarest of human beings—a supreme genius who lived to become a supremely rich man.

IV

VERDI'S PATH was paved with gold, but occasionally a sharp rock was injected into the pavement with the object of tripping him up. The Austrian censors, who found in his music a dangerous note of aspiration for Italian freedom, tried everything within their power to throw obstacles in his way. To be sure, they couldn't imprison him as they imprisoned the insurgent journalists and politicians and poets of Italy, since it was impossible to produce a legal proof of a concrete revolutionary thought expressed in the abstract language of music. But they employed every possible legal method either to forbid the production of his plays or to emasculate the plots in such a way that the plays appeared meaningless when produced. For example, they insisted on cutting the conspiracy scene—the very crux of the story—out of the revolutionary opera *Ernani*. In thus diluting the lifeblood of the plot they also compelled Verdi to water the strong wine of his music. In similar manner the censors tampered both with the words and with the music of *Joan of Arc, Macbeth, The Lombards* and *The Battle of Legnano*.

He encountered his greatest difficulty, however, when he tried to produce *La Maledizione*. This was in 1850, shortly after the unsuccessful revolution of 1848. Verdi had taken a courageous part in that revolution. He had set to music a patriotic poem commencing with the words, "Sound the trumpet, wave the black-and-yellow flag," and had sent it to his friend Manzoni (author of the famous novel *The Betrothed*) with the words, "May this hymn soon be sung, to the accompaniment of cannon, on the plains of Lombardy." That same year he had signed his name to a manifesto in which the Italian revolutionists had asked the help of France against Austria.

The Austrian censors were bent upon punishing Verdi for his insubordination. And their opportunity came when he submitted *La Maledizione* for their approval. They examined the opera and issued the following report to the director of the Fenice Theater in Venice, where the play was scheduled for production:

"His Excellency, the Military Governor of Italy, directs us to express his profound regret that the poet Piave and the celebrated Maestro Verdi should have found no better field for their talents than the revolting immorality and obscene triviality which form the argument of the libretto entitled *La Maledizione*.

"His Excellency has decided that the performance must be absolutely forbidden, and he instructs us at the same time to request you to abstain from making further inquiries in this matter."

Fortunately, however, there were among the music lovers of Italy a number of influential politicians, including the secretary of the military governor himself. Thanks to the intervention of these political supporters the ban was finally removed and *La Maledizione*, "corrected and expunged of its offensive revolutionary sting," received the official *nihil obstat*. It was produced at the Fenice Theater (March 11, 1851) under a new title— *Rigoletto*.

V

With *Rigoletto* Verdi had entered upon a new period in the development of his genius—a period of sixteen years in which he wrote nine operas: *Rigoletto, Il Trovatore, La Traviata, I Vespri Siciliani, Simone Boccanegra, Aroldo, Un Ballo in Maschera, La Forza del Destino* and *Don Carlos*. He now worked less rapidly but more carefully than he had worked in the past. His voice had become mature, and he was anxious to expend it only upon his best efforts. A new note had come into his music—a note of pity for the sufferings of his fellow men. Rebellion had been mellowed into regret; hope had given way to grief. Life at its best was pathetic—a striving for the stars and a groveling in the dust. Every human drama, whatever the course of its action, must come to a tragic end. From aspiration to frustration—that, in a phrase, was the keynote of mortal existence. His nation had longed for freedom, had failed; the individual longs for happiness and fails. The story of the human race is a somber epic of broken ambitions. Let us set this epic to music. Let us sing a sorrowful hymn to human failure.

This is the dominant note in the operas of Verdi's second period. And this is largely the reason for the popularity of such operas as *Rigoletto*, *La Traviata* and *Il Trovatore*. They strike within us a responsive chord of *self-pity* and *fellow pity*. As we listen to these operas in the theater we feel drawn together into a universal brotherhood—a family of equal shareholders in the common heritage of sorrow. We forget the melodrama of the plots in the genuine drama of the music. And the music of these operas, in a thousand different modulations, repeats the selfsame dirge—*we live, we suffer, we die*.

In spite of Verdi's material success during this second period of his production, his music was predominantly melancholy. It was a music that came out of the reflection of a mature mind.

VI

AND THEN CAME HIS OLD AGE and the third period of his production. He had taken a fling in politics, had allowed himself to be elected a deputy of the Italian Parliament and had found it not to his liking. And so he returned to his old love and wrote the three operas which have been justly acclaimed as the sunrise songs of the Italian musical renaissance.

He produced the first of these three operas, *Aïda*, in his fifty-eighth year. It was something new in Italian opera. For the first time the music flowed on continuously, like a living stream, instead of being divided into the stagnant pools of the old-fashioned arias, duets, choruses, trios and the like. The music and the drama of this opera are so closely intertwined as to form a perfect pattern of rhythmic beauty. *Aïda* is the practical demonstration of Verdi's credo that music must not only keep close to the words but must penetrate *through* the words to the subtlety of the thought that lies behind them. The spirit made flesh, the soul of music breathed into the body of poetry—this, in short, is the substance of *Aïda*.

[*202*]

Having given *Aïda* to the world, Verdi retired into silence. This opera, said his admirers, was his swan song. But they were mistaken. At the end of sixteen years he broke his silence with *Otello*, the supreme grand opera of Italy. And then, after another silence of six years, the old maestro of eighty astonished the world with *Falstaff*, his real swan song and Italy's supreme musical comedy.

For the composition of *Otello* and *Falstaff* Verdi was fortunate enough to secure the librettos of Arrigo Boïto. This poet, who as a librettist ranks with William S. Gilbert, succeeded in condensing the very essence of the Shakespearean dramas upon which these two operas are based. He transfused into his poetry not only the thought but the imagination of Shakespeare. Never before had Verdi's musical genius been challenged with librettos of such masterly technique and such living inspiration. And he was equal to the challenge. With the help of Boïto he succeeded in capturing both the tragic and the comic spirit of Shakespeare. In *Otello* and in *Falstaff* he translated immortal poetry into immortal music.

VII

But he was tired of life, this sad old man who in his last hours had learned to laugh. He had always stayed away from people— afraid of their cruelties and indifferent to their applause. As often as he could he had refrained from attending the performances of his operas. For he preferred the solitude of Sant' Agata to the plaudits of the crowd.

And now he felt no longer at home even in his solitude. For Giuseppina was dead. All his old friends were dead. And his young friends? They were too absorbed in the flood tide of their own ambitions to bother about anyone who was floating away on the receding current of life.

The world was leaving him behind and rushing forward without him. Rushing to what? New wars, new oppressions, new cruelties, new hates. Yes, and *new songs*. A strange satire of the gods, this world of ours—a world governed by brute force, a world inspired by divine music. In the final scene of *Falstaff* the actors advance to the footlights and inform the audience that "everything in life is a huge jest."

Such was Verdi's farewell to the world. When he died (at the age of eighty-eight), Boïto expressed his indignation at the jest of the Fates who had removed this maestro from life. "I have lost many of those whom I have loved, and sorrow has outlived resignation. But never before have I felt such hatred against death and such contempt for its mysterious, blind, stupid, triumphant, infamous power."

And Boïto had reason for his violent denunciation of death. For rarely had it taken away so great a genius and so modest a man. "In character," writes his biographer Bonavia, "he was surpassed by none." When the king offered him a title he refused to accept it. His talent, he thought, was an authentic enough stamp of his nobility. Yet even his talent he regarded as but a secondary reason for his claim to distinction. A friend once asked him which of his works he considered the best. To this question Verdi replied: "My best work is a home for destitute musicians that I have endowed at Milan."

GOUNOD

Great Compositions by Gounod

OPERAS:
Sappho, Ulysse, La Nonne Sanglante, The Mock Doctor, Philemon and Baucis, The Queen of Sheba, Mireille, La Colombe, Cinq Mars, Polyeucte, Le Tribut de Zamora, Romeo and Juliet, Faust.

OTHER COMPOSITIONS:
About 40 Sacred Songs, including the famous Nazareth.
Over 200 Secular Songs.
2 Symphonies.
3 String Quartets.
Meditation based upon Bach's First Prelude.
Funeral March of a Marionette.
Mass in G.
St Cecilia Mass.
Redemption.
Mors et Vita.
Requiem.

Gounod

Charles François Gounod

1818–1893

HE WASN'T A BAD CHILD, but he didn't attend to his lessons. Scribbled music all over his Latin notebooks. Hummed snatches of opera when his teacher tried to explain a problem in arithmetic. His mother, fearful for her child's future, appealed to M. Poirson, the director of the boarding school.

"Rest assured, Madame Gounod," said the director, "your child will not be a musician."

He had thought of a plan to cure him of his "bad" habit. With this plan in mind he called him into his office one day. "And so you want to be a musician, my boy?"

"Yes sir."

"Very well, then, take this poem and set it to music."

Gounod took the poem and glanced at it. "Adrift from the threshold of childhood . . ." A pretty rhythm. He looked up from the poem to his teacher's sarcastic face. "I'll see what I can do with it, sir."

Two hours later he came back with the musical score. "Here it is, sir. I hope you will like it."

M. Poirson looked at the music in amazement. "Come, Charles, sing it to me."

Gounod sang it in a clear, confident voice. When he had finished there were tears in his teacher's eyes. He drew the boy to him and kissed him. "You are right, my child. Music is your career."

II

IT WAS WITH RELUCTANCE that Gounod's mother agreed to a musical career for her son. Not that she was averse to music. Indeed, she was an accomplished pianist and had herself given lessons to her child on this instrument. But she was terrified at the dreary prospects of an artistic life. And she had reason for her terror. Her husband, François-Louis Gounod, had been a distinguished painter. Distinguished and poor. At his death he had left her destitute with her two children, Urbain and Charles. The younger of the two children, Charles, was only five years old at his father's death. But he was born with music in his blood, this younger son of hers. His maternal grandmother had been a singer and composer. From earliest childhood the boy had shown evidence of his inherited talent for music. "It is the will of Providence," she said, and resigned herself to the inevitable.

Gounod had won his point. The studies of harmony and fugue were added to his curriculum. And now that he was given encouragement in the pursuit of his first love, he began to apply himself more diligently to the study of the classics. So that at the age of eighteen he received his degree of Bachelor of Arts with honors.

His next objective was the Prix de Rome. The winning of this prize would mean a free musical scholarship at the Villa Medicis. Twice in succession he tried for this prize and failed. But he persevered, for this prize was "a matter of life and death for my future career." In his third attempt he succeeded.

GOUNOD

He arrived in Rome (January 27, 1840) at the age of twenty-one. His first impression of the Eternal City was unfavorable. "A filthy, drab, vulgar, provincial place." Little by little, however, he learned to revise this opinion. There was something mystical in the Roman atmosphere, and it struck a responsive chord within him. For Gounod, too, had a deep strain of mysticism in his soul. He wrote to his mother about the sacred thoughts that descended upon him in this city, "so grave, profound and austere, a city which speaks so softly that her voice can be heard only by ears attuned to silent meditation." He spent three happy years of study at the Villa Medicis, composing, practicing on the piano—"I have just enough 'fingers' to play tolerably well," he said—and cultivating the friendship of M. Ingres, the director of the French Academy at the Villa Medicis. Ingres had known and admired François-Louis Gounod. "Mon Dieu," he said when Charles had arrived at the Villa, "how closely you resemble your father!" Every Sunday evening Gounod was an invited guest at the salon of M. Ingres. The older and the younger man shared a mutual passion for the music of Haydn, Mozart and Beethoven. One night they became so absorbed in their discussion and their music that Mme Ingres was obliged to interfere. "Gentlemen," she said as she came into the room, "you had better stop your wrangling. It is almost time for breakfast."

In addition to his love for music Gounod had acquired another passion—a passion for painting. On one occasion, as he returned to the Villa from a walk, he came face to face with Ingres. "What's that you have under your arm?" asked the director.

"Nothing of importance, sir. Just a little album."

"Come on, Charles, let's see it." And despite Gounod's objections he opened the album to a skillfully executed copy of Masaccio's *Saint Catherine*. "By Jove," he cried when he saw this specimen of Gounod's work, "do you want us to bring you back here on the Grand Prix for painting?"

Painting, however, had become an occasional if fascinating mistress to Gounod. Throughout his life he remained "faithfully married" to his music. Every Sunday during his stay in Rome he attended the services at the Sistine Chapel, feasting his eyes on the frescoes of Michelangelo and his ears on the masses of Palestrina. It was under the influence of Palestrina that he wrote his own mass, an original composition required from every holder of a scholarship at the Villa Medicis.

Shortly after his arrival at the Villa he made the acquaintance of Fanny Hensel, the talented sister of Felix Mendelssohn, who was spending her vacation in Rome. Madame Hensel found him "still unripe, but possessed of a romantic and passionate enthusiasm. . . . Our German music produces upon him the effect of a bomb that has just exploded in the room."

The impressionable student composer and several of his fellow students at the Villa Medicis became ardent disciples of Fanny Hensel. With her superb playing she bewitched them into new visions of Mozart, Beethoven and her brother Felix. "She ushered us into fairy palaces where we indulged in many a musical carousal."

His studies in Rome completed, he went to Vienna. Here he made himself known to the various musical circles—Gounod was not the type to keep his lights hidden under a bushel—and received from the president of the Philharmonic Society a tentative commission to write a *Requiem* for the Feast of the Dead, which was to be celebrated six weeks later. "Are you sure you can finish the work within so short a time?" asked the president. "I'll try," replied Gounod in a tone that implied, "I can." He undertook the job and succeeded. The *Requiem* was performed on the appointed day to the surprise and delight of the music lovers of Vienna.

Overtures were made to him to remain in this city of "satire, sentiment and song." But he was anxious to go on to Berlin, where Fanny Hensel had promised to give him a letter of introduction to her brother Felix Mendelssohn, the conductor of the *Gewandhaus* in Leipzig.

Immediately after his arrival in Berlin he fell ill. To the physician recommended to him by the Hensel family he gave the following ultimatum: "Sir, I can afford to be sick only a short time. I give you just two weeks in which to put me under the earth or back on my feet."

The doctor accepted the challenge. Within two weeks Gounod was on his way to Leipzig.

Mendelssohn received him cordially. Although the regular season was over at the *Gewandhaus*, the maestro arranged for a special performance of his *Requiem*. After the performance Mendelssohn congratulated him. "My dear young friend," he said, "this piece reminds me of Cherubini."

"Thank you very kindly," replied the young composer. "But I hope someday to write a piece which will remind you of Gounod."

He left Leipzig in the spring of 1843. After sixteen changes of carriages and four days and nights of uninterrupted travel he arrived in Paris, pale and emaciated from his illness but over-bubbling with ambition. An old friend of the family, the Abbé de Dumarsais, offered him a position as organist of his church. Gounod accepted the offer on one condition—that he be recognized as the sole arbiter of the musical programs. "I expect to be the musical priest while you continue to serve as the ecclesiastical priest."

A few years of labor at the organ, and Gounod had had enough of obscure poverty. For a time, indeed, he had flirted with the idea of entering the priesthood. For that mystical strain in his nature wrestled occasionally with his ambition and inclined him to a life of self-sacrifice. He joined a society of "young evangelists" whose mission it was "to regenerate humanity through the medium of art." His art, however, won a decided victory over his evangelism. He turned from the pulpit to the theater. If he couldn't *regenerate* humanity, at least he could *amuse* it. And incidentally he could feed his own hunger for fame and fortune. No more masses for the dead. He would now write operas for the living.

He began to search for a librettist and found one in Emile Augier. Together they started to work on the pagan tragedy of *Sappho*—a strange subject for a man who had been so recently immersed in the mysticism of Christianity. But his paganism was merely the reverse side of the coin of his mysticism. "There is a common bond of sympathy between Apollo, the God of Light, and Jesus, the Saviour of Man." Gounod manifested a sacred emotion even in the most profane of his compositions.

The "profane" opera of *Sappho* was produced on April 16, 1851. It was a financial failure but an artistic success. At the end of the performance Gounod met Berlioz in the lobby. The latter was in tears. "Come, my dear friend," cried the young composer. "Show these tears to my mother. They will be the best commentary she'll ever read on my new opera."

III

ENCOURAGED by the reviews rather than the receipts of his first operatic attempt, Gounod offered his hand to the daughter of one of the professors at the Conservatoire.

Shortly after his marriage he composed another opera, *La Nonne Sanglante* (The Bleeding Nun). The opera, like its title, was sentimental, melodramatic, unreal. It dealt with the period of the Crusades under Peter the Hermit. The public cared neither for the period nor for the subject matter of the opera. After eleven performances it was withdrawn from the stage, never to be revived to this day.

Discouraged by his failure in the theater, he wrote two symphonies (in D and in E flat) and then plunged once more into his mysticism. He composed an oratorio on the biblical subject of the *Blind Tobit,* and then he secluded himself in the country and settled down like an anchorite to write the *Mass of St Cecilia.* His only recreation during the writing of this mass was the reading of St Augustine—a contrite penance for his pagan excursion into the theater.

He completed his penance—and went back to the theater. With a comic opera. It was a delightful version of Molière's comedy *Le Médecin malgré lui.* The opera was an immediate success, and the eyes of the world were once more turned upon Gounod.

Whereupon Gounod once more turned his eyes upon the world. The artist had again won a victory over the evangelist. He began to dream of more successful operas, greater conquests. He must hit upon a subject of universal appeal. Something that was bound to be popular and, too, something that would stir him to his best musical effort. Where could he find this sort of thing? It must be a worldly theme and yet with a religious background—a story of passion and compassion, an epic of sin and suffering and redemption, a panoramic picture of the misery of the Earth, the punishment of Hell, the glory of Heaven. In all literature there was but one such story—Goethe's immortal drama of God, Man and the Devil.

Gounod would write an opera on the story of *Faust.*

When *Faust* was first produced (March 19, 1859) Gounod was in his forty-first year—the customary peak year of artistic success. Yet *Faust* was not a success on its initial performance. The music, said some of the critics, was too dull. They recommended the omission of the garden episode and the soldiers' chorus—two of the most exquisite jewels upon the glittering necklace of his music. One of the reviewers suggested the scrapping of the entire opera. "In the music of Gounod, as in the words of Goethe, we are introduced to Herr Professor Faust, an old man who is bored with his studies, disgusted with his science.

[*213*]

This note of boredom and disgust permeates M. Gounod's opera from beginning to end." And then the reviewer went on with seven pages of "unreasonable reasoning" to prove that Gounod's *Faust* was bound to be a failure.

But the public thought otherwise. After an uncertain start the opera moved rapidly into the front rank of the world's permanent successes. "The critics," said Gounod, "are the sterile old maids of the artistic world, jealous of their confreres who have the potency to create."

He therefore disregarded the critics and went ahead with his work. Once more he banished himself to the countryside in order to escape from the distractions of the city. Assuming the name of "M. Charles" in order that he might remain incognito, he installed himself in a little white cottage at Saint-Rémy on the Rhone. Every morning at sunrise the peasants saw this mysterious stranger walking along the riverbank, a middle-aged man with a grayish beard and a faraway look in his eyes. He always came back from his rambles with bunches of flowers in his hands and garlands of music in his head. His only companion during this period was Mistral, the "shepherd poet of the Provence" who sat in his quiet fields of Maillane and dreamed those lyric dreams that were to win him the Nobel Prize in literature. It was here that Gounod planned some of his most inspired operas after *Faust—Philemon and Baucis, The Queen of Sheba, Mireille* and that "flawless masterpiece" which even the critics acclaimed, *Romeo and Juliet.*

And then, having reached the midday of his glory, he fell into sudden disgrace.

IV

The story of Gounod's disgrace—a misfortune due to no moral delinquency on his part—is the story of a weak man and a worldly woman. A refugee from Paris after the defeat of France in 1870, he went to live with his family in England. Here he was received with the greatest enthusiasm. Among those who wined and dined him was a young adventuress, Georgina Weldon, who with her equally adventurous husband held a brilliant salon at the Tavistock House, a place famous as the former residence of Charles Dickens. Gounod was carried away by the associations of Dickens and the beauty of Mrs Weldon—she was a tall woman, with a dazzling head of blonde hair, large, childlike eyes, an appealing mouth, white aristocratic hands and exquisite feet. Whenever he played for her she broke into a tempest of tears. She called him her master, her inspiration, her god. She offered him a shrine at the Tavistock House. He came to live there, and she laid her adoration as a daily tribute upon the altar of his genius. Lulled in the sweetness of her worship, he appointed her as his secretary, his adviser, his sole business manager. He signed away all his rights to this fascinating Circe of the British Isles. And like the followers of Ulysses he allowed himself to become more and more entangled in the web of her cunning deception.

At last his friends succeeded in rescuing him from her wiles. But not from her toils. Having lost his person, she refused to release his compositions, especially his latest opera *Polyeucte*, of which she had the only copy in existence. After several fruitless demands that she return this music he copied the entire opera of *Polyeucte* from memory.

But Georgina Weldon had still another card to play—her trump card. She sued Gounod for one hundred and fifty thousand dollars. On what charges? The following, among others:

". . . the defendant has lived at Tavistock House for three years, without having paid for his board and his lodging;

". . . he has been nursed, at the expense of his hostess, through an illness;

". . . he has broken his promise to engage Mrs Weldon for the leading role in his opera, *Polyeucte;*

". . . he has caused his hostess to undergo the expense of building an elaborate concert room at Tavistock House;

". . . he has inspired the publication of several newspaper articles in which Mrs Weldon has been depicted as an adventuress."

The trial dragged on for ten years, sapping his strength and his creative energy. The critics, always ready to descend like vultures upon a wounded creature, sneered that the London fogs had dissipated his talents. In the course of the trial Mrs Weldon was sentenced to a term in prison for criminal libel against another man. But all this was of no avail to Gounod. The English courts finally rendered a verdict against him and in favor of Mrs Weldon. The sum, fifty thousand dollars.

Crushed by this blow, Gounod took refuge once more in his mysticism. And this time he remained a mystic to the end. Fixing up his music room like a chapel with a huge organ, he would sit there for hours playing the religious cantatas of Bach, "the maestro of the maestros." And now there came to him the thought of the masterpiece of his own career, the oratorio *Mors et Vita* (Death and Life). In the preface to this work he explained his reason for placing the word *Death* before the word *Life*. "If life precedes death in the sequence of time, death precedes life in the sequence of eternity. Death may be the end of the *illusion* of life, but it is the beginning of the *true* life, the immortal life of the soul."

Saint-Saëns, in his celebrated *Portraits and Memories*, has this to say of Gounod's *Mors et Vita:* "In the distant future, when the operas of Gounod will be gathering dust in the archives of musical curiosities, his *Mors et Vita* will stand forth as a living illustration of the composer who brought glory to France in the nineteenth century." For this oratorio is "one of the world's famous love songs"—a song of Man's love for God, of God's love for Man.

He began one other religious work before he died, a *Requiem*.

But he never finished it. One afternoon in the autumn of 1893, as he sat down to his work, his head drooped over his desk. "Hush," said his wife to the other members of the household, "let us not disturb him. He is asleep. . . ."

"Death," he had said, "is the beginning of life."

BRAHMS

Great Compositions by Brahms

VOCAL:
German Requiem.
Cantata, *Rinaldo.*
Parzengesang.
Schicksalslied (Song of Fate).
Triumphlied.
Rhapsody (for voice and orchestra).
Numerous choral works.
Cycle of *Gipsy Songs.*
Many other songs.

INSTRUMENTAL:
4 Symphonies, in C minor, D major, F major, E minor.

2 Piano Concertos, in D minor, B flat minor.
Violin Concerto, in D major.
Concerto for violin, cello and orchestra.
Academic Festival Overture.
Tragic Overture.
3 String Quartets.
2 String Quintets.
2 String Sextets.
Several Sonatas for piano, violin, cello, clarinet, etc.
16 Waltzes.
Hungarian Dances, Ballades, Rhapsodies, Romances, Intermezzos, Fantasias, etc.

Brahms

Johannes Brahms

1833–1897

F ATE often chooses incongruous birthplaces and strange parents
for genius. Brahms was born in the slum district of Hamburg.
His father was a horn player in the band of the Hamburg
militia, good-natured, hard-dancing, hard-drinking Johann
Jakob Brahms. His mother was seventeen years older than her
husband. She walked with a limp, but her fingers were nimble
with the needle and with food recipes. An old maid at forty-one,
she had taken the young musician into her house as a boarder
and lured him into marriage within a single week through the
spells of her culinary magic. As William S. Gilbert might have
said, a well-baked pudding was the reason for the birth of
Johannes Brahms.

Frau Christiana Brahms kept her restless husband content
with her bilberry fritters and bore him two sons. For the first
three decades of their married life there was little disharmony
between them, and the children grew up in surroundings of
moral beauty for all the stench of the slums. The parents were
artists of the good life. They kept songbirds in their shabby
apartment and songs of sheer joy in their hearts. On their birth-

days they drank long and lusty toasts—wine for the father and eggnogs for the mother and the children. Many years later Johannes, who was still fond of his eggnogs, gave a friend his mother's old recipe—with an addition of his own: twelve eggs, four lemons, one pound of sugar and one bottle of rum.

The mysterious story of the human impulse toward divine expression began, in the case of Johannes, at an early age. His father was astounded one day to find that his son had absolute pitch. Immediate visions of a great musical future for the boy! Johannes would someday become "an even greater player than his father." And they would gladly take him into the Hamburg Philharmonic.

Johannes began to study the piano and was soon hailed as something of a child prodigy. An impresario offered to take him on a concert tour to America and to make a fortune for his astounded parents. But their sober-minded friends dissuaded the impetuous Jakob and his wife from venturing upon this short cut to El Dorado. Johannes remained with his teachers in Hamburg. These teachers were admirably suited to his talents. They not only gave him a mastery over the piano but they developed in him a sure grasp of the intricacies of rhythm, a facility in playing variations upon a musical theme and a genuine love for the German folk song.

But he was educated in more prosaic matters too. He had secured a job as a barroom pianist. At the age of thirteen he knew the inside of every tavern in the district. He was up at all hours of the night. The proprietors stimulated him with drinks to keep him awake at the piano. "Professional ladies" held him on their laps and aroused his passions. It seemed as if his delicate soul would stifle amidst these surroundings. Here, apparently, was a poet destined to live as a vagabond. But he challenged his destiny. His natural instinct for beauty clashed with his environment. It was a war of the soul against ugliness. It raged throughout his teens. No quarter was asked or given, and for a

time no decision was reached. At twenty he was a gifted vagabond. And then suddenly, within the space of a few months,
he entered the regions of recognized genius.

II

In 1853 Johannes Brahms was an unknown writer of hack songs.
So, too, was his older brother Fritz. Both sons of Jakob Brahms
had evidently inherited a modicum of music from the fractional
talent of their father. Fritz continued as a hack writer to the end
of his life and earned for himself the title of the "wrong Brahms."
Something happened to Johannes, however. He became the
"right Brahms." A popular violin player took notice of him and
invited him to come along with him on a concert tour as his
accompanist. Glad to escape from his surroundings, Johannes
accepted. Their journey took them to Hanover, where they met
the young virtuoso Joseph Joachim. Brahms had heard him
play the Beethoven violin concerto five years earlier, and that
occasion had been one of the landmarks of his spiritual career.
Now he opened up his heart to Joachim and played him some
of his own compositions for the piano. No one else he had ever
met could have inspired him to play these pieces with such
genuine feeling. Joachim listened to the music and recognized
at once the presence of genius. Here were original rhythms,
solid forms, fresh melody, passion untouched by the cynicism
of maturity. It was not the piano alone that sounded. It was a
whole orchestra speaking through the keys. And Joachim was
only a few years older than Brahms—still young enough to feel
a lover's thrill at the sudden proximity of a compatible soul.
   Joachim begged Brahms to visit his friend Robert Schumann
and to show him his work. For Schumann was the revered
master of the romantic school and a word from him could help
the young man mightily. At first Brahms was hesitant. He had
sent Schumann his work and the master had returned it without

even giving it a reading. But Joachim was insistent. And when in the course of his tour as accompanist he arrived in the Rhinelands, Brahms stopped off at Düsseldorf and came quietly to Schumann's house. Here he found no pompous old crank but a friendly fellow in the prime of life and mental vigor, surrounded by his adoring family. The young man sat down and played a few notes. Schumann interrupted him. "Clara must hear this," he said and he immediately summoned his wife. As Brahms played on, the eyes of the master became filmed with tears. He listened to the dreamy melodies of the *Sonata in F sharp minor*, the tender variations on the old German Minnelied, that inspiration of "unpremeditated craftsmanship" that he himself at forty-four had never been able to achieve. And as he listened his own generous spirit rose with a mighty throb and swore allegiance to this young man of twenty who had come here out of the slums of Hamburg. From that day onward Robert Schumann realized that his own art would come to no sudden end. For here was Johannes Brahms ready to carry it forward into regions of dizzier heights and more enduring beauty. He introduced Brahms to the best musical circles and gave him a permanent place at his table and in his heart. The young man found himself worshiped by the Schumanns and their friends. It was a challenge to his genius. What could he do but write music and more music for this master and his wife who had taken him into their intimacy? He dedicated his compositions to Robert Schumann and he fell madly in love with Robert Schumann's wife.

Clara Schumann was a noble and beautiful and gifted woman at that age when a woman is at her capable best to sway the souls of susceptible young men. And Brahms was most susceptible. Here, then, was a "concordance of discord" enough to perplex the heart of any musician. Clara Schumann was old enough to be his mother. She was the wife of the great man who had befriended him. And, as if the devil himself were taking a hand in the situation, Schumann suffered a mental breakdown and went to an asylum. He never emerged from it alive. The great mind, bowed down with the weight of genius and disappointment, never except for a few intervals was able to find its way out of the fog. And now he had entrusted to the boy he loved not only his music but his home, his children, his wife. Brahms underwent a terrific struggle for self-mastery. These people, Frau and Robert Schumann, were his idols. He must do everything in his power to lessen the burden of their tragedy. It was his talent that had once haunted Schumann, and now it was his talent that rescued Schumann's wife from despair. For when the moments of her grief became too poignant he sat at the piano and brought the vital message of music that to her was life. "I am developing a sense of beauty, don't you think?" he once told her. "When you see a lovely woman for a long time, a woman who is at once gracious and tender and pure, you cannot help being inspired by the spectacle."

Schumann lingered in his mental graveyard for two years. Sometimes he would recall his wife and their married happiness. Most of the time he was aware of nothing. Once when Brahms visited him Schumann recognized him. Together they discussed their music and their mutual love for Schumann's family. And the young man was filled with sadness as he stood before the ruins of his friend. A bitter, stormy stream of melody ran through his head.

Brahms was now only twenty-one, but he had already lived a lifetime. He took long walks with Clara Schumann in the Rhinelands. He talked to her of his passion. Clara listened and understood. She treasured his genius, his devotion, his youth. And how able she was to understand youth! A mother of six children, and a seventh child to come. In the eyes of the young Johannes she was transformed into a goddess. Every day she taught him to marvel at the nature of true love; every moment she showed him the beauty of self-denial. "My dear mother," he called her.

[225]

She must forgive him for his boyishness, for his anxiety to surrender without reserve.

The terrible two years were over. Schumann was gone. But the echoes of his music remained in Brahms's ears. They were stormy echoes that sounded like the dashing of the surf. They were undermining the very foundations of his resolve. Now the woman he loved was free! He wrote a sea poem. The elements of his passion rushed forth in a mad momentum.

And then suddenly all was quiet. He had found peace. He had summoned an iron will to control his emotion. There was no marriage with this widow. There was never in his long life to be a marriage with anyone else. The struggle was over. And he had emerged from this struggle with a leitmotif that was to dominate the theme of his music and his life. It was an Eleventh Commandment: *Control thy passion.* "Passion is not natural to mankind; it is always an exception, an excrescence." It must quickly subside or else it must be driven out. "Be calm in joy; be calm in pain." Be an old Greek philosopher garbed in the personality of a nineteenth-century musician. A tranquil, unperturbed Aristotle.

III

BRAHMS left Clara's side. Some say that she had been his mistress and that he had tired of her. Some believe that he was the father of her last child. Brahms took care not to throw any further light on the subject. Several years later, when he arrived at the height of his fame, he requested from Clara a number of letters he had written her during the two years following her husband's death. He destroyed them. Never in any of his subsequent letters did he speak to her of love. They remained close and tender friends and silent guardians of their memories. And he left behind a musical monument to this episode of his youthful ardor—a tempestuous concerto for piano in D minor.

Brahms had renounced the slavery of passion, but he still enjoyed the freedom of an occasional love affair in which he kept a careful watch over his heart. The first of these romantic episodes was with Agathe von Siebold, daughter of a university professor at Göttingen. The two lovers strolled through the countryside. They serenaded each other from the branches of trees. Agathe had sensuous dark eyes and soft black hair. "How delightful to run my fingers through this hair!" he told her. He wrote a sextet for strings in which the first and the second violins repeatedly call out her name as they sound the notes A-G-A-D-C-E. Yet his attachment to her was but a passing fancy. "I love you," he wrote to her after a separation, "but I cannot wear the fetters of marriage."

Brahms had the temperament of a bachelor. Be calm in passion! Drive it off! Every time he was on the point of losing his heart a new immortal passage was added to the scroll of his music. Modern psychologists would call it sublimation. Brahms called it the translation of emotion into song.

He was now a successful musician. Among his other duties—or rather pleasures—he conducted a female choir at Hamburg. These were delightful days. Most of the rehearsals in the summer time were out of doors. And under the soft skies the ladies fell in love with him. One of the young women he met at this time was a golden-voiced girl from Vienna. She cast a spell over him with her Austrian folk songs. She was much more fascinating than the reserved women of northern Germany. She came from a land of romance and fun. Soon she was followed by another charming visitor to Hamburg, a young woman who had sung in the Viennese opera house. If women like these came from Vienna, what was there left for young Johannes to do—but to go there himself?

In 1862 he visited the imperial city. And he made merry with members of the musical fraternity. In Vienna there were scholars who liked a little drink with their research and epicures who enjoyed a little scholarship between their drinks. Brahms,

who was fond of a good time in spite of his adherence to the
golden mean, found himself in ideal society. And needless to
say, the city was full of beautiful women. Once again he fell in
love—she, too, had a charming voice. Her name was Ottilie
Hauer, and she inspired some of his finest songs. She, too,
went her way, married and became a lifelong friend of his.
Brahms had the happy faculty of turning his young sweethearts
into old friends who comforted him in his declining bachelor
days.

During this period in Vienna he devoted himself to chamber
music and wrote piano quartets, a cello sonata and a horn trio.
He had gained an enviable reputation for himself among the
music-loving Viennese, but all along he had a secret desire to
come back to his birthplace. It was a matter of pride to him if
he could disprove the popular belief that a man is no prophet
in his own country. Specifically he hoped for an appointment
as conductor of the Hamburg Philharmonic Orchestra. In this
hope he was disappointed. His fellow townsmen passed him
over. He remained in Vienna where he received the leadership
of the Viennese choral society. Scrupulous in his artistic principles, he gave Bach's religious works such prominence on his
programs that one facetious critic remarked, "When Brahms
is really merry, he gets the chorus to sing 'The grave is my
joy.' " He gave music lessons in the aristocratic circles of Vienna
and again captured the heart of one of his young pupils, Elizabeth von Stockhausen. Later on she, too, married and became
one of his staunchest friends, leaving him a considerable sum of
money at her death. Afraid that her husband might misunder-
stand their early relationship, he returned the money which had
been sent to him concealed in a chest of music sheets. He explained that someone must have placed it in that chest by
mistake.

He was a pied piper who led women's hearts a merry dance.
And to only two women had he ever given his heart completely

—Clara Schumann and his mother. Frau Christiana Brahms, lame and homely and wholesome as ever, was in great trouble. Her husband, an erratic young blade of only fifty-eight, was beginning to tire of her seventy-five years. He began to cast his eyes elsewhere. For a time the couple fidgeted and fought, and then they separated.

Brahms wrote his father again and again, trying his utmost to bring him back to his nest. "It would please me mightily if I could think that you would return home. . . . Where do you take your meals? . . . Don't you want to spend even a single evening with mother?" But his father stubbornly refused to make any advances toward a reconciliation.

And before long there was no need of any reconciliation. Mama Brahms had passed on. Old Jakob shed a few tears and then wrote to his son of his plans for a new marriage. "She is a homely body, forty-one years of age, and she cooks and bakes divinely." An excellent bread mate for old Jakob Brahms.

Johannes was deeply moved by the death of his mother. He paid her the tribute of a *German Requiem*—the most impressive of his compositions to date. He had now attained the complete mastery of his art. He had developed a philosophy that would protect him through life against the changeful weather of events. For the sensible man there was nothing to be altered, nothing to regret. He must simply carry on and hold his head above the waves. Nothing to the end of his days would hurry him or slacken him unduly. He would keep the even temper of his way.

It was in this spirit of restraint that he wrote the *Requiem*. And when the first performance was announced nearly all his friends came to hear it. For it was a momentous event in the musical circles of Vienna. As he stepped upon the conductor's stand to lead the orchestra and the chorus in their solemn mass for the dead, he saw before him the wrinkled, homely, lovable old face of his mother. In the audience among the living sat Clara Schumann and her daughter Julie, who was now grown and who shared her mother's adoration for his genius. And somewhere, too, in the audience sat Joachim, proud that his prophecy about his young protégé had been so gloriously fulfilled. And there was his father, Jakob Brahms, none the worse for a couple of drinks. And when Johannes finished the *Requiem* there were tears in the old fellow's eyes.

IV

BRAHMS was approaching forty. His days of wandering between Vienna and Hamburg were over. He had settled down for good in the Austrian capital. He moved into a two-room bachelor apartment in Karlsgasse, near the Great Church and the busy city square; and here he remained to the end of his days. And as if to add a further symbol to his character as a hermit, he grew a beard. White and majestic it appeared in later life— a beard worthy of a Jehovah. Incidentally, it served to conceal his open collar. He hardly ever wore a tie. As he grew older his untidiness became more and more pronounced. At heart he was a peasant, and he loved the coarse clothes and the coarse laughter of the peasants. He wore a battered old hat that looked as if it had come out of an ash can. Cuffless flannel shirts were his adornment at the most formal of ceremonies. His frayed trousers barely reached down to his shoes. One evening at a party, when the parlor talk turned to stockings, he shocked a group of old Viennese ladies by remarking, "See how elegant *my* stockings are." And he raised his trouser cuff to show a bare ankle. He generally displayed a patch on the seat of his trousers and at the elbows of his alpaca coat. He rarely changed his clothes. He flung them helter-skelter into his trunk when he was called away on a trip and left them scattered on the floor when he went to sleep at home. No one ever saw Brahms put an iron to them. His friends were constantly apologizing for his appearance. They induced his tailor to cut him a pair of trousers the proper length, but when Brahms received them he slashed them back to shoe-top height. And he wasn't always accurate in his slashing. Very frequently one of the legs was longer than the other. Even as a young man, before he had become confirmed in his bachelor habits, he had shown the same carelessness about his physical appearance Once he had attended a party where everyone looked at him queerly. "What's wrong with my clothes?" he asked his mother when he got home. "Why," she cried, "you've gone and put on the coat from which I had cut off all the buttons!"

Whenever his pants tore he would stick the tatters together with sealing wax. "The only trouble was, the wax didn't hold very long. . . ." When he lost a pair of gloves in the dead of winter he couldn't bring himself to buy another pair. He was a grown-up Huckleberry Finn, a true son of his humble parents, a child of the slums. And as he aged in the disappointment of his spiritual aspirations he turned more and more to the solid qualities of food. He loved to eat. His stomach had developed a fondness for expansion. He cut a droll figure as he took his tubby little steps through the town in a large gray-brown plaid shawl that was flung about him like a sack and fastened at the throat with a huge safety pin. But he rarely showed himself in public. He spent most of his time with the music he loved. He hunched over the piano like a bear. The sweetest tones mingled with his own wheezes and grunts. He was lord and master in that little tenement of his which satisfied nobody but himself. The rooms were so arranged that a person entered by way of a dirty corridor and was compelled to go through the kitchen and the bedroom before he could reach the sitting room. And when he reached it there was no place to sit. For all the chairs were covered with music sheets and books. In a corner stood an old-fashioned trick armchair that Brahms coaxed his new acquaintances to try. The moment they sat down their feet were lifted toward the ceiling. He loved to play this prank especially on the ladies.

He was unconventional to the point of vulgarity. When the University of Cambridge offered him a doctor's degree in recognition of his music he sent his thanks on a crumpled post card. He did his own marketing and haggled about the prices like a veritable fishwife. He enjoyed nothing better than a huge plate of herring for his supper. He scrimped his money, smoked his cigars, gobbled his food, shocked the old ladies, outraged his friends. . . .

. . . And dreamt such dreams as had not been vouchsafed to anyone since the days of Beethoven. For the *First Symphony* of Brahms was the worthy sequel to Beethoven's *Ninth*. In his music, as in his character, Brahms was the legitimate heir of Beethoven. In both cases a gruff exterior concealed an enduring gentleness within. Beethoven and Brahms—the last of the musical trinity in B major—the two men who put the spirit of philosophy into the music of Bach. In the mathematical formulas of Bach perched beauty waiting for the philosopher to release her into the heavens. For the scientist alone and the poet alone could not set her free. The scientist musicians had constructed massive mausoleums of granite without any windows, and the poet musicians had produced fragile windows of stained glass but without any solid framework to support them. It took the philosophers of music, men like Beethoven and Brahms, to build houses for the living and not for the dead—mansions that are solid and at the same time full of air and vitality and enduring beauty.

Brahms built mansions to endure. It is hard to understand them at first. Their beauty consists not in the oddity of the decorations nor in the elaborateness of the surroundings. The solid masonry of the Brahms musical structure depends upon no mere sensationalism or deceit. The builder has no wares to show off. Only time can test the truth of his art. Brahms realized

[*232*]

the fact that music, for all its sensuous outer garments, is in its highest expression an affair of the mind. Only the most critical of intellects can possibly hope to possess the soul as well as the body of music. The senses alone are not enough to secure the possession. Indeed, a man with his senses impaired can still hope to reach its innermost spirit. Was not Beethoven deaf? Music is essentially an intellectual exercise—a superstructure of beauty based upon a foundation of thought. Brahms looked down upon passion unschooled by reason. His music is not meant, like the fragrance of the poppy, to glide into the uncritical senses of the voluptuary and to send him off into dreams. On the contrary, it is an exercise suited only for the critical mind. And the most critical of the critics was Brahms himself. He had a keen intellect and a cutting tongue. He was quick to see his own deficiencies and equally quick to point out the deficiencies of other people. At times his remarks were tipped with venom. Once at a banquet a number of toasts had been drunk to outstanding contemporary musicians. Among those at the table was Hiller, a fellow composer of Brahms. "And now," said Brahms, "having drunk to so many *living* composers, let us drink to a *dead* one. I lift my glass to Ferdinand Hiller!" On another occasion, when the ladies of the Viennese choral society were taking a passage in one of Haydn's oratorios too slowly, he asked them whether that was the way they had sung it under Haydn (who had died seventy years earlier). Upon leaving a drawing room on one of his most sarcastic evenings, he bowed ironically and said, "If there is anybody here whom I have forgotten to insult, I beg him to forgive my oversight."

But his gruffness, as we have seen, was merely the reverse side of his sentimentality. His music, like his temperament, concealed a tender soul within a granite body. And those could best understand his music who were best able to understand his character. He growled to keep himself from weeping. In the midst of a rehearsal of one of his pieces he sprang from his chair and walked across the room with clenched hands. "Stop that terrible music!" he shouted. His back was turned on the players. Tears were streaming down his cheeks. He was overcome with emotion, and this was the method he took to conceal it.

He was a study in contrasts. And perhaps the most remarkable contrast was that between the untidiness of his appearance and the precision of his mind. Externally he seemed to lead an unco-ordinated life. Internally the life was a perfect unit. With a sureness for true values, he characterized himself as a person who was carelessly thorough in his art, thoroughly careless in his personal habits. He littered his floors with his stockings and kept his soul in order. He was physically lazy only because he was mentally so intense. He concentrated entirely upon matters pertaining to his musical personality and let everything else go hang. His physical life was his dream life, ill organized, unsubstantial, lying on a subconscious level; while his mental life was his only true reality—rational, concrete, creative, fully awake. He saw his mistakes and took the utmost pains to correct them. He drove the chariot of his genius through the rocky path of discipline at a harder pace perhaps than any composer before or after him. He was a Hercules performing the labors of the soul. He wrote and rewrote, polished—and then destroyed. Twenty years of planning before he wrote down his *First Symphony*. Thirty-seven years after he had composed a trio in B major he rewrote it note for note. He developed almost a mania for meticulousness. What Mozart had dashed off spontaneously Brahms achieved only by the sweat of his creative brow.

A study in contrasts—a sad puzzle of a man. His neighbors shunned him, but the musical world honored him. A medal was struck in his likeness. At the Zurich Music Hall his portrait was hung side by side with those of Beethoven, Mozart and the other immortals. He received the Leopold Order of Merit from the Austrian emperor. His native city of Hamburg accepted him

[*234*]

into an honorary society in the fellowship of Bismarck and Moltke. Brahms, it may be interesting to note in passing, was a political jingo. Bismarck was his God, imperialism his national faith.

But his politics and his faith were but secondary interests with him. His chief vocation was his music; and his favorite diversion, even as he approached the frigid zone of old age, was an occasional flirtation with a pretty woman. The standard on his banner was *Frei aber Froh*, Free but Frolicsome. And the musical initials F A F formed the germ theme of much of his music. He regarded his musical compositions as the happy family of his children. And the favorite sons were his four giant symphonies. His friend and disciple, Hans von Bülow, called his *First Symphony* "the immortal *Tenth*." By that he meant to say that it was a sequel to Beethoven's *Ninth*. The *Second Symphony* was a woodland pastoral, the *Third* a Gothic architecture of form, the *Fourth* a mighty farewell blast. Close to his heart also was his strangest child—a morose, tempestuous hulk of a fellow —his *Second Piano Concerto* (in B flat major), with a really gentle streak beneath a ferocious scowl. And there was the winsome maiden, the *Clarinet Quintet*. With such wonderful children he needed few other companions.

And it was well that this was so. For one by one he lost his earthly friends. Elizabeth, an early love, succumbed to heart disease. And Hermine, the comfort of his middle age, passed on in the bloom of her youth. And then the baton fell from Hans von Bülow's grasp; and finally the dearest life of them all, Clara Schumann, went the way of the rest. Brahms was on his vacation at the time. He was so overwhelmed at the news of her death that he took the wrong train home. He traveled for two days until, worn out and shaking with his own advanced years, he stumbled to her grave and dropped a handful of earth upon the sacred dust.

His own great health was failing. At first no one could believe it. He was a vigorous walker, a vigorous eater, and he had muscles of steel. At sixty-four he still exercised strenuously, and he stood up against the landscape of old age like a sturdy oak. But without warning the body collapsed. The doctors diagnosed his illness as cancer, and before he had time to recover from his surprise it was over.

"I have not even begun to express myself," he complained on his deathbed. But perhaps—and who can deny it—he took along with him the unwritten music for a new and greater public?

TCHAIKOVSKY

Great Compositions by Tchaikovsky

VOCAL:
Several Operas, including *Eugen Oniegin, Pique-Dame, Jeanne d'Arc*.
Coronation Cantata.
2 Masses.
About 100 Songs.

INSTRUMENTAL:
6 Symphonies, of which the last 3 are the most famous.
Several Symphonic Poems, including *Romeo and Juliet, Manfred, Hamlet, Francesca da Rimini, The Tempest.*
Ballets: *The Lake of the Swans, Sleeping Beauty, The Nutcracker Suite, Snow-Maiden.*
Overtures: *Marche Slave, 1812, Italian Caprice.*
2 Piano Concertos.
Violin Concerto.
3 String Quartets.
Souvenir de Florence.

Tchaikovsky

Peter Ilich Tchaikovsky

1840–1893

Hᴇ ᴡᴀs ᴀ ᴄʜᴀʀᴍɪɴɢ ᴍᴀɴ, with a charming manner. He took his renown carelessly. He was in the habit of traveling incognito so that he would not be hounded to death by his admirers. He was fine looking. Young women fell easily in love with him. A wealthy patroness had supported him for thirteen years. A typical man of the world, to insinuate himself into the graces of one of the richest women in Moscow. He spoke and drank fluently. But no one ever saw him drunk. A gentleman to the finger tips. If ever there was a man to be envied, said his friends, here was the man.

Yet he was unhappy. Russian duchesses and American debutantes might outdo one another in feasting him and showering him with their adoration. But no thought of vanity, no breath of romance ever entered his heart. His tunes set everybody dancing—everybody but himself. He had no eyes for women, no ears for soft whispers of love. There had indeed been a marriage, but this marriage had ended in precipitate disaster. People said he was afraid of love, afraid of friendship, afraid of all human contact. Whenever he attended a concert of his

[*239*]

own music he sat in the upper gallery and doubled up so that no one could recognize him. Once he remarked to a friend, "Are you surprised that a man who has won success should complain of fate? Well, success can never compensate for suffering. . . ."

He was so lonely because he was so great. Like a statue placed upon a pedestal. He could look above the heads of the multitude, but he could not reach down to feel the touch of a human hand. A statue can inspire worship. But it cannot command love.

There was but one person on intimate terms with Tchaikovsky—Nadyezhda von Meck. Yet it was an intimacy of correspondence. The two admirers never met, although at times they lived but a few rods away from each other. Madame von Meck was a widow with a brood of children, conservative habits, a passionate love for music and a wealthy estate. She had heard a piano arrangement of his overture to *The Tempest*. Noble music! Somewhat melancholy to be sure, but this was only in keeping with her own melancholy temperament. She begged him to go on composing. She knew nothing of his life except what he told her in his letters. He was the son of an engineer . . . had been a student of law . . . had prepared for a government post but had "succumbed to the madness of music" . . . had studied under Rubinstein at the Moscow Conservatory . . . and now, at thirty-six, was "adrift on the sea of sound with no harbor of security in sight."

Madame von Meck undertook to supply this security for Tchaikovsky.

II

Tchaikovsky had a peculiar sensation ever so often when he walked through the streets or conducted at the Conservatory. He felt as if his head were about to fall from his shoulders. It was a bad case of nerves. Always heart cramps, always headaches and spells of indigestion. Wherever he went he carried about with him a bit of sodium bicarbonate. The first time it was recommended to him he had read the directions wrong and had placed half a teaspoon of water in a glass of bicarbonate. But he knew better after the distressing results.

At the Conservatory he was set down as an enigma. The young women were able to wheedle favors from all their teachers with the exception of Peter Ilich. He was impervious to their charms. Yet he was always the gentleman, even though cold and aristocratic and aloof.

His financial worries were over. Regularly he received his allowance from the woman who adored his music. And added to this allowance was the salary he got as instructor of harmony from the Rubinstein Conservatory.

Yet he remained, as always, unhappy. People were whispering evil things about him. They said that he was queer, that he was unable to love a woman normally but that he had love affairs nevertheless—affairs "not with women." To still those offensive rumors his brother had advised him to get married.

He agreed with his brother. It *would* be a good thing for him to marry, provided he could get the right woman. And as Tchaikovsky tried to find the woman, the woman found Tchaikovsky. She was an attractive, hysterical and aggressive young creature. They had met at the Conservatory and he had scarcely noticed her. But she had begun to bombard him with desperate letters, beseeching him to visit her. He came, he saw, and she conquered. "In the latter part of May, to my own surprise," he writes to his brother, "I became engaged."

Antonina Miliukoff was the name of his betrothed. She had threatened to commit suicide unless he married her. He had yielded out of sheer weakness, warning her that he did not love her, that he was poor, unsociable, irritable by nature and a hard person to get along with. They were married, and for a moment Tchaikovsky was content. At least he had stopped the gossip. . . .

The bride and the groom took a train out of Moscow for their honeymoon. For Tchaikovsky it was a period of torture. At first he had tried to calm himself in the belief that if he had made a mistake the bride at least loved him and would never willingly do anything to make his life unhappy. He had forced himself to chat with her in spite of his desire to crouch in a corner alone with his fears. Antonina had smiled bravely, unaware of the storm that was raging within him. Finally he told her the truth. "I must not mislead you. From me you can expect only brotherly love." Physically she was repulsive to him. She—and all women. He had tried to fight his nature with all his strength, but to no avail. Yes, Peter *was* queer.

The story of the subsequent days of his brief matrimonial venture is told in the letters he wrote to the woman who understood him and who worshiped his music. "Nadyezhda . . . here briefly is the record of all I have endured since the eighteenth of July, the day of my marriage." He told her that his wife was in no way to blame for the repugnance she inspired in him. After a week of marriage, however, he had hurried away from Moscow, allegedly for his health. He had asked Antonina to furnish an apartment which they were to occupy upon his return. He returned. "The terrible life dragged on for some days. I drank a good deal of wine. Antonina does not frighten me . . . She simply depresses me. Poor girl, she has done everything possible to make my life pleasant. And yet I look upon it all with the deepest disgust." The awful cry pounded in his inner ear, "I am abnormal!" He had tried hard to pretend that he was like other men. But what was the use? All Moscow would be talking! As she sat there smiling at him, doing everything for his comfort, pouring his tea, loosening his boots, he hated her with a mad overwhelming passion. He could take her small neck in his hands and twist it, so that no one would say to him again: "How is your Antonina, your pretty little wife? Why are you walking the streets at night alone? Why aren't you seen with her at the homes of your friends?" Good heavens, he could bear it no longer! He rushed out of his apartment and raced blindly through the dark streets of the city, with turned-up collar, hat covering his eyes. He found himself on the banks of the Moscow River. He waded into the icy waters, remained there immersed up to his waist and then stumbled home praying that he might catch pneumonia and die. Within twenty-four hours his relatives rushed to his bedside and found him delirious. The doctors held out a slight hope for his recovery. But they feared insanity if he did not escape from Moscow. He needed a long rest, alone. "He has gone through a great strain. Something has affected him dreadfully." His brothers pressed their lips. They understood.

III

THEY SENT PETER to a convalescent home on the shores of Lake Geneva. He had escaped from his intolerable existence. One thing was certain—he must never see his wife again. He must arrange for a separation. He must return to the sanity of his music. "With God's help, Peter," wrote Nadyezhda, "you will recover. . . . Music will again interest you and fill your life. . . . You will take up your work on our next symphony. *Our* symphony!" In a burst of gratitude at her generosity he had informed her that he was dedicating this new symphony to her. It was his *Fourth*, a symphony conceived in sorrow. "Dear, sweet Nadyezhda Philaretovna, perhaps I am mistaken, but I think this symphony is something out of the ordinary, the best thing I have done up to now." Nadyezhda sent him a sum of money to cover the expense of printing the music. She was willing to go abroad and to spread its fame all over Europe. Meanwhile she waited anxiously for the score so that she could devour it note by note. She had no doubt about its ultimate success, although it had not as yet been completed and she was unacquainted with any part of it. But Peter had written the music. It could be nothing but a melody from God.

Tchaikovsky was more dubious about the fate of his *Fourth Symphony.* "What will its story be? Will it live after the author has disappeared from the earth? I wonder."

He was away in Florence when the symphony was first produced in Moscow. For the longest time he got no news as to its fate. At last, however, Madame von Meck wrote him that the symphony had been well received, especially the third movement, the pizzicato, for which the composer had expressed great hope. But still there was no word from his conservatory associates. When a man has put his whole soul into a work he expects some recognition of his efforts—not necessarily praise, but at least acknowledgment. "I am deeply chagrined and amazed at the incomprehensible silence of everybody concerning the symphony," he wrote to Madame von Meck. "I had expected that this symphony would at least interest my musical friends even if it did not deeply move them."

Finally the official criticism came in the letter of a fellow teacher at the Conservatory. The first movement was too long. It produced the effect of a tone-poem to which the composer had tacked on three additional movements. The result was a hodgepodge instead of a symphony. "The trumpet fanfare in the introduction is too strongly programmatic. Every movement seems ready to burst out into ballet music—a stylistic error which spoils the general effect." Tchaikovsky answered this letter sharply. "Of course the symphony is program music"— he did not add that it was the musical expression of the terrible tragedy he had undergone—"and what's wrong with program music? My work is patterned after Beethoven's *Fifth Symphony*— not as to musical content but as to the basic idea. Don't you see a program in the *Fifth?*" Yes, Tchaikovsky's *Fourth Symphony* had a definite program. "There is in it not a phrase that I have not deeply felt; every note is an echo of the sincerest part of my nature." What of the pounding beat of the trumpet that introduces the symphony and is the germ of the entire music? It is Fate, that relentless blind force that forever obstructs the realization of man's hopes. "It is the Damoclean sword, that hangs over our heads in unremitting spiritual torment. . . . As our despair grows ever more stronger, we try to turn from reality and to sink into the illusion of dreams. . . . Little by little our dreams possess the soul. Here at last is happiness! . . . But no, this was only a mirage, and we awaken once more to the call of fate." Tchaikovsky's life had been an alternation between fantasy and reality, happiness and despair. Moods of exultation when he composed his music, thoughts of suicide when he was compelled to face the world—he with the woman's soul—and to pretend that he was a man. . . .

But it is not right for a man to be wrapped up forever within his own sufferings. There are moments when it is well to get away from ourselves, to forget our past sorrows and our future hopes, to drift into an impersonal sort of timelessness in which we experience no definite emotions but rather a succession of capricious arabesques, those intangible images that pass through the mind when one has drunk wine and feels the first touch of intoxication. The soul is neither gay nor sad . . . Suddenly there comes to mind the picture of a drunken peasant, a brief street song is heard . . . Suddenly a voice cries to us, "If you cannot find any joy within yourself, look for it in others. Go to the people. See—they know how to make the best of their time." If pleasure is not for Peter Tchaikovsky, let him turn away from his own gloomy thoughts and watch how others give themselves up to pleasure. A peasant festival. Forget your own sorrow in the spectacle of another's joy. "See how gay they are! And how fortunate to be ruled by such simple feelings!" This is the meaning of the *Fourth Symphony*. And this, to Tchaikovsky, is the meaning of life. Only by rejoicing in the joys of others can you overcome the sadness of your own fate.

IV

THE STRANGE FRIENDSHIP continued between Tchaikovsky and the woman who knew of his physical appearance only through the photographs he sent her, yet who knew his most intimate thoughts. With shrewd tact and womanly kindness Nadyezhda had won his complete trust. Never did she seek for any information beyond what he was willing to give. In his hours of despair she soothed him, listened to his complaints and gave him the courage to continue. And always she kept the wolf from his door. No other woman could have successfully pressed a financial allowance upon this proud and sensitive man. But she told Tchaikovsky that she was commissioning him to write his music for her and that she was merely paying him for his labor. When it came to finances Tchaikovsky was incredibly naïve. He never had enough money in his pockets, for whatever sums he received he almost immediately gave away. Once a friend asked him whether he was in the habit of investing his capital. At first he was amazed at the question. Then he burst out laughing. "I'll tell you where I made my last investment," he said. "In the Kokorev Hotel, where I stayed in Moscow. Where my next investment will be I can't say until I know my itinerary."

Because he was himself generous in his financial dealings with others, Tchaikovsky accepted without embarrassment the generosity of Madame von Meck. Nor was he bothered by the strangeness of their relationship. It was the relationship of a mother toward a son, and the bond that held them together was his music. But they must never meet, or the music relationship would be superseded by something too realistic, too material to make a further friendship possible. When Nadyezhda vacated her town home for a trip abroad she asked Tchaikovsky to visit it in her absence, to go over the books and to inspect her paintings, so that when she returned she would feel the atmosphere pervaded by his personality. And then, in the winter of 1878, she made an even bolder request from Florence where she was spending her vacation. She asked him to come to that city and to stay in a cottage she would prepare a few miles from her own. And before long they were carrying on a correspondence that traveled only across the lawn. He was a guest at her summer estate in the Ukraine. He gave orders to her servants; he drove in the coach she had set aside for him. Every day Peter walked to the village for the mail and passed her house, heard the sound of her children's voices. And was his apartment warm enough? And had he enough books and clothes? She had no thought but to make his stay comfortable. And still they never met. Occasionally Peter saw her from a distance at the theater. He knew her from her picture. Sitting up in the balcony, he would put the opera glass to his eye and watch the tall, proud woman in black who sat in the orchestra and conversed in an animated manner with her favorite daughter, Milochka. Tchaikovsky grew to love this little girl from a distance. "Tell Milochka," he wrote to her mother, "that she has a fervent admirer." The widow and her family took their daily walk past Tchaikovsky's cottage at exactly the same hour in the afternoon. Peter, shy as he was, would glance down upon them from behind his shutters and watch with anxious eyes lest they should look up and see him.

Never did she attempt to break in upon his privacy. His domestic life was sacred to her. On one occasion, indeed, she hinted that her daughter Milochka wished to come over to his cottage. For the little girl was burning with curiosity to meet this "Uncle Peter" about whom her mother was talking to her all the time. But Tchaikovsky, who was the gentlest soul alive, could be firm in his rights. "Forgive me, dear friend, and laugh at my queerness," he replied, "but I shall not invite Milochka to visit me. My relationship with you, exactly as it now stands, is my greatest happiness and the rock on which all my welfare rests. I do not want it to change even in the slightest respect."

Yet one day the inevitable happened. Peter and Nadyezhda, who had carefully arranged their schedules so that when one of them was outdoors the other would remain in the house, at last made a miscalculation and both of them were out at the same time. Their carriages approached each other along the street. As they passed, Tchaikovsky inadvertently looked up and straight into the eyes of Madame von Meck. For several long seconds they gazed at each other. Then Tchaikovsky bowed without a word. The widow returned the bow with equal formality and ordered her coachman to drive on. When Tchaikovsky reached home he wrote to Madame von Meck, "Forgive me for my stupid carelessness, Nadyezhda Philaretovna!" Nadyezhda, however, had been delighted at the meeting. "It convinced me of the reality of your presence so near to my house."

This was their closest approach to intimacy during their long summer idyll. This, and one other incident. Madame von Meck was celebrating the name day of one of her children. There was a party on the lawn, and Tchaikovsky was among those present. But he was uninvited and unobserved. He watched the merrymaking as he stood hidden behind a tree.

Shortly after this vacation which had brought them so "closely" together Tchaikovsky sent the widow the piano arrangement of his *Fourth Symphony*. Until then Nadyezhda had heard it performed once or twice by the orchestra. But here was her opportunity to become acquainted with the music at close hand. For forty-eight hours she "drank the full glory of the melody, refusing to eat or sleep." Then she wrote Tchaikovsky a letter in which she made a full confession. "I love you more than anyone else; I value you above everything in the world. If this knowledge bothers you, forgive me. I have spoken out. The reason is—your Symphony."

V

THOUGH living apart from his wife, Tchaikovsky was not yet free from the bonds of his marriage. Antonina refused to divorce him and hounded him with her continual demands for money. At times he was filled with an almost murderous fury. "I have learned," he wrote grimly, "how a man, not wicked by nature, can become a criminal!" Once more he began to suffer from his old neurotic spells—his sleeplessness, his loss of weight, his heart cramps, his nightmares. Only a strong glass of wine could relieve him at such moments. Every evening he took refuge in his wine, he admitted. "In the first stages of drunkenness I feel an absolute delight." Yet the stimulating effect of the drink wore off after a few minutes and he returned to his melancholy—and his music. "The thought that I am good for nothing, that only my musical work redeems my defects and raises me to manhood, in its truest sense, begins to overwhelm and torture me. The only means of escaping these tormenting doubts and self-flagellations is to start a new task. So I turn like a squirrel in a wheel . . . I fight as hard as I can. . . . My work alone saves me. And I work."

He wrote to Nadyezhda about his music—always about his music. "Words are useless to describe the emotion that comes over me when a new idea is conceived and begins to take definite shape. I forget everything; I am a madman, trembling and quivering in every fiber, with scarcely time to outline the sketches, so rapidly does one idea pursue another. Sometimes in the midst of this process an outside shock wakes me from the magic state of somnambulism. The bell rings, the servant enters, the clock strikes, reminding me that the business of the day must be attended to. . . ." His music, he tells us, translates him into an entirely different world—a world in which he can forget himself and become an impersonal instrument in the hands of a higher power. Do we find in his music a mirror of his own sad life?

No, replies Tchaikovsky. "My creative activity is objective . . . and those people are mistaken who believe that the artist can use his talent to relieve himself of the specific feelings of the moment. With no special reason for rejoicing I can experience a happy, creative mood; and conversely among the happiest surroundings I may write music suffused with darkness and despair. In brief, the artist lives a double life, his everyday human life and his artistic life, and these two lives do not always coincide." "It is not necessary to be happy in order to create happiness," said a wise man of the East. And Tchaikovsky proved the wisdom of this aphorism.

VI

1880. . . . . Growing fame. The composer with the cheerful face and the gloomy heart was forty. Though money had commenced to come in from sources other than Nadyezhda, he hadn't changed. He supported all the hungry musicians in Moscow. He took a trip to Paris and for a brief period scattered his worries to the wind. "You would laugh," he wrote to his brothers, "to see me walking the streets like a rooster in a new coat and a most elegant hat. . . . A mania for coquetry has seized me. I toy with the thought of buying myself a gold chain and a pin. . . . The money is flying, and I soon shall not have a franc left in my pocket." A few days later he left Paris and found himself stranded in Berlin. "In Paris," he wrote to Nadyezhda, "I managed my funds so cleverly that after paying my hotel bill I had not quite enough to take me back to Russia. When I got to Berlin I could go no further! So I wired Jurgenson (his publisher) to telegraph some money he owes me. I can't imagine why he hasn't answered." Nevertheless he added that his finances were in a most "brilliant" condition. Nadyezhda understood her optimistic dreamer and sent him the money for his hotel bill in Berlin and his fare for St Petersburg.

During his stay in Paris Nadyezhda had urged him to meet the "right" people. But he naïvely confessed that he was afraid of people. "All my life I have suffered from social contacts." Even when traveling on a train he would slouch in a corner of the compartment for fear that people might recognize him. He could not exactly define what there was in people that caused him so much pain, he declared. But society tormented him. "Anyone else in my place here," he wrote to Nadyezhda from Paris, "would already have made the acquaintance of the local musicians. It is a pity I can't do it." He admitted that he knew how his shyness had retarded his chances for success. And he claimed that he had tried to fight against this shyness with all his might. But he had given up the struggle. "Yes, now that I may hide in my hole and always be myself, since books and musical notation have become my only society, I am quite happy."

And at last he had broken through to success in spite of his shyness. His symphonies and his overtures had caught the fancy of musical audiences throughout Europe. His Slavic message had reached even the United States, where his music was played to packed halls. "From all sides," he wrote, "my music is received with sympathy. All morning I spend reading proof, and as I finish the sheets they are handed to the printer." Indeed, so fast were orders arriving that he feared he would not find enough time to supply the demand.

He had become a public figure. In order to avoid the continual stream of his visitors he nailed up a sign in his garden: "Peter Ilich Tchaikovsky. Receives Mondays and Thursdays from 3 to 5. Not at home the rest of the week. Please do not ring." He traveled all over the continent, and whenever he conducted his own works he was received with acclaim. To his instrumental music—he had now written several overtures and five symphonies—he added two successful operas: *Eugen Oniegin* and *Pique-Dame*. He wrote to Nadyezhda that he came home from every trip laden with laurels—"but only laurels. I don't know how to look after my pecuniary interests." He set out on a tour of triumph. London, Dresden, Paris, Geneva, Berlin, Hamburg, Prague, Leipzig. . . . But his glory failed to move him. "You, Nadyezhda," he had written to her at the height of his fame, "are the only person in the world who can make me profoundly happy." And he hoped with his entire soul that whatever inspired her feelings for him would never alter, never end, "because such a loss would be unendurable for me."

He was now close to the pinnacle of success. He had received an invitation to conduct a concert tour in six of the leading cities of America. Never had such an honor been accorded to any other Russian composer. Heaven at last, it seemed, had turned a smiling face upon him.

And then, just before he started for America, there came a sudden blow. A letter from Nadyezhda von Meck, written in a tone she had never before used. She told him in a curt and businesslike manner that her fortune was on the point of complete collapse, that from now on she would be unable to send him any money—as if this could possibly have made any difference to Peter Ilich!—and that their intimacy must come to an end. The letter concluded with a few casual words that were totally devoid of warmth: "Do not forget, and think of me sometimes."

Peter was stunned at the tone of the letter. He wrote a hasty reply. How could she possibly imagine that the loss of his pension would affect him? He begged her not to worry about his financial condition since his income had greatly increased from other sources. "But the final words of your letter, 'do not forget, and think of me sometimes,' have cut me to the quick. . . . Is it possible that you think me capable of remembering you only when I use your money? Can I ever for one second forget all that you have done for me, all that your friendship has meant to me and to my music?" For the life of him he couldn't under-

stand the reason for Nadyezhda's sudden coldness. There had
been no news in Moscow about the "complete collapse" of the
Von Meck fortune. On the contrary, the railroad in which this
fortune was invested seemed to be as strong as ever. Nadyezhda
must have other reasons, best known to herself, for her sudden
coldness. "Forgive this hasty scrawl," he added in the postscript
of the letter. "I am too upset to write clearly."

The blow had unnerved him. "She is tired of you and your
music," a voice kept telling him. "And now that you no longer
serve your purpose as her hired man, she wishes to get rid of
you. . . ."

Yet he hoped against hope that there had been some mistake.
She would surely send him another letter, explaining everything. Day after day he waited for that letter—and it never
came. He boarded the boat for America and reached New York
with its vociferous welcome. He became the idol of the New
World. Matrons, millionaires, educators, journalists, coachmen
—all bowed to him in obsequious homage. But this was empty
glory. He would have gladly exchanged it all for a single word
from Nadyezhda. He had aged rapidly in the last few months.
The reporters wrote that he was "an interesting-looking man of
about sixty," although he was only fifty at the time. Satiated
with his American adulation, he rushed back to Moscow. And
still no word from Nadyezhda. It was eight months since he had
written to her. And then at last there came a letter—not, however,
from Nadyezhda but from a mutual friend. "She is very ill, she
is terribly upset. She can no longer write to you as before. . . ."

Tchaikovsky sent an immediate reply to this letter. "Not for
anything in the world would I be the cause of adding to her
suffering. What hurts, troubles and, I may say, offends me
deeply is not the fact that she doesn't write, but the more bitter
fact that she has lost all interest in me. . . . What I urgently desire is that my relationship with her should not change, now
that I no longer receive any money from her. Unfortunately this

seems quite impossible, since Nadyezhda Philaretovna has evidently become quite cold to me. . . . It seemed to me that the earth would crumble to pieces under my feet sooner than that Nadyezhda Philaretovna's feelings toward me could change. But this has happened, and all my faith in people, all my trust in the world has turned upside down. My peace is gone and whatever happiness fate might have intended for me is forever poisoned. . . ."

To this last letter there was no response.

VII

Fate had reserved her greatest distinctions for these last sad years of his life. He was elected a member of the Académie Française. He went to England and received an honorary degree at the University of Cambridge. He traveled from one concert to another at a furious speed. "It seemed," wrote his brother Modeste, "that Peter had ceased to belong to himself. Some irresistible force had taken possession of him . . . a deep, inexplicable anxiety, a mood of despair that sought forgetfulness in distraction anywhere and everywhere. . . . One had the conviction that things could not go on longer as they were, that a change was coming, that something old and finished would shortly give place to something new and unknown." He was working, he had told his brother, on a new symphony, his sixth. It was to be a funeral dirge, a farewell song to a dead friendship. Its melodies were so lovely they had brought the tears to his eyes. "I believe it is the best of all my works to date; at any rate, I know it is the most sincere." But he must give it a special name—something to express the heart . . . the unbearable suffering he had undergone. *Tragic Symphony? Symphony of Tears?* No, too commonplace. And then his brother Modia, who knew him so intimately, suggested the word *Pathétique*. Bravo! *Symphonie Pathétique.*

[*254*]

VIII

THE *Symphonie Pathétique* was the last thing he wrote. It was the testament in which he bequeathed to the world the flame of his genius and the beauty of his sorrow. The symphony was completed. At this moment Russia was scourged by one of its frequent epidemics of cholera. Carelessly Tchaikovsky drank a glass of infected water. He contracted the disease. Four days he lay in agony, and on the fifth day he found rest.

A strange ending to a strange life. A genius to whom Destiny had given the gifts of a god and denied the powers of a man. What could have been the real thoughts of so sad and incongruous a personality, wondered the hundreds of worshipers who filed past the body as it lay in state. But two weeks later the *Symphonie Pathétique* was performed in all its glory, and those who listened bowed their heads and wept. For then they knew.

RIMSKY–KORSAKOV

Great Compositions by Rimsky-Korsakov

VOCAL:

Operas: *Snyegoorotchka (Snow-Maiden), Coq d'Or, Kasht-chei, Pskovityanka (The Maiden of Pskov), Mlada, May Night, Christmas Eve, Sadko, The Czar's Bride.*

Over 100 Russian Songs.

INSTRUMENTAL:

3 Symphonies.

Symphonic Suite, *Scheherazade.*

Spanish Caprice.

Easter Overture.

Serbian Fantasy.

Orchestral Prelude, *Nad Mogiloyu (At the Grave).*

Orchestrated numerous works of other composers.

Rimsky-Korsakov

Nikolay Rimsky-Korsakov

1844–1908

The best authority we have for the life of Rimsky-Korsakov is Rimsky-Korsakov himself. His autobiography is one of those rare phenomena—a book in which the author has succeeded in looking upon himself with an absolutely unprejudiced honesty. Like the fabled Irish recruit, Rimsky-Korsakov was able to step *out of* the ranks in order to observe his own maneuverings *within* the ranks. "*The Story of my Musical Life*," he writes at the end of his autobiography, "is without order, is unequally detailed throughout, is written in a wretched style and is often extremely dry. But, in compensation, it contains *nothing but the truth.*"

In following this autobiography we shall discover a man who was neither humble nor arrogant, neither modest nor boastful, but in all ways and at all times truthful. When he liked his own work he didn't hesitate to discuss its merits; when he disliked it he didn't hesitate to point out its defects. In every case he regarded himself as objectively as he regarded his friends. Even his enemies he observed with a scientific detachment and with no apparent trace of personal rancor. His character, like his music, had more of the perfection of science than the passion of art.

And yet, strangely enough, Rimsky-Korsakov was fundamentally an amateur rather than a professional musician. Indeed, not one of the so-called "Great Five Musicians" of Russia was a composer by profession. Cui was an artillery engineer; Moussorgsky, a lieutenant in the Preobrazhensky Guard; Borodin, a professor of chemistry; Balakirev, a clerk at the St Petersburg freight station of the Warsaw Railroad; and Rimsky-Korsakov, a petty officer in the Russian navy. Strictly speaking, these five men did not *play* music, they *played at* music. Their art was a relaxation, a sort of tasty dessert to the prosaic menu of their everyday life.

II

NIKOLAY Andreyevich Rimsky-Korsakov seemed from infancy destined to a prosaic life as a Russian sailor. His older brother, Voyin Nikalayevich, was a naval lieutenant; and his father, a retired official with a respectable pension, looked forward to a similar career for his younger son. Nikolay Andreyevich was only twelve years old when his father enrolled him (July 1856) at the Marine Academy in St Petersburg.

The monotony of the daily routine at the academy was enlivened by the Saturday night floggings that were administered to all those pupils who had failed in any subject during the week. Rimsky-Korsakov received his allotted share of these floggings.

He showed little interest in his studies and even less interest in music. On Sundays, at the insistence of his parents, he took piano lessons; but he never became a good player. Occasionally, however, "for the sake of fun," and out of a scientific curiosity to take things apart and to put them together again, he "composed music and assembled notes." Some of these compositions, he was pleased to observe, were "sufficiently coherent." But he paid little attention to them.

As time went on, however, his scientific interest in music

began to grow upon him. He was delighted to find that the symmetrical arrangement of his notes could produce a melodic effect upon the ear. He got into the habit of attending the operas at St Petersburg, and he amused himself occasionally by re-arranging the piano scores of some of these operas from four hands to two—all this, "so as to make the music easier for me to play."

One Sunday in November 1861 his music teacher took him on a visit to Balakirev. And on that day began his real interest in composition.

"Balakirev," wrote Rimsky-Korsakov, "produced an enormous impression upon me. A magnificent pianist, playing everything from memory; endowed with bold opinions, new ideas and, last but not least, a gift of composition which I literally adored. . . . Then, too, he was a marvelous critic, especially a *technical critic.*" In short, he had set himself up as the musical dictator of the younger generation in Russia. "He was obeyed absolutely, for the spell of his personality was tremendous." His influence "resembled some magnetic power." Under this influence the young musicians of Russia were taught to regard Beethoven's symphonies as "flabby," Chopin's melodies as "womanish," Mendelssohn's songs as "bourgeois." In the heaven of music there was but one God, Johann Sebastian Bach, and Balakirev was his prophet.

Rimsky-Korsakov attached himself to Balakirev and became one of his most ardent disciples. He accepted Balakirev as his "adviser and censor, editor and teacher." In some respects the influence of Balakirev was a fortunate thing for Rimsky-Korsakov, for it encouraged him to take up music as more than a mere plaything. It had turned an indifferent naval student into a serious composer. But in one important particular the guidance of Balakirev was bad. He transformed his pupils into mere satellites of himself. He compelled them to reflect the peculiar light of his own genius. Having had no academic training himself, he regarded such training as unnecessary for all other musicians. A knowledge of harmony, he insisted, was of no importance. "You must plunge boldly into the sea of composition," he said, "and learn to sink or swim. If you have the talent to swim, so much the better for yourself. If you are unfortunate enough to sink, so much the better for the world."

He employed this sink-or-swim method on his young pupil, Rimsky-Korsakov. The very first lesson he assigned to him was the writing of a symphony. "I asked him to give me a few preliminary lessons in harmony, whereupon he brusquely replied that he himself had no use for harmony and that therefore I, too, ought to get along without it."

Rimsky-Korsakov sat down to compose the symphony without so much as an elementary knowledge of the intervals and chords or the meaning of double counterpoint, cadence, thesis, antithesis or period. The result was a faithful copy of one of Balakirev's own compositions, *King Lear*. "I had particular difficulty with the string instruments, since the fingering and the movements of the bow were utterly unknown to me. I indicated interminable legatos, impossible of execution . . . But Balakirev himself had the most confused notion of violin playing."

Yet in spite of these handicaps Rimsky-Korsakov managed to complete the first movement, the Scherzo and the Finale. "The Finale in particular won general approval at the time." But he was unable to write the second movement—the Adagio. He wanted to cast it in the form of a cantabile (tuneful) melody. But melody was taboo to Balakirev, and Rimsky-Korsakov "worshiped Balakirev and obeyed him in everything."

III

SHORTLY after the composition of the symphony Rimsky-Korsakov was ordered on an extensive cruise as part of his training for service in the navy. He was a good sailor, but he disliked his job. For he lacked the qualifications that were regarded as indispensable to a naval officer. He possessed no executive ability; he couldn't give orders in a gruff voice; he was unable to threaten or to swear or to punish. "I confess," he tells us, "that I had none of these gifts." The Russian navy of the nineteenth century was no place for a man who had music in his soul. For those were the years of "rope ends and brutal blows on the mouth." Again and again, Rimsky-Korsakov informs us, he was obliged "to witness the punishment of sailors with 200 to 300 ratline blows on the bare back, in the presence of the entire crew." One of the officers on the training ship Prokhor used to greet the drunken sailors, as they returned from shore leave, with an uppercut to the jaw. "Great was his reputation for his ability to knock out teeth!" The commander of Rimsky-Korsakov's squadron, Admiral Lyesovsky, had achieved notoriety for a temper that was unmatched even in the Russian navy of that day. Once, in a fit of rage, he had rushed up to an offending sailor and bitten off his nose. "The entire moral atmosphere of the navy was filled with a nauseating stench."

In this atmosphere it was no wonder that even the gentleness of Rimsky-Korsakov's character had become tainted with a measure of cynicism. He had ceased to believe in a God who could permit such evils under the sun. But he tried to find solace in his music. His duties on shipboard were negligible. He had a great deal of time on his hands, and he spent much of this time on his music—and on the study of astronomy. The sea is a good vantage point from which to contemplate the glory of the heavens. The cruise had taken him to England, to the United States and then to South America. The spectacle of night in the southern sky inspired him to write one of the few poetical passages in his *Autobiography*. "The dark azure color of the sky by day would give place to a fantastic phosphorescence at night. As we sailed further south, the twilight grew shorter and shorter and the stars and the planets burst upon us with a sudden splendor.

[*263*]

What a radiance in the Milky Way, with the constellation of the Southern Cross! What a magnificence in Canopus, in the stars of the Centaur, in the blazing bright red of Antares, visible in Russia as a pale star on clear summer nights! Sirius, known to us in Russia on winter nights, looked here twice as large and bright. Soon all the stars of both hemispheres became visible. The Great Dipper hung low just above the horizon, while the Southern Cross rose higher and higher. The light of the full moon dipping in and out of the heaped-up clouds was simply dazzling. Wonderful is the tropical ocean with its azure color and its phosphorescent glow; wonderful are the tropical clouds at sunset; but the tropical night sky over the ocean is the most wonderful thing in the world."

For a time the squadron stopped at Rio de Janeiro. Here he found a veritable Paradise for a man accustomed to the icy winds of St Petersburg—"a tropical winter in June!" He reveled in the mildness of the climate, with the temperature ranging from sixty-five to seventy-five degrees. He rhapsodized about the green-blue waters of the bay and the gorgeous green tints of the mountains. He visited the Botanical Gardens, alive with hummingbirds in the daytime and fireflies at night. He took a trip to the Bamboo Valley, a long and narrow Gothic arch formed by the interlacing tops of the bamboo trees. He spent a number of days at the Brazilian emperor's palace in Petropolis, a city set like a jewel in the mountains; and from there he made excursions to the Imatorei Falls and marveled at their majesty. And all this time he forgot his music. For music, like wine, was to him but a stimulant against monotony. It was only when his life was drab that he resorted to the creation of beauty. "During my cruise to America," he writes, "my dreams of artistic activity had entirely faded . . . and I felt no sorrow over the dreams that were gone."

[*264*]

IV

HE RETURNED to the drabness of life at St Petersburg after a cruise of three years. Here he came once more under the influence of Balakirev and resumed his interrupted dreams. On one of his first visits to Balakirev's he met a newcomer to the circle, the talented and eccentric Borodin.

This interesting chemist musician was like a character out of Turgenev. More than anything else in the world he loved his crucibles and his piano; yet, equally fond of these two mistresses, he neglected them both. For he had many other interests in addition to his two main passions. He tried to bring about the establishment of medical courses for women; he participated in a number of societies organized for the purpose of supporting needy students; he allowed himself to be dragged off to any meeting for any cause whatsoever; and he boarded and lodged every stray beggar who came to him for charity. The floors of his little four-room apartment were always covered with his sleeping "guests." And his dining-room table swarmed with tomcats. These cats "paraded across the table, sticking their noses into plates and unceremoniously leaping upon the diners' backs."

A man of strong physique, Borodin ate voraciously but irregularly. "He could dine twice a day or go dinnerless altogether, both of which happened frequently." If he dropped in on a friend at dinnertime and the friend invited him to join the meal, he would readily accept the invitation. "Since I have already dined, I have sort of formed the habit; and so I don't mind if I dine again." On the other hand, there were days when he forgot to dine altogether. Late in the evening he would return home and join the family at tea around the samovar. "Where have you eaten today?" his wife would ask. And then Borodin would suddenly remember. "By Jove, I haven't eaten anywhere today!"

[*265*]

What with his lectures and his chemical experiments and his philanthropic preoccupations, Borodin worked harder than any other man of his acquaintance. Yet he slept very little, for his wife suffered from asthmatic attacks which kept him up every night. It was no wonder, then, that he found little time for his compositions. His friends felt that here was a great genius wasted. There were times even when they expressed the cynical hope that something would happen to him so that he might find himself with leisure on his hands. "I can only compose," he once laughingly remarked, "when I am too unwell to give my lectures. So my friends, reversing the usual custom, never say to me 'I hope you are well' but 'I do hope you are ill.' "

Next to Balakirev himself, Rimsky-Korsakov admired Borodin more than any other man in Russia. His talents expanded under the benevolent despotism of the one and the generous encouragement of the other. He began to take less and less interest in his professional work—he was now a midshipman on shore duty— and to devote more and more of his spare time to composition. He began to write songs, overtures and fantasias; and then, still ignorant of the principles of orchestration, he composed his first important work—the symphonic picture, *Sadko*. In his *Autobiography* he frankly discusses his talents and his limitations as depicted in this work. "On the whole," he tells us, "*Sadko* is pretty good; the general form is satisfactory; the dance themes are impressive; and the orchestral color is a miracle of beauty." Yet he confesses that it is largely imitative—"a thing of rags and patches. The Introduction is reminiscent of Liszt; the Allegro is borrowed from Glinka; the D major movement recalls Balakirev; and the Feast of the Sea-King is an echo of Dargomyzhsky. . . . It is easy to see that I knew nothing about the technical problems of orchestration when I wrote this."

With equal frankness he describes his next important work— his symphonic poem, *Antar*. "When I examine the form of *Antar*, after the lapse of many years, I can affirm that I did a good

[*266*]

job. . . . Where I got, at the time, the coherent logic of its structure, it is hard to explain. . . . The excessive brevity of the form
of Movements I and II is, to be sure, indicative of an inferior
imagination and an insufficient knowledge of technique. . . .
But speaking generally, the play of tonalities in the various
movements is interesting, beautiful and legitimate." Rimsky-
Korsakov had a perfect knack for dissociating his critical from
his creative ability. His intellect and his imagination were
almost like two distinct personalities. Unlike Wagner, he neither
blamed nor praised his work unduly; he merely *appraised* it
dispassionately.

This dispassionate appraisal of his shortcomings as well as
of his abilities stood him in good stead when he was appointed
Professor of Practical Composition at the St Petersburg Conservatory. "It was foolish and dishonest of me to become a
professor . . . For I was a dilettante and knew nothing. This I
frankly confess and attest before the world." He accepted the
offer with this unblinking recognition of his own inadequacy
and promptly set to work in order to make himself worthy of
the position. He undertook a thorough study of harmony and
counterpoint; he familiarized himself with all the string and
wind instruments; and in this way he became not only the best
teacher but also, as he humorously expressed it, the best *pupil*
at the Conservatory. In this way, too, he "untied his hands"
for his own work, so that within a few years he came to be
regarded as one of the most skillful exponents of orchestration
among the Russian composers of his day. Indeed, he was un-
officially appointed as the orchestral executor of almost every
great composition left unfinished at the death of its author. He
thus became in a literal sense a part owner, because he was a
part creator, of much of the musical wealth of Russia.

V

The year 1872 brought two happy events to Rimsky-Korsakov —the successful production of his first opera, *The Maid of Pskov*, and his marriage to Nadyezhda Nikolayevna Purgold, a woman of exceptional charm and equally exceptional musical talent. The following year he was appointed to the post of Supervisor of the Naval Bands. From that date onward his life was externally uneventful. Trips to the various bands, lectures at the Conservatory, winters at St Petersburg, summers in the bracing lake and pine regions of Russia, the education of his children and a continual stream of music colorful as the wild flowers of the steppes and melodious as the murmuring forests of Stelyovo —such was the perennial round of his activities. A serene and gentle and generous life. He was the patron of every young musician of talent. Occasionally he lost his temper, only to repent with his customary sincerity. "At times I was somewhat hotheaded. I remember that during a rehearsal of one of my concerts the orchestra's errand man Yuzegovich, who had forgotten to prepare something, got such a tongue-lashing from me that the musicians actually began to hiss me. . . . On another occasion, as I recall it, I yelled at the librarian of the Conservatory, Buslayeff, because he didn't bring the music on time. . . . Such fits of anger, in which I foolishly assumed the tone of a superior, were—I believe—the result of my training in the navy."

Little by little his interest in the navy, and in Russian politics in general, had diminished almost to the vanishing point. He became more and more absorbed in his music. Wealthy, respected, devoted to his family and loyal to his czar, he lived in a fairy-tale world of cloudless days and untroubled nights. And he depicted this fairy-tale world in his fairy-tale music—*The Snow-Maiden, The Spanish Capriccio, Mlada, Christmas Eve, Czar*

Saltan, Kashtchei the Deathless, Scheherazade—music in which goblins outwit the devil, broomsticks dance with pokers, genii rise from caldrons, mermaids sport with sea-gods and stars play at blindman's buff. Throughout his life he remained a child, with the child's fertile but unrealistic imagination. It was only on a few occasions that the bitter realities of life broke in upon the delightful dreams of his fancy. The death of his children, Masha and Slavchik, was a terrible blow, all the harder to bear because he was unused to suffering. And his dismissal from the Conservatory almost knocked the props from under his feet. For it disclosed to him a world of which he had been for many years blissfully unaware.

This is how his dismissal came about:

In 1905, during the abortive revolution of the Russian intelligentsia, the students at the Conservatory joined in the general restlessness. Rimsky-Korsakov, ignorant of politics but interested in the aspirations of youth, requested the students to state their grievances and then admitted that there was something in what they said. "The result of it all was that the Conservatory was closed, more than a hundred pupils were expelled and I was dismissed from the ranks of the professors."

The students, indignant at his dismissal, prepared a concert of his music. But the concert was broken up by the police. Thousands of sympathetic letters came pouring in to him from every part of Russia. He was hailed as a hero, a revolutionary, a savior. All of which brought nothing but embarrassment to the conservative little dreamer of his fairy-tale dreams. For revolution was farthest from his mind. He was interested not in rebellion but in justice. All he wanted was a world in which musicians like himself might be left alone to ply their art and to encourage their fellow musicians. Rimsky-Korsakov in the role of a crusader? The very thought of it was enough to make him blush. "My position," he complains, "had become unbearable and absurd!"

[269]

Fortunately the displeasure of the police was short-lived. His professorship was restored, and he was able once more to glide into his serene dreams after his sudden startling plunge into the nightmare of reality.

And thus dreaming, he wrote one more of his fairy-tale operas, *Le Coq d'Or*, and then he retired (at the age of sixty-four) to his dreamless sleep.

DEBUSSY

Great Compositions by Debussy

VOCAL:

Opera, *Pelléas et Mélisande.*

Cantatas: *L'Enfant Prodigue, Le Martyre de Saint-Sébastien, La Demoiselle Elue (The Blessed Damosel).*

Proses Lyriques.

Ariettes, Chansons de Bilitis, and several other songs.

Musical Prose Poem, *Christmas of the Homeless Children.*

INSTRUMENTAL:

Symphonic Poem, *La Mer.*

L'Après-midi d'un Faune.

Nuages.

Fêtes.

Sirènes (an orchestral nocturne with a women's chorus).

3 orchestral *Images.*

String Quartet.

Several piano pieces, including *Arabesques, Clair de Lune, Pour le Piano, Pagode, La Soirée dans Grenade, Jardins sous la Pluie, Reflets dans l'eau, Poissons d'Or, Douze Préludes, Hommage à Rameau.*

La Boîte à Joujoux (ballet for children).

Debussy

Claude–Achille Debussy

1862–1918

At seven he was a reserved, quiet, thoughtful little fellow who never played with other children. At fourteen he was a young man who earned his own living by giving piano lessons. At twenty-one he was an old cynic, disgusted with the world of men and concerned chiefly with the world of music.

He had never had any childhood. Or any regular schooling. His mother cared little for her children; and his father, the owner of a crockery store at Saint-Germain-en-Laye, was too busy with his earthenware to bother about the human affairs of his household. Fortunately, however, one of his paternal aunts adored Claude-Achille. She took him under her wing, taught him his letters and his notes and had him enrolled, in his eleventh year, at the Conservatoire.

His matriculation at the Conservatoire was like a prison sentence at hard labor. His father, seeing visions of wealth in his child's talent, exploited it to the limit of his endurance. It was all work and no relaxation. As soon as Claude had begun to earn his own money he was compelled to hand every last sou of it over to his parents. One day his mother caught him eating a bun at a pastry shop. She dragged him home, where his father gave him a sound thrashing for his extravagance.

His father had now sold his crockery shop and had moved to Paris, where he secured a job as a clerk in the Compagnie Fives-Lille. He was disappointed in his son, whose talent didn't turn out to be such a gold mine after all. The child was too perverse. He didn't mind his teachers. Every night when he returned home his father greeted him with a box on the ear. For he had developed unorthodox ideas about his music—a fatal defect for one who was expected to aim at popularity and financial success. The boy wasn't earning enough money with his lessons. He was a liability rather than an asset to his parents. It would be a good thing if somebody would take him off their shoulders.

And somebody did. Madame Nadyezhda von Meck had become interested in the young musician. She invited him to Moscow. This was a great relief to his parents and an important step in the development of his genius. For it enabled him to accustom his ear to the unfamiliar music of the Russians, Balakirev, Rimsky-Korsakov, Tchaikovsky, Borodin. In the evening he amused his hostess and her guests with his playing, and in the daytime he studied the possibilities of the "new" music. New music, new effects. Oriental harmonies. He became interested in the Greek scale with its six fundamental tones and in the bizarre modulations of the Chinese scale. Rich material for the building of new edifices of music. Arabesque towers of delicate design. Fairy palaces of unprecedented sound.

He experimented with these strange combinations of sound as he traveled with his patroness from country to country. And when he returned to Paris he submitted one of these "revolutionary" compositions in his candidacy for the Prix de Rome.

He was not unduly sanguine about his chances for carrying off the prize. For he felt no respect toward the judges. "Who are they anyhow, these judges?" he wrote. "What do they know about art? Are they quite sure that they themselves are artists?

From whence, then, do they derive the right to steer the mysterious barque of genius? By what scientific standards can they measure the relative merits of the various compositions submitted in the contest? It seems to me they would be wiser if they decided the winner by lot. . . ."

He was quite surprised, therefore, when he learned that he had won the scholarship. Surprised but not elated. For this recognition of his success was to him an indication of his failure. "My work, I am afraid, was too conventional," he said. Moreover, he was not too anxious to leave for Italy just then. He had conceived a passion for Madame Vasnier, the personable young wife of a wealthy old architect. His family and his friends, however, insisted upon his acceptance of the scholarship. It was too good an opportunity to pass up. Reluctantly he left for Rome.

His "enforced" studies in the Eternal City were extremely distasteful to him. Repeatedly he wrote to Madame Vasnier that he wanted to give up his scholarship and return home. But Monsieur Vasnier kept always advising him, with a solicitude that was a little more than fatherly, to remain in Italy and to attend strictly to his studies.

However, he didn't complete his studies at the Villa Medicis but returned to Paris before the three years were up. On his return he submitted to the Conservatoire the two pieces he had been obliged to compose as a prize scholar at the Villa Medicis. The judges examined these pieces and found them "unworthy of a man of talent."

Debussy was exultant. "Thank heaven," he said, "I have succeeded in writing something original at last!"

II

HE WAS NOW a taciturn young man of twenty-two—sharp features, piercing eyes, thick black curly hair flattened down over his forehead in the morning but disheveled into an unruly mane as the day wore on, strong bony hands, fingers that could strike the keyboard with hammerlike blows or caress them with feathery softness—a fighting anarchist, a gentle dreamer. He walked restlessly back and forth in his room as he composed, cigarette stub in his mouth, rebellious music in his heart. He was going to revolutionize the world of sound. "I shall never coop up my musical ideas within the cell structures of the old models," he said. "I shall give them space, freedom, life!"

He cared less than nothing for public opinion. "A few will probably appreciate my work. As for the rest, *ce m'est égal*, it's all the same to me whatever they may think."

But he worked hard for the appreciative few. "I drive my piano so relentlessly that it perspires like a human being." Always he sought to evoke from it the new cadence, the strange sequence of colors, the subtle combination of sounds, the echoes of enchanted voices coming from worlds unknown.

Yet his ear was also attuned to the voices of the world he lived in. Especially the siren voice of love. He had tired of Madame Vasnier. He had left her for the younger and more attainable allurements of Gabrielle Dupont, "Gaby of the Green Eyes." And then he abandoned Gaby for the still more alluring Rosalie Texier. Together he and Rosalie had read Maeterlinck's *Pelléas et Mélisande*—the haunting tale of the princess who comes from afar in search of happiness. They closed the book and fell silent for a time. And then Debussy looked into the violet-blue eyes of Rosalie. "Do you know, *ma petite princesse*," he whispered, "you are Mélisande."

"And shall I find my happiness?" she asked.

"Yes, if you will let me help you."

She touched his hand lightly as it lay on the closed book. "I believe I have found it already."

They were free lovers and free thinkers. But their families insisted upon the formality of a legal marriage, and they yielded.

And now that he was married he must think seriously of a

livelihood. His friends advised him to forget his "revolutionary madness" and to make a bid for popularity like a "sensible" musician. "Why don't you write simple music?" they urged him. "Like Massenet, for example."

"I'm sorry," he replied, "but I find it too difficult to write simple music."

Debussy could get no publisher for his compositions. He was obliged to content himself with giving piano lessons for his bread and butter. But though he was blessed with a superabundance of skill, he suffered from a deficiency of patience. He despised the stupidity of his pupils, and his pupils despised the acidity of their master.

He resented the necessity of stealing away so many hours from the realities of his dreams for the inanities of existence. His real work began after dark, when his teaching chores were over. Then he would sit down to his "breakfast"—at about five or six in the afternoon—and after a brief rest he would plunge into his night's composition.

It was thus that he wrote the music to *Pelléas and Mélisande*. His wife was his constant inspiration. Without her presence in the house he was unable to do his work. Walking from room to room "like a bear in a cage," he would continue for hours at a stretch to hum a tune until it had finally become registered in his mind. Then he wrote it down rapidly and resumed his restless march. His thoughts, like his habits, were irregular. He adhered to no orderly plan in the composition of this opera. For example, he wrote the fourth act before he started the first. He set all the other parts down in a helter-skelter fashion, yielding himself always to the inspiration of the moment.

For diversion he went to his favorite haunt, the Weber Café, where he drank either two glasses or one glass of wine, depending on the amount of money he had in his pocket. Most of the time it was one glass.

But his real pleasure came on Saturday nights. For then his

beloved cronies met at his house. Verlaine, Lalo, Chausson, Regnier, Mallarmé, Pierre Louis, Toulet—musicians, poets, novelists, haters of the old, admirers of the new, sworn disciples, every one of them, of Debussy's musical impressionism. And Debussy, in turn, sat at their feet as a humble disciple of their intellectual credo. He was anxious to make up for his lost schooling. When he had a few moments to spare he read—of all books—the dictionary! "The derivations and the definitions in the dictionary," he said, "contain more poetry, more philosophy, more history than any other book I know of."

He had become an expert in the subtle shading of words, just as he was an expert in the subtle shading of sounds. He found, to his surprise, that he could write as well as compose. He began to sell his articles on music to the various magazines—an avocation which he found more pleasant and often more profitable than his vocation of piano teaching. He developed a knack for epigrammatic criticism. With a single phrase he could transfix a composer like a butterfly on a pin. He expressed his contempt for "the goose-stepping, iron-helmeted music of Wagner." And Massenet he compared to a manufacturer of perfume. "It has a pleasant odor, but it is artificial." Of American music he complained that it was too mechanical. "Put an infant into a machine, and in five minutes you have a musician."

But his contempt for others was counterbalanced by a modesty toward himself. He rarely spoke of his music. He never regarded himself as a great man. He was genuinely surprised when he received the cross of the Legion of Honor. He accepted it merely because "it will give pleasure to my parents." Once he was acclaimed in a French magazine as "the great musical innovator." When this tribute was brought to his attention he smilingly remonstrated that he was quite unworthy of the honor. "I have been merely experimenting to satisfy my taste for the inexpressible."

Yet he didn't suffer from excessive humility. Nor from petty jealousy. His disparagement of his own work and his criticism of the work of other composers was the result of an honest evaluation. He was only too ready to acknowledge merit when he saw it. He was fair even to those whom he disliked. He couldn't stand the arrogance of Wagner, "the fortissimo chords of the trumpets . . . the beastlike cries of Tristan . . . the inhuman grandiloquence of Wotan . . . the bluster and blare of the music that keeps constantly shouting, 'I am the greatest of composers!' " But he summarized his estimate of Wagner's work in a sentence which is as penetrating as it is just: "Had Wagner been a little more human," writes Debussy, "he would have been truly divine."

III

TWO YEARS after the beginning of the twentieth century a new century in music began. For that year saw the production of *Pelléas and Mélisande*. This opera was a complete departure from the traditions of the past. No melodramatic effects, no elaborate changes of scenery, no ballets, no choruses, no duets. Merely one long, simple recitative, quiet like a deep river, varied like the innumerable ripples that play under the moonlight. Not a single "catchy" tune, for Debussy didn't care for popularity. Not a single concession to the public taste. Instead, an enchanting stream of music that carries the hearts of the initiated few away to those

> Charmed magic casements, opening on the foam
> Of perilous seas, in faery lands forlorn.

Yet in the opinion of the leading critics this opera is not the best of Debussy's works. It is in such pieces as the *Sea*, the *Afternoon of a Faun*, the *Nocturnes* and his prose poem, the *Christmas of the Homeless Children*, that he exhibits the most characteristic qualities of his genius. "The prose poem alone," writes Jean Lépine, "would have been sufficient to insure his immortal

[279]

fame." It was a product of the World War. He wrote the words on a winter's day in 1915, and he composed the music on the following day. It tells the story of the little French children who have lost their homes as a result of the German invasion.

"They have wrecked my house."
"My brothers are dead."
"They have broken my doll."
"They have stolen my bed."

Refugee children, lost in the inferno of the battlefield. It is Christmas Eve, but for them there will be no Christmas celebration. Nothing but cold and hunger and fear and the uncertainty of the future.

"What shall we do?"
"Don't know. Do you?"
"Where shall we go?"
"Anywhere, anywhere,
away from the foe."

But there's no escape from the foe. The German soldiers are everywhere, in Belgium, in France, in Russia—"all over the world!"

"They have burned the schoolhouse and murdered our teacher."

"They have burned the church and murdered God."

But perhaps God isn't dead yet. Perhaps He is stronger than the Germans. Let us pray to Him and see.

"Please, dear God, try to give us once more our daily bread." Note the pathos of the word *try*.

And then a passionate appeal to the spirit of Christmas. "Noël, Noël, don't ever again come to the houses of those wicked men. . . . Take pity on us, Noël, and punish them!"

The simple little poem ends with a prayer which today, as in 1915, re-echoes in millions of hearts: "Bring victory in the end to the children of France!"

[*280*]

IV

RECOGNIZED in his lifetime as the "father" of the new music, he remained to the end an *impoverished* father. His "children" praised him and left him to shift for himself. To a great extent this was his own fault. For instead of courting publicity he shunned it. When *Pelléas and Mélisande* was first produced in London it aroused a veritable tempest of enthusiasm. For fifteen minutes there was a continual demand that the composer step before the curtain. And where was he? In his hotel room, nonchalantly reading a book. Later on, when he heard of the public's disappointment at his nonappearance, he dryly remarked: "They want me to scrape and bow before them like a dancer."

He expected no immediate reward for his work. "The artist in modern civilization," he said, "will always remain a creature whose usefulness will be recognized only after his death."

He was resigned to his "preordained" poverty. He refused to advertise his music "like a newsboy shouting his papers on the boulevard." He understood little of business transactions, royalties, advances, contracts. "Art," he said, "should be divorced from commercialism. . . . The idea of marketing a musical composition like a tub of lard or a barrel of beer is to me as sad as it is ridiculous."

He despised the materialism of the world. He shunned the company of businessmen, of *most* men. But not the company of women. And that was his greatest weakness. He knew the pleasure of love but not the duty of faithfulness. Several women had come into his life—come and gone. Madame Vasnier, "Gaby of the Green Eyes," and others too before he had married Rosalie Texier. And now he was growing tired of Rosalie, his "Lily-Lilo," as he had affectionately called her. A chance meeting with Madame Emma Bardac, the music-loving wife of a money-loving banker, and his marriage vows were completely forgotten. There was an elopement, a scandal, an attempt at suicide on the part of Rosalie and finally a divorce. He married Emma Bardac—and began immediately to cast longing eyes in other directions.

But his time for loving, and indeed for living, was nearly over. He was stricken with cancer, and the last few years of his life were years of torture. At first he tried to hide his illness from his friends. Why bother them with his troubles? Hadn't they troubles enough of their own? But the suffering became acute, and he underwent two operations. To no avail. He became "a walking corpse." His days of pain were further saddened by the destructive advance of the Germans. Yet he never gave up hope for his country. "The German arrows," he said, "are cut out of rotten wood. They are bound to collapse in the end." France, he said, might be temporarily defeated. But she would never die. "The Germans may destroy French lives, but they can't kill French thought." He wasn't afraid of the outcome of the war. "What I am afraid of is the outcome of the peace that will follow the war."

Prophetic words!

V

ON THE LAST DAY OF HIS LIFE (March 25, 1918) all sounds had been muffled in the vicinity of his house. But in the distance there was an incessant noise—the pounding of the German guns. He had disliked the aggressive music of the Germans—their fortissimo chords, their grandiloquent shouting, "their bluster and blare and arrogant air." He had always preferred the quieter cadences of French art. Once a friend had told him proudly that he would be remembered as the founder of modern music. "I would rather," he said, "be remembered as a musician of France."

PUCCINI

Great Compositions by Puccini

OPERAS:
Le Villi, Edgar, Manon Lescaut, La Bohème, Tosca, Madame Butterfly, The Girl of the Golden West, The Swallow, The Cloak, Sister Angelica, Gianni Schicchi, Turandot.

OTHER COMPOSITIONS:
Sinfonia Capriccio.
2 Minuets for Strings.
Hymn to Rome.

Puccini

Giacomo Puccini

1858–1924

As a child Giacomo Puccini hated music. Like Bach, how-ever, he sprang from a family of musicians. Like Bach, too, he was apprenticed to an organist. But he showed no interest in his work. His father put gold coins on the keys, and when the youngster reached out his fingers to clasp them he struck the tones demanded of him. Thus, even at an early age, Puccini found gold at his finger tips. And throughout his life as often as he touched music he touched money.

His childhood hours of practice, however, were periods of painful memories. For whenever he struck a false note he would receive from his teacher such a vigorous kick in the shins that ever afterward the sound of a false note sent his reflexes into action and his foot into the air with a jerk. Some of his other boyhood memories at his native village of Lucca were of a more pleasant nature. For example, he performed at the organ of the local church and stole the tin pipes to buy some cigarettes. In the midst of a solemn Sunday hymn he would improvise a lively dance tune and set the hearts of the congregation a-waltzing. But he soon grew tired of playing the organ. One day (in 1878) he walked to Pisa to hear a performance of *Aïda*, and he decided to leave the church for the opera. He was twenty at the time.

II

HE PACKED HIS BELONGINGS and went to seek his fortune in Milan, the city of a thousand spires and a million aspirations. Young men with brains gathered here from all parts of Italy. The cafés featured spicy wines and spicy women. The musicians devoted themselves to the technique of composition and the art of love. And everybody sang—a gay and tuneful chorale to the goddess of joy.

Here Puccini commenced his studies in the opera. There was a ringing of bright new harmonies in his ears. But to his chagrin they were *theatrical* harmonies. "If only I could be a purely symphonic writer," Puccini was accustomed to say in later life. "But that was not for me. . . . Almighty God touched me with His little finger and said: 'Write for the theater—mind you, only for the theater.' "

During his student days at Milan he lived in the Bohemian circles where the conventional thing was to be unconventional. He was poor in his pocket and makeshift in his habits. A black, ill-smelling stove in a squalid attic. The meals consisted of soup and beans. He treated his poverty cavalierly with the assurance of youth. Someday he would write an opera about the hungry garret dwellers and he would turn their sufferings and their grumblings into a beautiful song. The Song of the City.

In the meantime he heard a voice from the woodlands. He wrote an opera (*Le Villi*) about the peasant folk who lived in the Black Forest of Germany. He submitted it in a contest and failed to win a prize.

This was a bitter disappointment. His desire to achieve fame —he was already twenty-six at the time, and youth is a period of impatience—had been spurred all the more intensely as a

[*286*]

result of the sensational success of his friend and fellow composer, Pietro Mascagni, a man with whom he had often shared his most intimate thoughts and his choicest wine. One of Mascagni's operas had carried off the first prize in a similar contest. The name of this opera was *Cavalleria Rusticana*. The entire continent was talking about it. Puccini had attended the opening performance and had been moved to tears at the tumultuous applause—tears of happiness at his friend's good luck but also tears of grief and envy. For he was yet to make his mark. He wrote a second opera around a mediocre libretto and still found nothing but obscurity for his pains.

And then suddenly he followed the way of Mascagni to the stars.

III

WITH the successful production of *Manon Lescaut* Puccini's personality as a man and as an artist had reached a clear definition. He was an easygoing man, an easygoing artist. He did not think of himself as endowed with a noble mission. There was nothing sanctimonious about his self-evaluation. He received his gifts lightly and became a master entertainer rather than a serious teacher. The stream of his genius ran swift but not deep. His melody was a sort of chloroform that sweetened the senses and put the intellect to sleep. The narcotic of his music, however, was destined to enchant the world.

He continued his success with the seductive lotus flowers of *La Bohème, Tosca, Madame Butterfly* and *The Girl of the Golden West*. He had become a popular song writer on a large scale. He was a fashionable Don Juan with clean-cut features and just enough genius to make him irresistible. No woman was safe from his charms. And no woman wished to be safe. He was the cynosure of every married woman's wandering eyes. One of them left the arms of her husband permanently and lived with Puccini for eighteen years. And then when the husband had

[*287*]

passed on beyond his marital rights her union with Puccini was legalized. Yet there was hardly a breath of scandal attached to the affair, for Puccini had such a proper manner in his improper morals.

He loved his Elvira, the woman who had so readily surrendered herself to him. But this didn't prevent him from sipping the joys of other loves wherever they were offered. "Monsieur Butterfly," his friends called the composer of *Madame Butterfly*. "He sips each flower and changes every hour." And to this the master replied, "On the day I'm no longer in love you may order my burial."

He was not the owner of his morality. It was a public trust in which the entire world of his worshipers had an interest and from which many of them received dividends. His private life gave rise to many an amusing anecdote. One will suffice. While staying at a fashionable hotel in Vienna during the height of his fame he received a call in his room. A handsome young lady had come to see him. He was clad in his pajamas and somewhat embarrassed. But the young lady seemed quite at her ease. She entered the room, accompanied by a lad with a music book. She explained that she was an admirer of the composer and that she would like to stay and talk with him for a while. She added that the master needn't be disturbed, since her brother was on his way to a music lesson. Whereupon she dismissed the lad. Puccini excused himself and retired into his bedroom to dress. When he returned to the sitting room fully clothed he found the young lady fully unclothed. "A mad woman," he thought. And he was ready to telephone the hotel manager. But then he decided that it was dangerous to fight against madness—especially a mad mind in a beautiful body.

Puccini was forever hounded by this rather desirable lunatic fringe. But his chief delight was solitude. He was most happy when he was able to retire to his villa amidst the pines of Viareggio. Here in the long, low-ceilinged parlor, while a few friends chatted at a bridge table in the corner, he would sit at the piano, hat on head, puffing vigorously at a cigarette and striking his notes as the theme of a new song ran busily through his mind. The chatter of his friends, the thick smoke rising to the ceiling and music bubbling out of his finger tips—this was his idea of solitude, of heaven on earth.

Beyond the piazza stretched the body of the lake, silver against the night sky. Through this water he had churned his motorboat over many a league. In the woods he had traveled after game with his gun. And here at the piano, as he sat weaving his dreams and watching the water and the woods, he felt himself at once a creator and an intimate part of all creation.

It was an evening in November 1895. His friends, as usual, were drinking and chatting at the bridge table. And Puccini was at the piano. Every now and then, when the conversation lapsed, Puccini would look up and beg them to continue. For the silence annoyed him. It was only when he heard their reassuring gibes and their laughter that he could resume his composition. Finally he struck a chord with decisiveness and looked up. "It is finished," he remarked quietly. They all crowded around him to listen to the final scene of the opera they knew he was engaged on—a story of Paris, the Latin Quarter and the Bohemians. "Gentlemen, I would like to introduce you to Mimi. She is a little grisette who sells her body for fine clothes and a carriage. But she is immortal, for she loves with a heart that can break. I will play you the death scene which I have just completed." They were overcome with emotion when they heard the music. "You, too, will be immortal along with Mimi," remarked one of his friends.

Puccini smiled. "Perhaps."

"What is this opera called?" asked another friend.

"The name of this opera," replied Puccini, "is *La Bohème.*"

IV

BECAUSE of the tremendous popularity of his operas and the sensational quality of his music Puccini was likened to a writer of dime novels. Against this charge Puccini offered no defense. He admitted that he was but a secondary instrument in the orchestra of operatic creation. He was fascinated by the rich plenitude of Verdi's tone. Wagner, too, cast a spell over him—a spell of despair. When he glanced at the score of *Tristan* he exclaimed with chagrin: "This terrific music reduces me to nothingness . . . I am only a mandolin player. . . ." His own music knew little of cosmic power. It spoke not the language of gods but of human beings—pitiable and weak human beings. "I do not understand the music of Wotan," he said, "but I know the song of little Mimi. It pierces my heart."

The libretto of *La Bohème* is based upon a novel written (in 1847) by Henry Murger. It is the story of the young starving Bohemians in the Latin Quarter of Paris. Puccini had led this sort of life as a young man in Milan. There are a million Latin Quarters within the frontiers of youth. The opera of Puccini is simple and human. Here we have a humble subject set to noble melody—a musical counterpart of the democratic trend in the art and the literature of the nineteenth century. An opera need not be the stage for an epic, it may be the setting for an idyll; it need not deal pompously with cosmic issues, but simply and unpretentiously with everyday things. "The music of Puccini's operas must not be sung with the throat only, it must be sung with the heart."

Grand opera is a strange phenomenon in Italy. It is as indigenous to the diet of the Italians as olive oil and spaghetti. And the Italians regard their music as they regard their food. It is a vital element of their daily existence. A bad opera is poison to them and they treat the composer accordingly. During one operatic offering a number of enthusiastic critics bombed the auditorium and killed a number of the audience. Small wonder that every time Puccini was about to witness a first production of his music he said he felt like a criminal attending his own execution. Just before the presentation of *Tosca*—the opera which followed *La Bohème*—he consulted the police officials on measures to insure the public safety, and he was advised that if any disturbance arose the orchestra would strike up the national anthem and quiet the unruly element in the audience. The Italian audience, in contrast with the German audiences at Bayreuth, never treated the opera as a continuous drama. At any moment in the midst of the action the author in his street clothes might be summoned from the wings to take his bow, together with the performers in costume—especially at the end of a popular aria. And if a conductor refused to encore a death scene that struck the fancy of the house, he was likely to be pelted with rotten fruit. It was not unusual for the fickle audience to call the actors thirty or forty times to the footlights with deafening applause and then to go home with the declaration that the opera was "foul." *La Bohème* had been only a moderate success at its first performance, although the audience had dragged the actors from their dressing rooms at the end and forced them to go through Mimi's death scene in their street clothes minus their wigs. Arturo Toscanini had conducted the opera at that performance. Later on he did much to bring it to the attention of the world. "When that fellow gets a score into his hands," Puccini said of him, "he digs into it like a miner in order to explore every corner."

Yet there were times when Puccini's criticism of his fellow musicians showed less discernment. During one of the rehearsals of *La Bohème* he told a friend of his that he was compelled against his will to listen to a tenor who sang the part of Rudolph very poorly. "What's his name?" the friend wanted to know. "Enrico Caruso," replied Puccini.

This was, of course, snap judgment. For later Caruso was acclaimed not only as the greatest Rudolph but also as the foremost singer of all Puccini's operas. And the two became intimate friends.

V

IN 1902 Puccini began the composition of *Madame Butterfly*, the story of which is based on a play by John Luther Long and David Belasco. The librettists were Puccini's friends, Illica and Giacosa, the men who had previously associated with him on *Tosca* and *La Bohème*. *Madame Butterfly* is perhaps the most popular of Puccini's operas. This story, "woven of musical moonbeams," deals with the unhappy fate of the Japanese geisha girl who has married a bluff American naval officer. One wonders where the comedy ends and the tragedy begins in the life of the pathetic little creature who is doomed from the start by her youthful freshness and innocence. In the lightest of her musical moods we can hear the somber undertone of approaching doom.

Madame Butterfly, perhaps the finest of Puccini's operas, was hissed off the stage by the fickle Milan audience on its first performance. The spectators booed and catcalled. The hall rocked with jeers. Puccini stood in the wings defiant. "Splendid! Louder, you beasts!" he muttered in his teeth. "Shriek, yell, sneer at me!" All along he had told his friends that this was his best work. "It is I who am right, I! You shall see! It is the greatest opera I have ever written!" The critics called it "Puccini's fiasco." But the composer stuck to his guns. After some revision and further rehearsals he produced it again. And the echo of a new masterpiece rang around the world.

VI

IN THE TWENTY YEARS that were left to Puccini after the completion of *Madame Butterfly* he wrote several additional operas but only one other masterpiece—*The Girl of the Golden West.* The Indian summer of his life was warm and serene but uneventful. The best harvest of his music had already been gathered in. The composer of melodrama, he led an existence that was anything but melodramatic.

And yet in the ending of his life there was a dramatic touch. In his sixty-seventh year he was at work on *Turandot,* an opera whose Chinese atmosphere was designed as a contrast to the Japanese atmosphere of *Madame Butterfly.* He was interrupted in his work by a throat ailment—a recurrence of an old irritation he had incurred when he had swallowed a goosebone at a banquet. The doctors were now called in to examine his throat and found a malignant tumor. He was put under the care of one of the leading throat specialists in Europe. Radium treatments were applied and with excellent results. He was recovering from his cancer—when he died suddenly of a heart attack.

Fate—the master of the surprise ending to the drama of human life.

SIBELIUS

Great Compositions by Sibelius

7 Symphonies.
Several Symphonic Poems, including *Finlandia, Kullervo, En Saga, Tapiola.*
String Quartet in B flat major.
Canzonetta for Strings.
Violin Concerto in D minor.

Suite, *Belshazzar's Feast.*
Several "Songs" for piano.
Valse Triste.
Incidental music to *King Christian II, The Tempest.*
Karelia Suite.
Scènes Historiques.

Sibelius

Jean Sibelius

1865–

H IS FATHER was a physician in Tavastehus, a village in the interior of Finland. He came of a stock that was predominantly Swedish, yet the psychology of the Sibelius family was that of the Finnish middle classes.

He was born in 1865. Three years later his father, the kindliest and most sociable man of the village, died in the line of duty. He had been infected with the typhus germ while attending his patients. Thenceforth the children of the family—two boys and a girl—were looked after, indeed were dominated by, their mother and their two grandmothers. The children were some-what pampered by their feminine environment, but they grew up and out of it unspoiled.

The boy had been named Johann Julius Christian, but when he reached manhood he called himself Jean after an adventur-ous uncle who had gone to sea and died of yellow fever in Havana. His childhood experiences were pleasant enough. He spent much of the time with his female relatives on the coast and developed an intense love for the sea. At that time Finland

[*297*]

was under the domination of the czar. Russian troops were garrisoned in the little country and got along surprisingly well with their Finnish hosts. Many an individual friendship had been struck up between the conquerors and the conquered. Indeed, one of the closest boyhood chums of Sibelius was a youngster by the name of Kostya, the son of a Russian colonel. Yet Sibelius, in common with the other children of Finland, was brought up to hate Russianism even though he liked Russians. It was in his childhood years that he imbibed the spirit of that impassioned anthem he was to write later on—his national Declaration of Independence, *Finlandia.*

He showed an early but by no means precocious musical talent. At five he ran his fingers over the keyboard of the piano and sought for new harmonies and tunes. But his attachment for the piano was lukewarm. His one devotion was the violin. (Throughout his life the violin was to remain the dominant instrument of his music.) Together with his brother and his sister he formed a family trio. Very often the children went to the homes of musical friends with whom they were able to play quartets. Jean got to know several of the Mozart and the Haydn quartets by heart, and he found great delight in their sculptural style. Before long, however, he began to compose his own chamber music for these domestic concerts—and then something in the nature of a miracle happened. Within the space of two years, and without any formal training, he commenced to express himself in a musical language of his own. Casting off the influence of the classics, he developed a new idiom, an individual interpretation of his Northern landscapes of sea foam and forests and mountains. And, too, there was even in this early music another characteristic accent—a Sibelian passion for freedom.

So completely absorbed was Sibelius in his music and his dreams that he paid scant attention to his school lessons. "Good gracious," the kindly schoolmaster would remark with a sigh when he questioned him suddenly and received an absent-minded answer, "Sibelius is in another world again!" Sibelius was indeed in a world many leagues of imagination removed from the world of the classroom.

II

LIKE SCHUMANN and Tchaikovsky, Sibelius was destined for a legal career. To please his relatives he enrolled at the University of Helsingfors; but at the same time, to please himself he entered the Helsingfors Musical Academy as a special student. "If you ask me what I learned at the University," he remarked many years later, "I can say with a clear conscience, nothing." On one occasion he had become so bored with a prescribed textbook that he had put it, with its pages open, upon the window sill where the sun could get at it and had then promptly forgotten about its existence. Month after month the book lay there until its pages grew yellow from the heat. Finally an uncle visited Sibelius to find out how the young "student" was getting on with his work. He walked over to the window, took one glance at the book on the sill and said with a sigh: "After all, Jean, it would be best for you to devote yourself entirely to music. . . ."

Sibelius resigned from the University and threw himself heart and soul into his music. His formal education had offered him merely the instruments through which he might assimilate his experience into the wealth of his ideas. His primary instincts needed no schooling. They were direct. For example, he would walk along the shore and the sour smell of flax and hemp that had just been taken out of the water would come to him. And the odor would set his musical sense into motion. He would screw up his nose, make a wry face and jot down the theme of a capriccio. Or else he would take an icicle in his hand. "How lovely it is to feel the moisture of the melting ice!" And now the

[299]

tactile senses were aroused and sent the germ of music into his system.

But it was his visual sense that was particularly strong. His moods always suggested themselves in colors. And there was moreover in his mind a definite association between color and sound, so that a musical composition assumed a kaleidoscopic pattern, a convenient, aesthetic image which he could not only hear but see. One of the friends of his student days remarked that to Sibelius every musical key had a different hue. "The key of A major was blue; C major, red; F major, green; and D major, yellow."

During his formative period at the Helsingfors Academy of Music Sibelius was fortunate enough to find a teacher who was neither a genius on the one hand nor a pedant on the other. This man was Martin Wegelius, an honest musician who refused to place discipline above talent or talent above discipline. Aware of his own limitations, he was too sensible to overwhelm his pupil and to transform him into his satellite. Although he himself had a predilection for Wagner, he was unable—and indeed unwilling —to impose this predilection upon the independent mind of Sibelius. He did nothing to discourage the individualistic taste of the younger man.

Sibelius spent three years with this teacher. He found him helpful but uninspiring. And since his classwork was of necessity dry and routine, he did most of his best composition in secret. He paid lip service to the classical forms and studiously copied out the assigned fugues and contrapuntal passages. But in the shelter of his room he composed to his heart's content, using his own style and his own methods. While studying under Wegelius he wrote three important pieces—a theme and variations in C sharp major, a quartet in A minor and a string suite in A major. The first piece was a thoroughly conventional exercise, the sort of thing that was required of the conservatory student after his three years of technical study. Wegelius was delighted with this

[*300*]

result of his teaching. But the last two works sprang not from the teaching of Wegelius' school. They were unacademic, original, free. The more discerning critics of Helsingfors paid sincere tribute to these two pieces and declared that their young composer had already struck an authentic new note in the modern music of Finland.

III

SIBELIUS was fortunate in his environment. He had never suffered the acute maladjustments and distorted psychology common to a child prodigy who, because of his abnormal musical precocity, must sacrifice his normal physical growth. Sibelius had matured musically by easy stages, and he had arrived at his manhood with a healthy body as well as a vigorous mind. His would not be the fate of Mozart, Schubert, Chopin. During his student days he had made the acquaintance of an unhappy virtuoso of that type—a pianist by the name of Busoni. "This young friend of mine," wrote Sibelius, "had grown up as an infant prodigy and had spent his youth in hotels in practically every city of Europe. He came into contact with the outdoors for the first time in Finland. In the early stages of our acquaintance he was very much surprised at the great benefits I had been able to draw from my communion with nature."

The slow and healthy development of Sibelius' talent was characterized by his relatively small output up to the age of twenty-four. Several of his contemporaries had written considerably more in the same period of time. But today few of their works are worth mentioning. They supplied the demands of the moment. But there was little of artistic unity or of vital integrity in their attempts at their so-called modernistic music. With Sibelius the growth of the soul was slow but it was vigorous, organic, alive.

And now that he had completed his conservatory training he desired to achieve additional technical skill and further experience in life among new peoples in new lands. He took his first trip beyond the borders of Finland to Berlin. Here he apprenticed himself to a deliberate and conscientious study of the masters. He no longer scorned the science of his craft. "Practice in technique seems to me today to be as important for the composer as practice in anatomy is for the surgeon." At times, to be sure, his patience almost failed him as he labored constantly on the theory of fugues. "I could not resist the feeling that I was like an excavator digging up the skeletons of the past." Yet dig them up he did. Sibelius was destined to become one of the great paradoxes in modern music. For this man who scorns to imitate the music of the past for its own sake and who believes wholly in expressing his own time in the mode best suited for it is, among contemporary composers, the most eager to preserve the eternal and fundamental traditions of music. It is he who has kept on writing symphonies when the ultramodernists have long since given up the symphonic form.

Sibelius continued to study the symphonic and the other classical forms not only in Berlin but in Vienna. When he arrived in Vienna the epic battle between the schools of Brahms and of Wagner was at its height. But Sibelius found his own peace of mind in the midst of the battle, for he championed neither school. Vienna was the headquarters of Brahms—tart, gruff, untidy and smelling everlastingly of tobacco. Busoni attempted to secure for Sibelius an introduction to the master. But the master wouldn't waste his time on an unknown musician. "What can he do?" he asked Busoni, and when the latter told him that Sibelius had written a "good quartet" Brahms shrugged his shoulders. He was not interested.

But Hans Richter, the distinguished conductor of Wagnerian opera, was more accessible. He gave Sibelius a hospitable reception and the benefit of his own expert advice. Up till now the young composer had made a thorough study of the medium of chamber music but had not as yet tried his hand at composi-

tions for full orchestra. Richter recommended a teacher of instrumental composition, and Sibelius took lessons from him.

At that time, also, Sibelius made the acquaintance of the
third member of the musical trinity at Vienna—Karl Goldmark,
the composer who after Brahms and Bruckner reigned supreme.
Goldmark, an amazingly shrewd businessman, was at the height
of his fame and his fortune. Nevertheless he found the time to
supervise and to correct Sibelius' work. He was frank in his
opinion. "A queer bird," he called the Finnish composer. A
queer bird, indeed. The song of the Northland forests was
strange food for the city-bred soul of Vienna.

As for Sibelius himself, he cared as little for the contemporary
music of Vienna as the contemporary musicians of Vienna cared
for his own music. He returned home, relieved to find himself
once more in his native environment. Fascinated as he was by
the turmoil of life in Berlin and in Vienna, he could live nowhere but in Finland. Here alone, with its rugged climate and
its glittering skies, could he do his best work. Finland was his
blood, the marrow of his bones, his very heart. He had come
home hungry with a yearning for articulate patriotism. He
wrote a symphonic tone-poem based upon a myth from Finnish
antiquity. He performed this work—*Kullervo*—under his own
baton and created a sensation. With it Sibelius had "arrived"—
at least in his own country. He was at the time only twenty-six.
In the flush of success he married Aino Jarnefelt, the daughter
of a Finnish general, and honeymooned with her on the Karelian
Isthmus. Here was a perfect place to study "the aboriginal
language of music," to familiarize himself with the ancient folk
songs of his native land.

When he returned to Helsingfors he accepted a position as
teacher in the Musical Academy and a similar post in the orchestral school of the Philharmonic Society. The orchestra was
placed at his disposal. It proved a worthy laboratory of musical
experimentation, for he was to spend his entire life wrestling

with the problems of the orchestra. Again and again he told his friends, "You must judge me by my orchestral works." And then he would add with a smile, "I write piano pieces in my moments of relaxation. As a matter of fact, the piano does not interest me; it cannot sing. A complete song can be sung only by the orchestra."

And a flood of orchestral songs came pouring from his pen. National songs. Fighting songs for freedom. He owed his early success not only to his genius as a composer but to his consecration as a *patriotic* composer. He had become the articulate voice of Finland in her struggle for political independence.

In 1897 the Finnish government awarded the youthful composer a yearly pension of four hundred dollars. It was not enough to release Sibelius from all his financial worries but it served to relieve him of his heavier teaching duties. Now he was free to devote most of his time to his composition and to give a few hours to the instruction of his most advanced students.

His teaching was methodical, thorough, yet informal. On sunny afternoons he would enter briskly, puffing with animation on a cigar, and with a twinkle in his eye he would observe the students at their textbooks on harmony. It would be a pity if the young ladies' cheeks were to lose their country color. "It is so beautiful outside. Would you care to take a walk in the fresh air and look at the town?"

His love for nature—or, to put it in its broadest sense, his love for life—was a religion with him. Music was but one of the mirrors for the reflection of life. *Contemporary* life. Tradition for him was not a rigid formula of consecrated judgments, dogmatic axioms that have become fastened between the pincers of the present and the past; it was rather a projection of the vivid spirit of the past into the vivid experiences of the present. The greatest of the classics are alive today because they were alive in their own day. The eternal is both classic and modern at the same time.

In discussing composition with his pupils, Sibelius never tired of remarking, "No dead notes. Every note must live!" He told his pupils that he couldn't teach music in the usual sense. He taught—and he wrote—after a formula of his own, the musical credo of classical modernism. In spite of his constant growth and experimentation this musical credo of Sibelius' has remained substantially consistent throughout his career.

Sibelius staked his entire spiritual life upon the judgment of his own soul. He was not influenced by the conventional values of others, especially of the professional critics who made it their business to estimate the infinite in art through their own finite spectacles. "A statue has never yet been set up in honor of a critic," he once remarked dryly. His attitude toward composition, as we have seen, was "orthodoxically unorthodox." Around him were many so-called "modernistic" composers who used the orchestra for a display of their musical pyrotechnics. They sought to dazzle by their brilliance. And this sensationalism had become the convention in contemporary music halls. On the other hand there was a long line of composers, more subdued but equally conventional, who assiduously followed the letter rather than the spirit of the great masters. Thus handicapped by their bridles and their blinkers, they had plodded their way through life looking neither to the right nor to the left.

And so there had sprung up two groups of uninspired musicians—the modernists, who were branches without roots, and the classicists, who were roots without branches. The work of both groups was equally dead. In order to be alive, said Sibelius, a musical composition must reach downward into the soil of the past and spread upward into the sunlight of the present.

This is precisely what Sibelius tried to do—to bind the past and the present into an orchestral unit of organic life. And this is what transformed him from a regional into a universal genius. His name first became known to the outside world when he wrote his *Finlandia*, the tone-poem expressive of Finnish national hopes. But what interested music lovers everywhere in this tone-poem was not its *local* but its *world-wide* aspiration for freedom. The music was a battle cry for independence that re-echoed through all the capitals of Europe. So, too, were most of his other compositions—stirring hymns to the sunrise of a new day. The day of social regeneration.

IV

PERSONALLY Sibelius had no reason to be a rebel. The world was kind to him. His struggles were mental and not material. He was happy in his home life. He had a faithful wife, and a mistress—his orchestra. "You know," he once remarked, "I am not legitimately married to the orchestra. I am its lover." And he was a most devoted lover. He dealt constantly with the problems of orchestration. "The orchestra," he told his pupils, "is a huge and wonderful instrument that has everything—except the pedal. . . . The composer who really understands this fact must create an artificial pedal to fill the gaps in this otherwise sonorous instrument." He must produce a continuous current of music; otherwise the various parts will sound like ragged little urchins splashing in the mud. It is the function of the piano pedal to produce the homogeneous stream of tone color, to emphasize and to harmonize the infinite number of overtones that vibrate in the timbre of the notes. In the orchestra you can achieve the same effect. Suppose the beginning of a chord is given to trumpets, trombones, horns and woodwinds, all fortissimo. A diminuendo will follow as the stronger instruments are dropped, thus leaving the weaker instruments to carry on into gradual pianissimo. "It will be like a thought born under a heavy sky and slowly trying to reach into purer regions." His ear was very sensitive to overtones. He could catch them as he lay in a field of rye and heard the breeze sweeping over it. He loved especially the "still, small voices" of nature. In his delicate conception of the orchestra's function he sharply criticized what he called the "rude, brutal, vulgar" music of Richard Wagner. "He always shouts, 'I love you, I love you!' To my mind, love is something that you should whisper." This reflects Sibelius' entire attitude toward refinement in art. It is indeed his entire personality. He despised undisciplined loudness. When you shout about your love for others you are merely advertising your love for yourself. He advocated self-restraint. Commenting on Anton Bruckner, the romantic composer whose genius ran wild under the whiplash of his ego, he had this to say: "Writing scores was for him like sitting in the organ loft of a church with all the keyboards in reach. He simply used the different registers, without thinking of their instrumental individuality." Sibelius didn't believe in a vulgar display of emotion. The harmony of restraint is necessary in the tones of the orchestra as well as in the feelings of the human heart.

In the opinion of Sibelius the two greatest geniuses of the orchestra were Mozart and Mendelssohn. And he might have added that the overtures to *The Magic Flute* and the *Midsummer Night's Dream* were his own musical Bible. Both Mozart and Mendelssohn had solved successfully what Sibelius called "the difficulty of materializing absolute idealism." There is often a great gulf—said Sibelius—between the ideal themes that run through the composer's head and the audible sounds that reach the ear of the concertgoer in their final form. The limitations of the orchestral instruments generally defeat the composer. His idealism is conquered by the material difficulties of life. "There are in music as in life all sorts of obstacles to the effective expression of our ideas. And orchestration, like life, is a hard struggle for existence." All the more credit, then, to those who can clothe their ideal dreams in the material garment of sound with a minimum loss of beauty. This Mendelssohn did. And Mozart too. This was Sibelius' great struggle in the midst of a material life without struggles.

[*307*]

V

As soon as he was financially able he moved away from Helsingfors and lived in the country. Here, close to nature, he could bring his dreams closer to realization. Tomasby, near the Tusby Fens. Vast, peaceful fields going down to the lake. The best milieu for his work. Here he instructed his pupils, and when they trembled before their tasks and told him that they were only beginners he answered, "So am I." And here he wrote the supreme chapters of his musical experience—the symphonies.

Once he had met Gustav Mahler and the two had discussed the definition of a symphony. Sibelius had stated that he admired the true symphonic style because of its severity and because of the profound logic that demanded an inner connection between all its motifs. "No," disagreed Mahler. "A symphony must be like the world. It must embrace a little of everything without discrimination." Whereupon Sibelius retorted: "If we understood the world, we would realize that there is a logic of harmony underlying its manifold apparent dissonances."

Every note, every shade of melody has a definite logical meaning in the music of Sibelius. One of the best interpreters of his symphonies, the Helsingfors conductor, Robert Kajanus, attributed his own success to the fact that he understood the mind as well as the music of Sibelius. He used to steal in unobserved whenever Sibelius rehearsed his symphonies. One day Sibelius caught him. When asked to explain his intrusion Kajanus stammered, "I wanted to see your mind in the process of thinking." A Sibelius symphony, believed Kajanus, represents a definite system of philosophy; and a single deviation from the composer's plan would spoil the entire thought. "You know," he remarked to a friend, "I once gave Sibelius' *First Symphony* without the score. Everything went well, and I even received congratulations on the performance. But afterwards I was struck with re-

[*308*]

morse, thinking that I might have omitted some shades, even if nobody had noticed. I promised myself never to conduct any of his work by heart again."

Sibelius' *First Symphony* was written at the age of thirty-six, when he had thoroughly mastered all the other forms of music. The work is built along orthodox classical lines, with the usual four movements. The first movement is a Mozart allegro, the second an expressive cantabile, the third a scherzo, the fourth an epic finale ending on a note of triumph. Yet so unique is the harmony that many in the audience called the work revolutionary when it was first performed. Others, less extravagant in their praise, noted for all of Sibelius' restraint a kinship to the Slavic melodies of Tchaikovsky and the same propensity for the music to break out into waltzes. The mood, however, is not one of alternating exultation and depression as in the case of the Russian composer. Instead there is here a spirit of heroism and tremendous courage—and at the same time an absence of warmth. "When we see the granite rocks of our Finnish coast, we know why we are able to treat the orchestra as we do!" Gaunt, overpowering outlines, heroically tragic against a solid archaic background. This is a symphony of romance in its truest sense—the romance of a Northern people with a somber good heart. In many respects this work is the last of a dynasty of symphonies and perhaps one of the best. It is the archetype of the traditional heroic symphony in which the nineteenth century abounds. It is the child of Beethoven's *Eroica*, the nephew of Brahms' *Fourth*, the first cousin of Dvořák's *New World Symphony*. It is the conclusion of a time-honored style.

The *Second Symphony* of Sibelius, on the other hand, marks the beginning of a new style. It is still constructed in the traditional four movements, but the handling of the thematic material is now completely revolutionized. In the earlier symphonies, for example, the themes would be stated in an exposition, analyzed in various fragmentary combinations and then put together again in a recapitulation. But in the opening movement of this symphony the entire process is reversed. The fragments of the theme are introduced in the exposition. At first they seem like scraps of disjointed melody having no connection with one another. But soon they are developed into the whole theme and broken up again into musical atoms in the recapitulation. Nothing like this treatment has ever been known to music, this "breathing of life" into musical segments, this process of organic cell creation which multiplies into living organisms. Before our ears the seed develops into the flower, the flower absorbs the rain and the dew and then the entire plant is dissolved into dust while the new seeds take up the process all over again. The slow movement of the symphony is also quite new. Never was the melancholy of life more honestly or more graphically expressed. And as if to show the world that he is still mindful of the old traditions, Sibelius returns to the conventional forms for the scherzo and the final movement. Indeed, for all its elaborate force and embroidered tapestry, the finale is built up on a simple allegro theme as old as Mozart.

The *Third Symphony* marks still another step in the experimental progress of Sibelius. It is written in three movements. There is no slow movement proper, nor is there any scherzo. But the second movement is suggestive of both. As an illustration of Sibelius' continual effort toward greater precision it is interesting to note that each symphony is shorter and more compact than its predecessor. The *First Symphony* contains 160 pages of score; the *Second*, 145; the *Third*, only 70. And each symphony is scored for fewer instruments. The *First Symphony*, which is full and resplendent and which represents Sibelius in his more orthodox mood, is scored for the full orchestra. The *Second* is scored for the full orchestra minus the harp. The *Third* is scored with still greater restraint. The bass tuba, which played a dominant part in the first two symphonies, is here omitted. Indeed, almost the entire accent in the *Third Symphony* is based upon the strings.

It is almost like a return to the chamber music of which the composer used to be so fond in his earlier days. The musical pigment is much lighter, more impressionistic. The trumpets are conspicuous by their absence. From the elaborate texture of a Velasquez painting in music the new sound picture has the supple, transparent suggestiveness of a Franz Hals. There is not the same complexity of themes as in the earlier symphonies. There is a complete return to the old classical simplicity. The atmosphere is not the somber, mysterious restlessness of the *Second* nor the epic heroism of the *First;* it is flooded with sunlight and fun.

The *Fourth Symphony* is even stranger by contrast. No one unacquainted with the facts could have believed that the man who composed the first three symphonies was also the composer of the fourth. And yet there is no one else who could have written it. For it is a profound and unique personal expression. It belongs to a world of its own—a world which no other musical composition has ever been able to invade. It is as different from the earlier works of Sibelius as it is from the works of any other man. If the *Third Symphony* showed a tendency toward compactness and an inclination to get down to the bare essentials of music—if the *Third Symphony,* as the English critic Cecil Gray has put it, "represents the result of a slimming treatment, a reduction of the adipose tissues and somewhat opulent curves of the symphonic muse as she appears in the first two examples," the *Fourth* is the outcome of sheer asceticism. The first movement, which is based entirely upon a theme of four notes in the strings, is over in thirteen pages. The idiom is new. The tone is haunting and somber and suggestive. There never was a more compact movement nor one that told so much. The second movement, a graceful allegro, is fifteen pages long and entirely impressionistic. It is a full philosophical essay written in musical shorthand. This music is remarkable not so much for what it says but for what it leaves unsaid. The third movement, largo, is nine pages long. And in this narrow compass "a theme is built up out of nothing before our eyes." Such self-denial in music had never been heard before. The final movement, too, is written down to scale. It develops a complete and colorful theme but it contains not a single superfluous note.

This symphony is approximately a third as large as the *First*. And yet nothing essential is missing. Indeed, it is potent with meaning. Sibelius wrote it at a time when the other composers of the day, Strauss, Debussy, Ravel, were indulging in orchestral orgies, lounging in the upholstery of rich melodies that were meant to entice the audience with their voluptuous appeal. But this composition of Sibelius' stands out as a protest against what he regarded as the insincerity of the time. It is a chaste creation of austere genius. It portrays the relentless power of an overwhelming fate.

This work was composed in 1910. It was five years before Sibelius wrote another symphony. During this time he had been honored throughout Europe and he had paid a triumphant visit to America. And then the World War broke out. The faith of many thinking men was staggered. Sibelius had already reached the depths of pessimism in his music. Even before the war he had been profoundly shocked at the spectacle of man's inhumanity to man. But, curiously enough, the war restored his faith. It takes a great tragedy to prove the moral fiber of mankind. "This life that I love so infinitely" was crashing around him. And yet, "civilization is strength, and not weakness. Look at the great nations of Europe and what they have endured! No savage race could have survived the sufferings that they have undergone. It is their civilization that has given them such vitality and courage." He believed profoundly in civilization. And in this belief he emerged from the purgatory of his earlier visions. Already he had caught a glimpse of the mountains that he would ascend. "God opens His door for a moment and His orchestra plays the *Fifth Symphony*." This symphony is a return to triumph. It is Olympian. The ghost of the *Fourth* has been laid. This new music is rich and sonorous. It is a sequel to Beethoven's *Fifth*. It heralds the joyous destiny of man; it is an affirmation of his courage and his persistency and his hope. In spite of the devastated fields of Flanders, Sibelius proclaims with renewed strength, "I *do* believe in civilization!"

Never in all his long life did he flinch from the sincerity of his art. "This art," he observes, "stands out as a protest against the compositions of today. Nothing, *absolutely nothing*, of the circus about my work." The more he saw of modern life, he confessed, the more classical became his attitude toward art. In 1924 he wrote his *Sixth Symphony*, which was characterized by its great restraint after the outburst of the *Fifth*. Once again his mind had resumed its even keel, his spirit had regained its tranquillity. And (in 1925) he followed this "masterpiece of tonal control" with his final tour de force, the *Seventh Symphony*. Always the experimenter, Sibelius wrote this new symphony in only one movement—one vast ocean of innumerable ripples stretching in a single singing body from shore to shore.

Sibelius stopped his symphonies at the magical number of seven. And in these seven symphonies he displayed a versatility equaled only by Beethoven. Not only is Sibelius among the most unique of composers, but each of his seven symphonies is unique in itself—a musical entity different in character from any of the others. As in the case of Beethoven and of Shakespeare, we find ourselves asking the question: "Can one human mind encompass such a diversity of thought?" And yet in all the diversity of Sibelius we find a unity of purpose—an almost unbroken development from extravagant brilliance to unadorned simplicity, from poetical exuberance to intellectual restraint. Sibelius has been called the last musical exponent of the old classics. Perhaps it would be more correct to say that he is the first musical exponent of the new mathematics. Sibelius has stood forth as the Bach of the twentieth century.

[*313*]

He is an old man now. His finest work has been done. After the war he went through the ravages of the Finnish Revolution and later experienced the Bolshevik terror. But he emerged unperturbed. The scars of his struggle were all mental. For there were new paths of art to be hewn, new obstacles to be met and new songs to be written. He is now, as he remarks, a "young-old apprentice of seventy-five," still experimenting reverentially with "the mathematics of the scale." And over a bottle of claret and a good cigar he sounds his testament: "Let no one imagine that composing grows easier with the years if the composer takes his art seriously. The older the artist, the greater the demands he imposes upon himself. . . . One is always faced with fresh problems."

STRAVINSKY

Great Compositions by Stravinsky

VOCAL:
Comic opera, *Mavra*.
Japanese Lyrics.
Choral Works: *Apollon Musagète, Oedipus*.

BALLETS:
Le Chant du Rossignol, L'Oiseau de Feu, Petrushka, Le Sacre de Printemps, L'Histoire d'un Soldat, Pulcinella, Les Noces.

OTHER COMPOSITIONS:
Octet for Winds.
Concertos and Sonatas for Piano.
Capriccio for Piano and Orchestra.
Concerto for Violin.
Symphony of Psalms.

Stravinsky

Igor Stravinsky

1882–

STRAVINSKY is not only a great composer. He is the supersales-man of a fantastic product, a new type of unmusical music, an unconventional, startling and therefore captivating harmony of discords. In the music of Stravinsky the most irreconcilable of sounds are joined in amazing wedlock, resulting frequently in family quarrels and clashes of melodic interest.

Stravinsky is the high priest of the bizarre. Yet there was nothing bizarre in the sounds that he heard as a child—the simple songs of the peasant women as they returned from the fields, the whistling of a half-witted vagabond who amused the children with his antics, the chattering of the birds in the trees. His earliest musical hero was the quite conventional Tchaikovsky, whose *Symphonie Pathétique* was the musical gospel among the fashionable circles of Russia during Stravinsky's childhood. He was brought up in an atmosphere of traditional music. His father was the famous bass of the St Petersburg Opera. Igor read the scores in his father's library until he had learned most of them by heart. He became a skillful pianist, completed a course in the law school and gave up a government position for a musical career.

He brought some of his compositions to Rimsky-Korsakov. The master weaver of orchestral harmony was not impressed. He took a fancy to Stravinsky's personality, however, and offered to give him lessons in the principles of orchestration. The older and the younger musician became close friends.

Upon the death of Rimsky-Korsakov the pupil wrote a *Chant Funèbre*. It was a clever piece of "pictorial" music. "All the solo instruments," remarks Stravinsky, "filed past the tomb of the master in succession, each laying down its own melody as a wreath . . . against a deep background of tremolo murmurings that simulated the vibrations of bass voices singing in chorus."

His head was bristling with musical effects. New rhythms, new combinations of tones. Such talent could not long go unrecognized. And the man who first recognized it was Diaghilev, that unique Russian combination of mysticism and realism, the poet politician with golden visions in his head and golden promises on his tongue. A fantastic man for a fantastic business. Diaghilev was the director of the famous Ballet Russe.

The ballet had supplanted opera as the supreme music festival of Russia. Dancing in pantomime to the music of sensuous dreams had taken the artistic centers by storm. It was fine to see young girls "weaving music with their feet," and young men with the bodies of Apollo simulating the gestures of a dying faun. The scenery was rich, the audience was rich, and the managers had become fantastically rich.

But in spite of its material foundation, or rather *because* of its material foundation, the ballet had developed into a truly beautiful form of art. For Diaghilev was ready to pay the highest prices for the best talent. His aim was to combine two great arts into one greater unit. And so he took the poetry of motion and the poetry of sound and transfused them into that superb form of art, the Imperial Russian Ballet.

[*318*]

The poetry of motion. It burst upon the public in the form of Vaslav Nijinsky, the dancer with the incredibly beautiful limbs. It was whispered that he was a pagan god come to life, that he had descended from the heights of Olympus to dance before men. Russia sat in adoration at his feet. The wealthy classes showered him with their gifts. The women went into ecstasies of hysteria at his approach.

Diaghilev loved this Pan of the Russian stage. Loved him immoderately, as did everybody who had come into contact with the bewitching beauty of the young man. Diaghilev had a strong, domineering mind. Nijinsky had the mind of a child. The ballet master took him into his power and raised him to international fame. In return he insisted upon the possession of Nijinsky, body and soul. Nijinsky followed his master as if he were in a trance. Diaghilev kept a zealous watch over him. Though the dancer had captured the hearts of all the young women in Russia, he was prohibited from associating with any of them save under the censorious eye of his master. And the undeveloped mind in the beautiful body did not question, only obeyed.

It was into this fantastic society of the Russian ballet that Stravinsky was thrust at an early age.

II

DIAGHILEV REALIZED that here was a young composer with extravagant ideas who could supply his ballet with the sensational music it needed. He commissioned Stravinsky to write the music for the ballet of *The Fire Bird*. And Stravinsky turned out a sumptuous score. Then he had a vision. "One day I saw in imagination a solemn pagan rite: sage elders, seated in a circle, watched a young girl dance herself to death. They were sacrificing her to propitiate the god of spring." Out from the wilds of Africa to the semiwilderness of Russia. The beating of the tom-tom. A good idea for a ballet, thought Diaghilev, who had an eye and an ear for such things. The music must be savage. Could Stravinsky write music that would be sufficiently bloodcurdling? The audiences' hair must stand on end! "I'll do it," agreed Stravinsky. And he more than succeeded. "He stood the audiences on their heads."

The ballet, *Sacre du Printemps* (Rites of Spring), was produced on May 28, 1913. What reached the ears of the audience on that occasion has reached the ears of the public many times since. But the first shock is always the greatest. If Stravinsky had been a musician before that date, as one of the critics put it, he was a musician no longer. He had assumed the duties of a witch doctor of sound. It was a law unto itself, this new composition into which "music occasionally enters as an accident. But when it does enter, it is beautiful music to be sure."

Some people, however, were not so sure. At the first performance they let their fists fly. Others in an instant became enthusiastic champions of the new order and met the opposition with their own fists. One patron, out of sheer disgust, slammed the head of a man sitting in front of him; "but the victim was in such ecstasy that he continued to listen unperturbed, without feeling the blow." At the conclusion of the performance there was a riot. The police were summoned. Diaghilev turned off the lights. Stravinsky followed Diaghilev to a taxi. They drove on and on without speaking until they finally reached a park. There under the first gray streaks of dawn they took out their handkerchiefs and mopped their faces. "I didn't see the subsequent performances of the *Sacre*," remarks Stravinsky, "because a few days after the notorious first night I fell ill . . . and spent six weeks in a nursing home."

III

STRAVINSKY had broken completely away from the traditions of the past. But on the other hand he had no false notions about his

[*320*]

mission as a musical Messiah. He cared nothing about the so-called "art of the future." He wrote, as he frankly confessed, for the present. He was interested in pleasing, or rather in startling, the audiences of his own day. He shattered the indifference of the public with a new explosive, a combination of elemental chords that didn't mix.

Above all, he hated the complacency of the public, its un-critical acceptance of the old—and, to the ears of Stravinsky, defunct—musical idols. He attended a Wagner festival at Bay-reuth and found it about as exciting as a funeral. "The place," he writes, "was like a crematorium, and a very old-fashioned one at that. Every moment I expected to see the gentleman in black who had been entrusted with the task of singing the praises of the departed. The order for the audience to devote themselves to contemplation was given by a blast of trumpets. I sat humble and motionless, but at the end of a quarter of an hour I couldn't bear it any longer. . . . At last the 'Pause' arrived, and I was rewarded by two sausages and a glass of beer. But hardly had I found the time to light a cigarette when the trumpet blast sounded again, demanding another period of contemplation. . . . Then there were more sausages, more beer, another trumpet blast, another period of contemplation, another act—Finis!"

No, this sort of preserved inspiration wouldn't do. The kings of the past were dead. Long live the music of the present! The complex and formless music of a complex and formless age. People were mistaken when they expected music to express something. Music shouldn't really evoke any feelings at all. "Any emotion is an illusion. The only property of music is its intellectual structure. Music is meant to be admired, not to be enjoyed."

With this in mind Stravinsky set about to perfect his technique —of which he had a great abundance. Unskilled in melody, he indulged in counterpoint with fanatical zeal. Don't coddle your audiences; make them toil. Labor is the surest way to happiness.

[*321*]

There is nothing so pleasurable as painful music. Life is always so tragic; let's for a change make it grotesque. Thus spoke the man whose knowledge of orchestration and of the potentialities of every instrument was unsurpassed. Stravinsky went to Italy and studied the mechanical pianos and the orchestrinas of the streets for their whimsical and unexpected melodies. He met Picasso, and there sprang up an immediate bond of sympathy between the cubist composer and the cubist painter. For both of them subscribed to the same aesthetic credo—from form through formlessness to form. Having rejected the old simple patterns, they were groping their way through chaos to more complex and, they believed, more satisfactory patterns of their own.

Picasso painted a portrait of Stravinsky. The customs authorities confiscated this portrait and held it against him for evidence. For with all the angles and curves it looked like the secret map of a military objective made by a spy. "It is merely the map of my face," explained Stravinsky. But to convince the authorities he was obliged to write to the British ambassador in Rome who understood something about the art of Picasso.

At this point Stravinsky came under the influence of ragtime. Immediately he realized the rhythmic opportunities of this new field of exotic music. To be sure, it had failed to win the respect of the pedants. But it appealed to the primitive passions of mankind. It was naked, unashamed, alive. To the devil with the prudes! "Is it respect or is it love that urges us to possess a woman?" It was in this spirit, he tells us, that he composed his *Ragtime* "for eleven instruments—wind, string, percussion and a Hungarian cymbalum."

But with characteristic originality he got at the kernel of the jazz form and threw away the shell. The emotional qualities that set the hips swaying were not for him. For he had decided inexorably that music must be intellectual rather than emotional. Understand the passions of others? Yes. But succumb to

[*322*]

them yourself? Emphatically no! It was out of sheer technical curiosity that he was interested in the novel rhythmic combinations of jazz. The curiosity of the man was unquenchable. He wasn't the least bit thrilled at the voluptuous beauty of the muse. He was far more concerned in studying the vertebrae of her spine. He was not a poet of tonal emotion, he was a scientist of tonal color.

Still on his quest for new combinations of tonal color and "tired of the dominant part played by the string instruments in orchestral music," Stravinsky wrote a symphony scored only for woodwinds. And then he tried a still more outlandish effect by scoring a composition for a mechanical pianola, an electrically driven harmonium, an ensemble of percussion instruments and two Hungarian cymbalums. But even these experiments did not completely satisfy him. On one occasion he collected an orchestra of kettledrums, bells and xylophones. The chief virtue of this orchestra, said Stravinsky, was the fact that "none of the instruments gives out a precise note."

But for all his experimental modernism, Stravinsky never really despised the classics. He had the greatest respect for Beethoven. But he objected to the basis upon which Beethoven's reputation rested. "People praise him for his moral ideas. However, these ideas are merely side issues." Sociologists and moralists have adopted the man for their own. Yet these "publicity mongers of liberalism in all the bourgeoisie democracies" who make him a revolutionary, a Jacobin, a humanitarian, "have not made him thereby a great musician." You write sonnets, Gertrude Stein would tell us, not with ideas but with words. In the same way, maintains Stravinsky, you write music not with philosophy but with notes. A false theory, perhaps, but an interesting basis for unique experimentation in artistic expression.

On this basis Stravinsky wrote his "Experimental" piano concerto. It met with such marked success that he became a concert pianist for the express purpose of performing it in public. This

[*323*]

he did about fifty times in the course of the next ten years. The piece was so involved that when he tried to play it from memory at the Paris Opera House he forgot how the second movement began and sat in embarrassment until Koussevitzky, who was conducting at the time, whispered the notes of the opening chords.

Stravinsky's reputation was now world-wide. The younger generation idolized him. He came to play his music in America, the land of "skyscrapers, traffic lights and Negroes." Like many another composer who had arrived from Europe with snobbish ideas about our "inferior" culture, he went home generously remunerated and favorably impressed with America's genuine love for beauty. After all, he confessed, an absolute monarchy and a corrupt aristocracy are not necessary for the cultivation of a great national art. Perhaps the beauty of the Old World is dying only to be reborn in the New World across the sea.

Stravinsky likes America. For America likes Stravinsky. There has been no stranger bond of communion than that between this politically reactionary, Greek Orthodox product of Russian czarism and the freedom-loving liberals in American musical circles. The American mind is inventive. It is fascinated by novelty in art as well as in science. And Stravinsky is always novel, always experimental, always unique. He can always be expected to do the unexpected.

The genuis of Stravinsky is like a pendulum that sways between two extremes. When he is tired of being ultramodern he can become ultra-ancient. Anything so long as it is ultra. One day he decided he would compose music to a Latin script. Latin was a dead language. Its words were to most people meaningless. And that is precisely what interested him in this language. "For the text thus becomes purely phonetic material for the composer." His music, like his words, could then afford to be meaningless—an archaic ritual to an outmoded religion. It would possess the lofty dignity and sacred frigidity of a religious consecration to a dead god. He could hardly fall into the pitfalls of sentimentalism with Latin for a text. And this man hated sentimentalism with a hatred that makes one suspect he was very sentimental at heart.

This is how the oratorio, *Oedipus Rex*, came about. It was an irrational attempt to recapture the rationalism of the ancient pagans. Stravinsky admired the classical contours of the Greek statues and tried to project their spirit into his music. But he captured none of their beauty; he succeeded only in capturing their marble coldness.

IV

In 1930 Serge Koussevitzky asked Stravinsky to write a symphony on the occasion of the fiftieth anniversary of the Boston Symphony Orchestra. And Stravinsky went about it in his characteristic fashion. "The symphonic form as bequeathed to us by the nineteenth century held little attraction for me." It was his business, as always, to produce something different. He decided to combine the orchestra with a chorus into a sort of symphonic oratorio. And he chose the Psalms as his text. The resultant *Symphony of Psalms* is a strangely moving work for a handful of people. The vast majority of music lovers, however, find in this work no message, no meaning, no understanding. For, they maintain, Stravinsky is becoming less and less of a poet and more and more of a professor. He is sacrificing his artistry to his eccentricity, his heart to his mind.

To this latter charge Stravinsky would plead guilty. The greatest music, he believes, must appeal to the mind and not to the heart. He makes a frank plea for the credo that "music must not be enjoyed." With him it is a conviction. In all art he sees an eternal war between two principles—Apollo and Dionysus, reason and emotion. Most people assume ecstasy to be the goal of art. "But the one goal should be objective aloofness, order, the austerity of form." Most people look for art to express a message.

But they are wrong. "If I have displeased my audiences by veering away from the colorful music of *The Fire Bird*, I cannot help it. What delights me leaves them indifferent, and what still continues to interest them holds no further attraction for me. For that matter, I believe there was seldom any real communion of spirit between us." He doesn't blame people for being amazed by "a language in which all their aesthetic values seem to be violated." But their attitude will not make him deviate from his path. He will not give in to those "who in their blindness do not realize that they are asking me to go backward."

Yet to many music lovers his earliest work is his best. Once in his early days he had a vision about a puppet at a fair suddenly endowed with life. For a while the puppet danced and realized the joys and sorrows of love, and then it died like any human creature. Stravinsky's music about this puppet was colorful and ironic and surcharged with emotion. *Petrushka*, the doll who suffered like a mortal. This ballet is perhaps the highest peak of Stravinsky's music. For here he spoke in a language effective, different, original, yet clear enough to be understood and felt. The mechanical puppet had been brought to life for a few electric moments against the glittering pageantry of a bazaar, had danced and loved with an intense passion and then —what irony!—had died from an excess of human feeling. So too the muse of Stravinsky, mechanical by nature, had for a few moments acquired a heart and poured out the music of human feeling. But then the heart died from an excess of its own emotion. And today Stravinsky's muse is once more a clever mechanical puppet without a heart.